On Course to Desert Storm

CONTRIBUTIONS TO NAVAL HISTORY... NO. 5

On Course to Desert Storm:
The United States Navy and the Persian Gulf

Michael A. Palmer

Naval Historical Center
Department of the Navy
Washington, D.C. 1992

∞ The paper used in this publication meets the minimum requirements of American National Standard for Information Sciences—Permanence of Paper for Printed Library Materials, ANSI Z39.48–1984.

Library of Congress Cataloging-in-Publication Data

Palmer, Michael A.
    On course to Desert Storm : the United States Navy and the Persian Gulf / Michael A. Palmer.
        p. cm. — (Contributions to naval history ; no. 5)
    Includes bibliographical references and index.
    ISBN 0–945274–09–2 (pbk.)
    1. Persian Gulf Region—Relations—United States. 2. United States—Relations—Persian Gulf Region. 3. United States. Navy—History—20th century. 4. Persian Gulf Region—History, Naval. 5. United States—Foreign relations—1945– I. Title. II. Series.
DS326.P37   1991
956.704'3—dc20   91–33206

To my mother and father

Secretary of the Navy's Advisory Committee on Naval History

(As of 1 January 1991)

William D. Wilkinson, *Chairman*
CAPT Edward L. Beach, USN (Retired)
David R. Bender
John C. Dann
RADM Russell W. Gorman, USN (Retired)
Richard L. Joutras
VADM William P. Lawrence, USN (Retired)
Vera D. Mann
Ambassador J. William Middendorf II
VADM Gerald E. Miller, USN (Retired)
Clark G. Reynolds
Daniel F. Stella
Betty M. Unterberger

Contributions to Naval History Series

Michael A. Palmer, *Origins of the Maritime Strategy:*
   American Naval Strategy in the First Postwar Decade   1988

Thomas C. Hone, *Power and Change: The Administrative*
   History of the Office of the Chief of Naval Operations,
   1946–1986   1989

Gary E. Weir, *Building American Submarines,*
   1914–1940   1991

Tamara Moser Melia, *"Damn the Torpedoes": A Short*
   History of U.S. Naval Mine Countermeasures,
   1777–1991   1991

Michael A. Palmer, *On Course to Desert Storm:*
   The United States Navy and the Persian Gulf   1992

The Author

Dr. Michael A. Palmer is an assistant professor of history on the faculty of East Carolina University's Maritime History Program. He is the author of several books on maritime strategy and operations and has published widely in maritime and naval journals. Between 1983 and 1991 he worked at the Naval Historical Center in Washington, D.C., in both the Early History and Contemporary History branches. During this time he wrote *Origins of the Maritime Strategy*, the first volume to appear in the Contributions to Naval History series. Dr. Palmer earned his Ph.D. at Temple University in 1981. He resides in Greenville, North Carolina, with his wife and two children.

Contents

	Page
Foreword	xiii
Preface: A Line in the Sand	xv
Acknowledgments	xxi

PART ONE: An English Lake, 1800–1945 1
   1. Americans: No. 2 Englishmen in the Gulf 3
   2. The Second World War and the Persian Gulf 11

PART TWO: Establishing a U.S. Military Presence in the
   Persian Gulf, 1946–1950 19
   3. The Iran Crisis of 1946 21
   4. The Oil Scare of 1947–1948 29
   5. Establishment of the Middle East Force 35

PART THREE: Assuring Access to Adequate Oil Supplies,
   1950–1981 41
   6. Arab Nationalism and the Defense of the Middle East ... 43
   7. The United States and Iran 49
   8. War, Intervention, Crisis, and War 61
   9. The Nixon Doctrine and the Twin Pillars 75
  10. The Carter Administration and the Gulf 89

PART FOUR: The United States, the Gulf, and the
   Iran-Iraq War, 1981–1988 101
  11. "Not While This President Serves": The Reflagging Decision ... 103
  12. The United States and the Tanker War 121

Conclusion 135
Appendixes
   A. Operation Praying Mantis, by Hans S. Pawlisch 141
   B. Middle East Force Chain of Command 147
   C. Commanders, Middle East Force, 1949–1988 148
Abbreviations 151
Notes 155
Bibliography 181
Index 193

Tables

		Page
1.	World, U.S., and Persian Gulf Petroleum Production (in 000 metric tons)	30
2.	U.S. Petroleum Exports and Imports (in 000 barrels)	32
3.	U.S. and Soviet Ship-Days in the Indian Ocean, 1968–1973 (surface combatants and auxiliaries)	76
4.	U.S. and Soviet Port-Calls in the Indian Ocean, 1968–1973	77
5.	Iranian and Iraqi Arms Expenditures and Imports, 1969–1978 (million/dollars)	78
6.	Growth of Middle East Force, 1978–1988	97
7.	Increases in U.S. Navy Strength in the Indian Ocean, 1976–1988	97
8.	Notional Central Command Forces	107
9.	Attacks by Iran and Iraq on Ships in the Persian Gulf, 1987	121
10.	Attacks by Iran and Iraq on Ships in the Persian Gulf, 1988	132

Illustrations

Photographs with NH numbers are held by the Naval Historical Center, Washington, DC 20374–0571; those with 80–G, 306–PS, USA C, K, and USN numbers are held in the Still Pictures Branch, National Archives, Washington, DC 20408–0001; and those with DN numbers are from the Department of Defense Still Media Records Center, Washington, DC 20374–1681.

	Page
Ticonderoga in Venice	5
Rear Admiral Robert W. Shufeldt	7
Allied ships off-load war supplies in Iran, 1945	13
President Roosevelt and King ibn-Saud	15
Saudi entourage on deck of destroyer *Murphy*	16
Loy Henderson, Director Near Eastern and African Affairs	23
Battleship *Missouri* off Turkey	26
Secretary of the Navy James Forrestal	33
Carrier *Valley Forge* in the Persian Gulf	37
Captain Harry D. Felt and Captain Ernest M. Eller	38
Rendova in Bahrain	45
George McGhee, Assistant Secretary of State	47
Arab-American Oil Company refinery	50
President Truman and the Shah of Iran	52
Iranian Prime Minister Mohammed Mossadegh	55
Carrier *Lake Champlain* in Aden	57
Navy evacuation crews at work in the Suez	65
Marine landing at Beirut, Lebanon	68
Middle East Force command ship *Valcour*	71
Liberty after Israeli rocket attack	73

	Page
Damage inflicted by the rocket attack on *Liberty*	73
President Nixon and Vice Admiral Isaac C. Kidd	81
U.S. Naval Support Activity, Diego Garcia	84
Soviet F-class submarine	85
President Jimmy Carter	90
Soviet guided missile frigate off Lebanon	93
Carrier *Midway* in the Indian Ocean	96
Sea Stallion helicopters in the rescue mission to Iran	99
Indian Ocean Battle Group	104
U.S. Navy and Soviet aircraft over the Arabian Sea	108
Small seaplane tender *Duxbury Bay*	110
President Reagan and Caspar Weinberger	113
Guided missile frigate *Stark* after Iraqi attack	114
View of *Stark*'s damage	115
Modern Middle East (map)	118
Operation Earnest Will (map)	120
Tanker *Bridgeton*	123
Illusive and *Mount Vernon* at anchor off Sitrah, Bahrain	125
Self-defense force on board *Okinawa*	125
Iranian command and control platform burning	127
Destroyer *Chandler* in the Persian Gulf	128
Minesweeping operations in the Persian Gulf	128
Mark III patrol boat	130
Crane on the barge *Hercules* preparing to lift boats	131
Iranian frigate *Sahand*	133
Samuel B. Roberts returning to home port	134

Foreword

It is most appropriate that this study, *On Course to Desert Storm*, is appearing at a time when the Persian Gulf is of special concern to the United States. Michael Palmer's purpose is to go behind the recent headlines associated with the crisis that began when Saddam Hussein invaded Kuwait in 1990. The author explains the military and political factors that affected American policy in the region and led to the establishment of the U.S. Navy's Middle East Force in 1949. He then traces the evolution of this small force over the ensuing decades. Dr. Palmer shows that the Navy periodically sent major reinforcements to the region during the era of tension and war that followed the abdication of the Shah of Iran in 1979. Starting in the late 1970s these reinforcements included American carrier battle forces, which thereafter became a familiar sight in the North Arabian Sea approaches to the Persian Gulf.

Dr. Palmer's broad grasp of naval history makes him exceptionally well qualified to write this far-reaching history. His previous writings include an important study of an undeclared naval war that an infant U.S. Navy waged from 1798 to 1801 against France. The author also contributed a distinguished study of the development of U.S. naval strategy in the years following the Second World War. While preparing *On Course to Desert Storm*, Dr. Palmer visited the Joint Task Force, Middle East. The opportunity to gain first-hand knowledge of U.S. naval operations in the Persian Gulf added immeasurably to the author's understanding of the subject matter covered in this book.

Among those who contributed to Dr. Palmer's work were a number of authorities from outside the Naval Historical Center who kindly reviewed and commented on the manuscript. These readers included Vice Admiral Gerald E. Miller, USN (Retired), who serves as a member of the Secretary of the Navy's Advisory Committee on Naval History; Captain Peter M. Swartz, USN, a former member of the Advisory Committee; Dr. Nina Noring, a historian with the Department of State; Mr. Jeffrey Cairns, an analyst with the Central Intelligence Agency; and Lieutenant Commander Joseph T. Stanik, USN, of the U.S. Naval Academy's history department.

Within the Naval Historical Center, Dr. William S. Dudley, the Senior Historian; Dr. Edward J. Marolda, Head of the Contemporary History Branch; and Sandra J. Doyle, the Center's senior editor, and her assistant, Akio J. Stribling, deserve special recognition for their contributions to this project.

Despite the assistance offered by these and other individuals, Dr. Palmer is solely responsible for the views and conclusions expressed in *On Course to Desert Storm*. His opinions do not reflect the position of the Department of the Navy or of any other agency of the U.S. Government.

Dean C. Allard
Director of Navy History

Preface
A Line in the Sand

In the late winter of 1990 President Saddam Hussein of Iraq initiated an anti-Western propaganda campaign. In mid-February he called for the withdrawal of the U.S. Navy's Middle East Force from the Persian Gulf waters it had cruised for nearly half a century. In March, despite world outcry, the Iraqis executed an Iranian-born British journalist accused of espionage. In April Saddam threatened to burn half of Israel if the Jewish state struck at Iraq as it had in 1981 when Israeli F–16s bombed Saddam's Osirak nuclear reactor. These threats—combined with disturbing reports of Iraqi efforts to develop a super cannon, increase the range of Soviet Scud missiles, and purchase atomic detonators—sent shock waves through the Middle East and the West.

In midsummer, Saddam turned his attention to the gulf Arabs, accusing Kuwait and the United Arab Emirates of trying to hold down petroleum prices and weaken Iraq by overproducing oil in collusion with the United States. Saddam needed to increase his oil revenues if he was to pay off the Western and Arab banks and governments that had loaned billions to Iraq during the eight-year war with Iran. He also had to maintain the momentum of his country's planned economic expansion and to keep nearly a million men under arms. By 21 July, 30,000 Iraqi troops had massed along the Kuwaiti border to underscore Saddam's seriousness. As the crisis in the gulf developed, Americans were by no means of one mind regarding an appropriate policy towards Iraq. Some U.S. experts believed that Saddam was a regional and international threat; others considered the Iraqi dictator to be a local bully intent only on shaking down the gulf sheikdoms for some extra cash. Some in Congress were issuing clarion calls about the butcher in Baghdad, while others beat a path to Saddam's capital to expand American commercial opportunities in Iraq. By spring the Bush administration was considering taking a tougher stance against Iraq because of its use of poison gas against Kurds and its human rights abuses. But on the eve of the Iraqi invasion of Kuwait a few months later, State Department officials were before Congress fighting against legislative restrictions on United States-Iraqi trade.

Whatever the state of American concern over the situation in the gulf, the United States could do little without the cooperation of the threatened gulf Arabs. But despite Saddam's bellicosity most Arab leaders cautioned the United States against any move that might appear provocative, with Egyptian President Hosni Mubarak taking the diplomatic lead in an effort to broker an Arab solution to the crisis. Only the United Arab Emirates requested an overt display of American assistance. In response, the Bush administration announced on 23 July that the U.S. Navy's Middle East Force (six ships already on alert) and U.S. Air Force tankers would conduct exercises with the air and naval forces from the United Arab Emirates, the first maneuvers ever to combine U.S. and emirate units.

At the Organization of Petroleum Exporting Countries meeting in Geneva on 25–27 July, the Iraqis gained the higher prices and lower production quotas from Kuwait and the United Arab Emirates that Saddam demanded. While these discussions were underway, Hussein met in Teheran with the American ambassador to Iraq, April Glaspie. She made it clear to the Iraqi president that although the Bush administration would take no position on inter-Arab border disputes, the United States would not countenance the resolution of such disagreements by force. Saddam appeared to relent. He agreed to send emissaries to an Arab summit at Jidda in Saudi Arabia and promised to refrain from any military move while diplomatic discussions continued. But the talks held on 31 July at Jidda lasted only two hours and produced no results.

In the meantime the Iraqi Army had concentrated about 100,000 men along the Kuwaiti border. At 0200 (local time) on 2 August, Saddam's troops stormed into Kuwait, overruning most of the country by the end of the day. The emir and the royal family, along with some troops and aircraft, fled to safety in Saudi Arabia.

The United States, Western Europe, the Soviet Union, most of the Third World, and a majority of the Arab states promptly condemned the invasion. On 2 August the United States froze Iraqi assets, imposed a near total embargo on trade with Iraq, and began orchestrating a worldwide diplomatic effort to pressure Saddam. That same day the United Nations Security Council passed Resolution 660 calling for Iraqi withdrawal from Kuwait. Frenzied diplomatic activity to convince Saddam to pull his troops out of Kuwait continued for the next five and a half months.

Even as it was managing the diplomatic response to the Iraqi invasion, the Bush administration also had to ensure that Saddam's army did not continue its march into Saudi Arabia. As troops poured into Kuwait and moved south, the possibility of an Iraqi invasion of Saudi Arabia remained a matter of grave concern in Washington and the Saudi capital of Riyadh. Saddam denied reports that he was preparing to strike again, but he had made similar denials in July regarding Kuwait and could not be trusted. Preventing Saddam from exporting petroleum required not just a blockade of Iraqi and Kuwaiti ports, but also a shutdown of the oil pipelines that carried Iraqi crude across Turkey and Saudi Arabia to ports on the Mediterranean and

Red seas. But neither Turkey nor Saudi Arabia were likely to halt the flow of Iraqi oil without guarantees of American support. Turkey, a member of the North Atlantic Treaty Organization with a strong army and a defensible frontier, was relatively safe from attack and would probably be satisfied with diplomatic and economic commitments from the United States. But the Saudis, whose armed forces were small, would probably require an American military presence, either to deter Saddam or to blunt an Iraqi drive, which, if not already planned, might follow a Saudi shutdown of pipelines carrying Iraqi oil. If the Saudis refused to halt this flow of Iraqi crude across their country, the United States would face the prospect of enforcing a trade embargo against Iraq by blockading Saudi ports.

By 6 August the Kuwait crisis came to a head. The Iraqis maintained that they had been invited into the territory of their southern neighbor by the so-called Interim Government of Free Kuwait. Although Saddam announced to the world that his troops would soon withdraw, reinforcements continued to stream into the country. On the fourth Saddam had named his cousin—Ala Hussein Ali, who had been implicated in the gassing of the Kurds in 1988—as the head of a provisional Kuwaiti government. On the fifth, amidst reports of Iraqi troops massing on the Saudi frontier, efforts to find an Arab solution to the crisis had collapsed with the cancellation of a planned summit to be held in Jidda. Presidential spokesperson Marlin Fitzwater commented: "[The Iraqis] are close enough to the Saudi border to indicate cause for concern, but we don't know what their intentions or motives are."

On the sixth the United Nations passed a second resolution calling for a near total trade embargo against Iraq. In Washington, the Bush administration announced its policy objective: immediate and unconditional Iraqi withdrawal from Kuwait, restoration of the power of the legitimate Kuwaiti government, safeguards for all Americans in Kuwait and Iraq, and freedom of navigation and the unimpeded flow of oil in the gulf.

After meeting with his senior national security advisers during the weekend of 4–5 August at Camp David, Maryland, President Bush sent Secretary of Defense Dick Cheney and Commander in Chief of the U.S. Central Command, General H. Norman Schwarzkopf, to Jidda to meet with Saudi Arabia's King Fahd. The President had decided to send American ground and air forces to Saudi Arabia if Fahd requested American assistance. Back at the White House Bush told the press that the Iraqi occupation of Kuwait would not be permitted to stand. When asked what the United States would do to prevent the installation of what the President had termed "a puppet government," Bush replied: "Just wait. Watch and learn."

Cheney and Schwarzkopf arrived in Jidda on Monday, 6 August. That evening they met with King Fahd and other Saudi officials for about two hours. The king reminded the Americans of the long-standing nature of the U.S.-Saudi relationship and recalled the February 1945 meeting between his father, King Abdul Aziz, and President Franklin D. Roosevelt. He felt confident that he could trust the Americans to defend Saudi Arabia and then to withdraw from the Arabian peninsula when the crisis ended. Fahd, however, could not be sure that Saddam Hussein would either halt his forces at the Saudi border or withdraw from Kuwait. After discussing the diplomatic and military options, he requested American military assistance. Secretary Cheney immediately informed President Bush of the Saudi decision by secure telephone. The President in turn directed the deployment of American ground and air forces to the Persian Gulf. Lead elements left the United States early Tuesday morning, 7 August. The Ready Brigade of the 82d Airborne Division began leaving Fort Bragg and Pope Air Force Base in North Carolina at 0300 on Wednesday, 8 August. At a press conference later that day, President Bush warned: "A line has been drawn in the sand."

With the exception of the limited use of naval facilities in Bahrain, the United States lacked any major base in the region. Between 2 and 8 August only American naval forces and a handful of U.S. Air Force tankers and E–3A Sentry AWACS aircraft were on the scene. The Navy and Marine Corps team led what became the largest buildup of naval forces since the Second World War. Middle East Force was already on station in the gulf. As Chairman of the Joint Chiefs of Staff General Colin Powell made clear during a press briefing that day, U.S. Navy aircraft from the carriers *Independence* (CVA–62) and *Dwight D. Eisenhower* (CVN–69), on station in the North Arabian and Red Seas, respectively, would cover the airlift in its initial stage. The first heavy mechanized units deployed to Saudi Arabia were Marines of the 7th and 1st Marine Expeditionary Brigades. The men were airlifted from bases in California and Hawaii to Saudi ports, where they "married up" with their equipment, which had arrived from Diego Garcia and Guam in the vessels of Maritime Prepositioning Ships Squadrons 2 and 3. By the time Desert Storm commenced—16 January 1991 (EST)—the Marines had deployed the corps-sized I Marine Expeditionary Force (1st and 2nd Marine Divisions and the 3rd Marine Air Wing) and a pair of amphibious Marine Expeditionary Brigades (the 4th and 5th)—to the theater. The Navy moved more than 120 ships including six carrier battle groups, two battleships, and a thirty-one-ship amphibious force to positions in the eastern Mediterranean, Red Sea, Persian Gulf, and North Arabian Sea. Navy personnel totaled about 75,000. More than 73,000 Marines were deployed ashore, and another 18,000 were afloat.

Support of U.S. and allied operations in the theater throughout Desert Storm necessitated a massive logistical effort. At its peak early in the operation, a veritable air bridge connected the United States and Europe with the Arabian Peninsula. Every ten minutes a transport plane landed at the U.S. air base in the Saudi gulf coast city of Dhahran, but the bulk of the equipment and supplies—over 90 percent—came by sea. The Navy's Military Sealift Command employed nine Maritime prepositioning ships, eight fast sealift ships, and ten afloat prepositioning ships among the 250 ships that carried over 18 billion pounds of equipment and product to Arabian ports before the cessation of hostilities.

Between August 1990 and January 1991 the ships and aircraft of the U.S. Navy cooperated with Allied naval forces in extensive maritime intercept operations. By mid-January these operations had challenged 6,913 merchant ships and boarded 803 of these ships. The operations, critical to the early stage of the effort against Iraq, demonstrated the allies' solidarity and determination in a politically acceptable and effective form before recourse to outright military confrontation with Iraq.

The failure of the U.N. embargo and the allied naval blockade to convince or force Saddam to withdraw from Kuwait led to the transition from Desert Shield, the operation deployed to protect Saudi Arabia, to Desert Storm, the operation designed to drive Saddam from Kuwait. Although the U.S. Air Force dominated the air campaign, and the U.S. Army controlled the ground effort that followed, the Navy-Marine Corps team made substantial contributions to the Allied effort. About 400 Navy and 200 Marine aircraft participated in the combined air effort. Navy ships and submarines launched hundreds of Tomahawk cruise missiles against well-defended Iraqi targets. Amphibious forces threatened Saddam's left flank with attack and tied at least five Iraqi divisions to the coast. When the ground offensive began, the two Marine divisions ashore spearheaded the drive to liberate Kuwait in cooperation with Arab forces and the Tiger Brigade of the U.S. Army's 2nd Armored Division. Other American, British, and French units conducted a decisive sweeping maneuver around the Iraqi right that led to the destruction of the Iraqi Army in the Kuwaiti theater and the liberation of Kuwait in a 100-hour ground war that carried American troops to the Euphrates River. Forty-two Iraqi combat divisions of Saddam Hussein's "desert-wise," "battle-hardened," "veteran" army had been destroyed.

For the United States the six-week military effort to expel the Iraqis from Kuwait was far less tortuous than the six-month domestic political struggle that had preceded Desert Storm. Many Americans were confused by the policies of the Bush administration and taken aback by the scale of the American commitment to the Persian Gulf. Why was the United States supporting a small, oil-rich sheikdom? Were we risking a bloody fight with the Iraqis to secure the flow of oil from the gulf, protect human rights, stop aggression, or ensure American jobs? Why was the United States taking the lead in defending oil resources that were of far greater importance to the Europeans and Japanese? Why were we confronting Iraq when, only two years before, we had "leaned" towards Iraq during the final stages of the Iran-Iraq War? How could the United States deploy such massive force to a region halfway around the world?

The purpose of this study is to address these issues in a historical framework, with a focus on the U.S. Navy. Neither the United States nor its Navy are strangers to the Persian Gulf, and questions about the nature and the extent of American involvement in the region are not new. Over the course of two centuries, our nation has developed commercial, strategic, and petrostrategic interests in the Persian Gulf,* and U.S. naval ships have steamed the gulf's waters for over forty years. But although the world has undergone recent and significant changes since the end of World War II, most of the major impulses that brought the U.S. Navy to the Persian Gulf in the late 1940s remain fundamental factors underlying American policy in the early 1990s.

Given the limited length of the books in this series, Contributions to Naval History, I could not provide the reader with a detailed account of over four decades of Middle East history and relevant American foreign policy. I have attempted, therefore, to look at those events that brought the United States to the Middle East in the first place, survey the factors that led the United States to deploy military forces to the Persian Gulf and the Indian Ocean in Operations Desert Shield and Desert Storm, and examine the impact of those forces on American policy and of American policy on those forces. Events that occurred elsewhere in the Middle East are dealt with only to the extent that they affected events in the gulf. I am not a historian of the Middle East writing about the U.S. Navy, but a historian of the U.S. Navy writing about the Middle East.

Until Desert Shield, U.S. military forces in the Middle East were principally naval in character. In the wake of Desert Storm, most American ground and land-based air units will likely withdraw from the Gulf, leaving naval forces behind to demonstrate continued U.S. resolve. Accordingly, I suspect that a U.S. presence in the region will remain a significant part of this nation's overseas commitment. For this reason, this book is dedicated to the men and women of the Middle East Force—"the Arabian Gulf Yacht Club"—who are likely to be cruising the gulf's often-dangerous waters into the twenty-first century.

Of course, the views expressed in this book are my own and not those of the Naval Historical Center, the U.S. Navy, the Department of Defense, or any other U.S. Government agency.

Michael A. Palmer

---

*I use the term "petrostrategic" to differentiate between the period of interest early in the twentieth century, when American oilmen sought access to the petroleum of the Gulf for purely commercial and entrepreneurial reasons, and the post-World War II period during which Western Europe, East Asia, much of the Third World, and the United States became increasingly dependent on the Middle East for energy.

Acknowledgments

I conceived this book in June 1988 during a research trip to the Persian Gulf. As a historian I was pleased to find that the majority of American military personnel I spoke with knew that the U.S. Navy's Middle East Force had been patroling gulf waters since the late 1940s. But I quickly realized that few understood why the United States had first sent its ships to the gulf, how the force's mission had evolved over the decades, and why American men-of-war were still there. I decided to write a book that would address those questions.

Over the next three years I researched, wrote, and revised the manuscript, quickly discovering the complexities of trying to describe even the most simple occurrence that took place in the Middle East. I also confronted the difficulty of writing about events that, in some cases, were so recent that their details are often shrouded by the veils of classification. I also found myself contending with a moving target. No sooner had I completed the chapter covering the 1987–1988 tanker war when a new conflict began in the gulf.

Nevertheless, thanks to the assistance of many people, I managed to complete the manuscript. I need to thank the Naval Historical Center's archivists, especially Judith W. Short, Kathleen M. Lloyd, Regina Akers, and Bernard F. Cavalcante; John E. Vajda and the ever-changing staff of the Navy Department Library; Drs. Edward J. Marolda and Gary E. Weir, my comrades in the Center's Contemporary History Branch who read the initial draft; Director of Naval History, Dr. Dean C. Allard, and Senior Historian Dr. William S. Dudley, who commented on the second draft; Captain Peter M. Swartz, USN, Special Assistant to the Chairman of the Joint Chiefs of Staff, Nina Noring of the Department of State, Jeffrey Cairns of the Central Intelligence Agency, and Lieutenant Commander Joseph T. Stanik, USN, of the U.S. Naval Academy, who read the third draft; Dr. Hans S. Pawlisch, the historian of U.S. Central Command, who allowed me to include his account of Operation Praying Mantis as an appendix; Ella Nargele, the Naval Historical Center's declassification officer, who smoothed the release of the manuscript through the always daunting security-review process; Midshipman John Keppler of the University of California, Berkeley, who conducted the photographic research; and Charles R. Haberlein and Ed Finney of the Center's Photographic Section. My gratitude goes to the Naval Historical Center's senior editor, Sandra J. Doyle, who together with Akio J. Stribling did a masterful job guiding the book through publication, and also to the staff of SSR, Incorporated, who edited the manuscript, typed the final copy, and indexed the book.

And finally, I would like to thank Rear Admiral Anthony A. Less, USN, who as Commander Joint Task Force Middle East played host to Captain Charles Chadbourn, USNR, Senior Chief Terry Mitchell, and myself in June and July 1988. Thanks to Admiral Less, his staff, and the personnel of Joint Task Force Middle East, I was able to approach this history with a much clearer picture of the nature of operations in the Persian Gulf. I hope that future commanders of the Middle East Force, their staffs, and the U.S. Navy's men and women deployed to the gulf will find this short history half as interesting and useful as I found my trip to be.

PART ONE

An English Lake, 1800–1945

U.S. interests in the Middle East region are as old as the republic itself. At the end of the American Revolution in 1783, Yankee traders started to seek out distant corners of the globe not yet dominated by the major European mercantilist powers. With these traders pursuing dreams of riches to the markets of the East Indies, China, and Japan went the diplomats, usually accompanied by the men-of-war of the U.S. Navy.

The numerous American merchantmen and naval squadrons that sailed and steamed to the Pacific during the nineteenth century did so around Cape Horn and across the Indian Ocean, the principal transit route to the East before the opening of the Panama Canal in 1914. Not surprisingly, enterprising Yankees developed markets on the Indian subcontinent, along the East African coast, on the Arabian Peninsula, and in the Persian Gulf.

The development of the oil industry in the Middle East early in the twentieth century further fueled existing American interests in the region. Subsequently, two world wars demonstrated the strategic importance of the Persian Gulf where so much of the world's supply of oil was to be found.

1

Americans:
No. 2 Englishmen in the Gulf

During their first 125 years of independence, Americans were only vaguely familiar with the Persian Gulf. Indeed, the nation was over a century old before the first American man-of-war doubled the Strait of Hormuz.[1] Yankee traders, sealers, and whalers were quick to reach the waters of the Indian Ocean, and the merchants of Salem, Massachusetts, dominated the trade in the ocean well into the nineteenth century. Few, however, chose to pursue commercial opportunities in the gulf proper.

In 1800 the frigate *Essex*, under the command of Captain Edward Preble, became the first U.S. warship to pass the Cape of Good Hope into the Indian Ocean. In 1833 Master Commandant David Geisinger brought a two-ship squadron—his own sloop-of-war *Peacock* in company with the schooner *Boxer*—to Muscat, along the Omani coast. Geisinger's assignment was to provide transportation and a small show of force for an American diplomatic mission to the East. "Special Agent" Captain Edmund Roberts, a Salem merchant, represented the commercial community interested in trade east of the Cape of Good Hope. One of his principal tasks was to negotiate a treaty of amity and commerce with Sultan Saiyid Said of Muscat.[2] Roberts found the sultan eager to trade with Americans. The treaty signed by Roberts and the sultan on 21 September 1833 established the United States' first tie to a Persian Gulf state, a diplomatic relationship that has endured into the 1990s.

Muscat was an important commercial entrepôt for the Indian Ocean trade, but the truly dominant maritime power in the Indian Ocean was Great Britain. British merchants came to the Indian Ocean and the Persian Gulf in the sixteenth century seeking not the imperium of the Portuguese, who preceded them, but commercial opportunity,[3] and Britain gradually displaced Portugal as the major power in the region. A successful British-Persian assault on Hormuz island in 1622 finally broke the Portuguese grip on the gulf.[4]

British commercial dominance in the form of the India-based East India Company survived both French and Dutch challenges over the next two centuries. Not until General Napoleon Bonaparte's French army landed in Egypt in 1798, did the British, concerned about the security of India, start seeking formal diplomatic and military ties with gulf states. Muscat's location, midway between the exit of the Red Sea and India, and the Saids' control of the Gulf of Aden made the sultanate the immediate object of British attention. The perceived French threat to the Indian subcontinent first drove

An English Lake

the East India Company into a treaty relationship with Muscat.[5] During the nineteenth century the British increasingly intervened in the affairs of gulf states and established ever more formal procedures to secure an environment conducive to commercial activity.

Throughout the nineteenth century and into the twentieth, the region remained an area of tremendous instability. Trading patterns changed dramatically, in part because of the dominance of Europeans, in part because of political conditions around the gulf littoral. European steamers and commercial companies gradually displaced Arab dhows and traders in the Indian Ocean. Britain's successful campaign to end the slave trade, however well intentioned, further disrupted established commercial patterns. The ebb and flow of Wahabism—fundamental Sunni Islam championed by the Saudis—threatened the political existence of the maritime Arab chieftains around the periphery of the Arabian peninsula and increased the piracy to which the gulf was prone. Dynastic instability frequently led to internal strife, economic decline, and ultimately the establishment of a British protectorate. Expeditions to suppress gulf piracy and diplomatic and military support of threatened states led Britain into ever deeper involvement in the gulf.

Not surprisingly, when the British heard exaggerated rumors of a far-reaching American treaty with Muscat negotiated by Roberts, they questioned the sultan. But the British found nothing offensive in the actual agreement and the treaty survived, principally because of British indulgence.[6]

As the American-Persian treaty negotiations were to demonstrate in the 1850s, such forbearance would not have been forthcoming had the provisions of the treaty gone beyond simple commercial opportunity. The Americans, who had reached a similar accord with neighboring Turkey in 1830, were now anxious to sign a commercial treaty with Persia and to gain a consulate at Bushire to facilitate what had become a growing trade within the gulf.[7] The Persians in turn viewed the United States not only as a potential commercial partner but also as a force for countering the imperialist pressures of the Russians and British.

For several centuries, as the British were steadily expanding their position in the gulf around the periphery of the Arabian Peninsula and in India, the Russians were pushing south from the steppe into Transcaucasia and Central Asia. Throughout the seventeenth and eighteenth centuries Russia's southern expansion came primarily at the expense of the Ottoman Turks and the Khanates of Central Asia. In a series of wars fought between 1722 and 1828, the Russians secured their position in the Caucasus. By 1881 Persia's entire northern border fronted Tsarist Russia.[8]

Faced with this new threat from the north and the old British threat from the south, the Persian leadership searched the horizon for a counterweight. The United States appeared to fit the bill. Under the treaty proposed by Persia in 1855, the United States would agree to defend the Persian coast against all attacks and to assist the efforts of the Shah's naval force to capture those islands in the gulf, including Bahrain, claimed by the Shah.[9]

The British considered the proposed treaty, a copy of which they secured, a sure recipe for Anglo-American war. Fortunately the Americans had neither the means nor the desire to commit themselves to such a treaty, concluding instead a traditional commercial treaty with Persia in 1856. The Persians nevertheless asked the Americans to send a warship to the gulf as a show of strength.[10]

It took nearly a quarter-century for the United States to respond. In December 1879 Commodore Robert Wilson Shufeldt visited the Persian Gulf in *Ticonderoga* en route to Asia and his ultimately successful mission to open Korea to American commerce.[11] When *Ticonderoga* passed through the Strait of Hormuz, it became the first American man-of-war to sail into the gulf. Shufeldt visited Bushire and Basra and steamed seventy miles up the Shatt-al-Arab. Shufeldt found that Muscat, under the rule of Sultan Turki ibn-Said, was no longer an important independent power.[12] The commodore also discovered that American commercial interests remained strong, constituting two-thirds of Muscat's trade.[13] More opportunities abounded despite the American government's unwillingness to provide diplomatic and military assistance.

Shufeldt reported on conditions in the gulf. "There is no place in the world where the physical manifestation of power is so necessary for the diffusion of the knowledge of the moral power of a civilized Nation as among

Ticonderoga anchored in Venice, c. 1865–1869.

An English Lake

the semi-barbarous and barbarous peoples that dwell upon these shores."[14] He also found that few knew of the existence of the United States, and he reported that the dominant British were less than eager to foster American competition.[15] Great Britain, Shufeldt recognized, had made the gulf an "English Lake."

Despite manifestations of British power, Shufeldt viewed the British imperium as a facade. Arabs, Turks, and Persians appeared willing, even eager, to see another power replace Britain in the gulf. The American commodore also foresaw that a future challenge in European waters might weaken the British empire in the East, perhaps fatally. He hoped that Americans would pursue their own interests and challenge Britain commercially and diplomatically and not "continue to play the role long ago assigned to us in China—of No. 2 Englishmen?"[16]

Shufeldt was also among the first Americans to look beyond mere commercial interests to broader strategic or geopolitical concerns, observing that Persia was a focal point of the Anglo-Russian imperial struggle in the region.[17] A quarter-century later, a more vocal American naval officer, Alfred Thayer Mahan, similarly outlined the importance of the Persian Gulf[18] especially the significance of Turkey and Persia as bulwarks against Russian expansion—a proto-Northern Tier.* Absent from Mahan's strategic observations on the Persian Gulf was but one major consideration—oil!

The industrial revolution changed the face of the world. By the turn of the century machine power had replaced most of the power formerly supplied by humans, animals, wind, and water. Coal, which had long since replaced wood, was now being supplanted by petroleum. Although it could not have been apparent to Mahan writing in 1900, industrialization in Europe, North America, and Japan, along with the growing demand for oil to fuel that industrialization, would by mid-century make the Persian Gulf region critically important to the world.[19]

The strategic significance of the region steadily increased even early in the century. Of the world's industrial and military powers, only the United States and Tsarist Russia were major producers and exporters of oil.[20] The remaining powers were, therefore, forced to rely on foreign, usually American imports, or to look abroad for new sources of oil.

In May 1901 Englishman William Knox D'Arcy gained an oil concession from the Shah that covered the whole of Persia except the five northern provinces. The first major strike at Masjed Soleyman seven years later heralded the beginning of the oil age in the Persian Gulf. In April 1909 the

---

*"Northern Tier" is a term coined by Secretary of State John Foster Dulles to describe those states in the Middle East that lay close to the southern border of the Soviet Union. States frequently included in the various definitions of Northern Tier include Greece, Turkey, Iran, Pakistan, and Afghanistan.

No. 2 Englishmen

During his visit to the Persian Gulf in 1879, Rear Admiral Robert W. Shufeldt recognized the opportunities for Americans to challenge the commercial and diplomatic domination of the British in the region.

newly established Anglo-Persian Oil Company (APOC) began work on a pipeline to move oil from the fields to the gulf for shipment. Construction begun on a refinery at Abadan in 1910 was completed three years later.[21]

Petroleum also became associated with a particular facet of the might of a modern industrial state—sea power. On the eve of the First World War the desire for a secure supply of oil for the Royal Navy drove the British government into formal involvement in the management of APOC. Admiral Sir John "Jackie" Fisher was the Royal Navy's main proponent of oil as the replacement fuel for coal in warships. His advocacy of petroleum earned him the sobriquet "Oil Maniac" as early as 1886.[22]

Fisher recognized that oil-fueled ships were cleaner, faster, more easily refueled and maintained, and had superior endurance.[23] Technological advances like Rudolf Diesel's 1892 internal combustion engine made petroleum especially useful for smaller vessels such as torpedo-boat destroyers and submarines. Even the mammoth dreadnoughts constructed after 1904 could use oil to produce steam to propel the ship.[24] If the British were to maintain their naval advantage, they would have to lead or at least keep pace with this technology.

The problem was supply: Britain had no known oil reserves of its own. Fisher's appointment to the Royal Commission on Fuel Oil in 1912 led to a recommendation that the government establish storage facilities and refineries, construct tankers, and secure control of a source of oil. In August

An English Lake

1914, on the commission's recommendation, the British government purchased a controlling share in APOC for £2.2 million.[25]

British concern about having access to oil and maintaining the security of its position in the gulf extended beyond Persia. In 1912 the British entered into an agreement with German and Dutch interests to jointly develop the oil resources of the Ottoman Empire, principally in the area that would become Iraq after the empire's dissolution. Elsewhere in the gulf Britain pressured the local sheiks and emirs to refrain from granting oil concessions to any non-British company.[26]

While the United States had no need for the petroleum of the gulf, by 1900 American petroleum giants were interested in developing Middle Eastern resources for purely commercial reasons. The Ottoman Empire, long the focus of U.S. commercial and missionary activity, now became a target of the fledgling American oil industry. Retired Rear Admiral Colby Chester led an American syndicate that negotiated a railroad, mining, and oil concession with Constantinople, although the Turks failed to ratify the agreement before the outbreak of the First World War.[27] Standard Oil Company of New York obtained licenses for oil exploration in northern Anatolia and Palestine, but here too the war intervened before drilling began.[28]

The First World War accented the importance of oil, especially American oil, to the industrial world and heightened interest in the potential of the Persian Gulf. Armies with their motor transport and air forces with their aircraft joined navies in their increasing reliance on petroleum.

In the Middle East, the Ottoman Empire's alignment with Germany and Austria-Hungary brought it defeat and dissolution. British imperial operations in Palestine and Mesopotamia drove the Turks from the Red Sea and Persian Gulf coasts of the Arabian Peninsula. Despite early setbacks the Mesopotamian campaign shielded British positions in the gulf and protected APOC interests in southwestern Iran, where oil production and refinery capacity increased 400 percent during the war. By 1918 the German threat had disappeared; the Russian peril also receded, at least temporarily, amidst revolution and civil war.

British power flowed into the resulting vacuum, with Palestine, Iraq, and Kuwait coming under Great Britain's influence and control. Other than France, entrenched in Lebanon and Syria, no foreign power could threaten Britain's seemingly supreme position in the Middle East.[29]

Great Britain attempted to make the most of its victory and adopted a determined national oil policy that sought to secure control over what was now recognized as a vital strategic resource.[30] APOC expanded its concession through further agreements with the Shah in Persia.[31] In Iraq the British considered their former concession with the Ottoman Empire still valid and pressed for further oil-field development. Anglo-French cooperation in the Middle East, embodied in the 1915 Sykes-Picot agreement to divide the Ottoman Empire, became apparent at the San Remo Conference of April

1920. French companies were granted a 25 percent share in the Turkish Petroleum Company, soon to become the Iraqi Petroleum Company (IPC), in return for an agreement to support the construction of a pipeline from the northern Iraqi fields to the Mediterranean across French-controlled Syria.[32]

British actions in the Middle East, especially the San Remo agreement, infuriated American diplomats and the oil industry. At the end of the war representatives of American oil companies returned to Palestine and Mesopotamia and found themselves excluded from commercial activity. APOC officials plus the Soviet refusal to allow the transport of crude oil through the Caucasus to the Black Sea frustrated American efforts to gain a concession in the northern provinces of the Persian empire.[33]

Although Americans after the war were in a panic about how long their oil reserves would last (ten years according to official government estimates), the administrations of Woodrow Wilson and Warren G. Harding failed to develop a resolute petroleum policy and allowed those wartime measures that had coordinated business and government oil activity to lapse.[34] American diplomats at Versailles refused the requests of the American oil industry to press for concessions during the peace negotiations, preferring to wait until the fate of the Ottoman Empire was decided. American diplomatic efforts on behalf of the oil industry were limited to outraged protestations of British behavior, declarations of America's Open Door policy, and a refusal to recognize the legitimacy of the IPC.[35]

The United States had been an "associated" rather than a fully allied power during the Great War and had never declared war against the Ottomans. In addition the United States had not ratified the League of Nations Treaty under which the mandates of the Middle East were administered. Thus the British, who had borne most of the cost of defeating the Turks, saw no need to share the spoils of war with the Americans.

Despite the American reluctance to play a major role in world affairs, the United States remained an international power. As a result, Middle East doors did open to American oil companies during the 1920s.[36] Faced with a resurgent nationalist Turkey that seemed intent on recovering the oil-rich Mosul province, Britain eventually sought American involvement in the development of the petroleum industry in Iraq, to which Mosul was ultimately given.[37] Most important, British oil companies lacked the capital to develop the vast area they had staked out.

Between 1922 and 1928 British and American oil companies negotiated the terms of the latter's involvement in Iraq and, with the acquiescence of the State Department, bought into the British-dominated IPC. Following the settlement of the boundary dispute between Turkey and Iraq that led to new agreements between the IPC and the Iraqi government, and major oil strikes in 1923 and 1927, several American oil companies signed the infamous Red Line agreement on 31 July 1928.[38] The accord established a multinational cartel within the area bound by a red map-line around the former Asiatic territories of the Ottoman Empire, an area that included much of the Arabian Peninsula. For the United States, the agreement marked the end of its fight not to recognize the IPC as well as a setback for the government's Open Door policy. Nevertheless, American oil companies did establish themselves in the Persian Gulf, principally through their own efforts.

Eager Americans also sought concessions in Kuwait, Bahrain, and the Arabian Peninsula itself. British companies held the concessions to explore for petroleum throughout the region, but efforts to find British companies willing and able to purchase these rights often failed. Capital-rich American firms were soon on the scene with ready cash.

As a result, American companies were instrumental in the development of the petroleum industry throughout the Persian Gulf.[39] By the early 1930s the oil industry in Bahrain, which had become a strategic base for British military forces in the gulf, was firmly in the hands of the United States.[40] Gulf Oil Corporation became a partner in the formation of the Kuwaiti Oil Company.[41]

The most significant American penetration into the region came in the formerly British-dominated, politically divided Arabian Peninsula.[42] In the early 1920s the monarch, Abdul Aziz, known as ibn-Saud, needed cash to consolidate his hold over the tribes of his newly established Saudi Arabian state and looked eagerly for loans and the royalties that came with oil development. In 1923 a British consortium negotiated an oil concession with ibn-Saud for Al-Hasa in the northeastern part of the peninsula along the Persian Gulf but failed to exercise its rights. Following the 1932 Bahrain strike in a formation that geologists believed extended into the adjoining Al-Hasa region, the bid to develop Saudi oil resumed; Standard Oil of California (Socal), already operating in Bahrain, won a sixty-year concession for the newly formed California-Arabian Standard Oil Company.[43]

Between the world wars the petroleum industry in the Middle East expanded enormously. Oil production in the Persian Gulf region increased 900 percent between 1920 and 1939. Iraq, Bahrain, and Saudi Arabia joined Iran as major producers. Less than 5 percent of non-U.S.-produced oil had come from the gulf in 1920; by 1939 the figure had grown to 14 percent.[44]

American corporations increasingly fueled the region's development. Britain may have held a monopoly of military power in the gulf, but American capital challenged the British economically during the 1920s and 1930s. British-dominated Iran remained the source of about two-thirds of Persian Gulf oil, but American participation in the IPC and control of the oil concessions in Bahrain and Saudi Arabia demonstrated a growing American presence. The fact that the petroleum concession for Bahrain, the strategic center of the British position in the gulf, fell into American hands perhaps best illustrates the point.

2

The Second World War and the Persian Gulf

During the First World War British imperial forces had been able to defend the Middle East. Between 1939 and 1945, however, internal and external threats compelled Britain to rely on American and Soviet forces to redress the imbalance of power in the region.

The Second World War revealed the inherent weakness of Britain's strategic position in the Persian Gulf. Early in the war, pro-Axis sentiment in Iran and Iraq threatened the security of Britain's major sources of oil. British and Indian army forces crushed the short-lived Iraqi coup of May 1941 at the expense of the campaign in Libya against the Germans and Italians.

The Axis invasion of the Soviet Union in June made overland communications through Iran of great importance. A friendly Iran was indispensible to the Allied war effort, and the presence of German advisers in the country led to a crisis that summer. When the reigning monarch, Reza Shah Pahlavi, refused to expel the Germans, British forces invaded from the south while Soviet troops invaded from the north. The Allies forced Reza Shah to abdicate in favor of his son, Mohammad Reza Shah Pahlavi, who signed the Anglo-Russian-Persian Treaty of January 1942. The treaty legitimatized the joint occupation but also guaranteed the territorial integrity and political independence of Iran.

External threats also imperiled Britain's position in the Middle East. Between June 1940 and December 1942 the British faced threats from the north, where the Germans nearly broke through Soviet positions in the Caucasus; the west, where German-Italian forces in Libya menaced Egypt; the south, where Italian-controlled Ethiopia and Somalia fronted the Gulf of Aden and the Red Sea; and the east, where Japan's army invaded India, and the Imperial Japanese Navy sortied into the Indian Ocean.[1]

By early 1943 the British had secured their position in the Middle East but, unlike the experience of the First World War, they did so only with major assistance from their allies. Russian troops were entrenched in northern Iran. American sea, ground, and air forces had engaged the Axis in North Africa and had arrived in the Persian Gulf to secure the overland lend-lease route to the Soviet Union.

Despite the importance of oil to the prosecution of the war, early threats to Britain's position in the Middle East impeded the development of the petroleum industry in the Persian Gulf region. Fears that the oil fields might be overrun by Axis forces, lack of capital (especially in the case of

An English Lake

Britain), and the interruption of overland and sea communications slowed and, in some cases, reversed development trends. Decreased production and reduced royalties exacerbated tensions between the Allied powers and the gulf states, especially in Iraq and Iran.[2]

Qatar, Oman, Kuwait, and the Trucial States, all latecomers to oil development and reliant on British capital, also suffered.* British-dominated companies capped wells and postponed development. Only late in the war did Kuwait, where the consortium included capital-rich American concerns, resume production.[3]

Bahrain and Saudi Arabia, where the controlling interests were American, fared much better.[4] Stephen Hemsley Longrigg, an IPC official at the time and historian of Middle East oil development, noted that the marked decline in oil production in British-dominated areas "gave throughout the Middle East an impression . . . that the tempo of American development far exceeded the British."[5] Only in late 1942 and early 1943—with the Allies cut off from oil supplies in the southwestern Pacific, the Middle East secure, the Mediterranean reopened to sea communication, and the Western Allies' economies and military forces expanding—did demand for Persian Gulf oil force increases in production.

While the war threatened and weakened Great Britain's strategic position in the Middle East, the global conflict started to bring about a revolution in American oil policy that ultimately increased U.S. economic participation in the Persian Gulf and, for the first time, direct military involvement as well. Using bureaucratic controls established during the Great Depression, the administration of President Franklin D. Roosevelt oversaw a massive wartime effort to increase the production of petroleum products both at home and abroad.[6] Harold Ickes's Petroleum Administration for War (PAW), a further development of earlier bureaucratic regulatory agencies created by Roosevelt during the 1930s, made the government the arbiter of the oil industry. For the first time the U.S. government had a national oil policy linked to its foreign policy.[7] Moreover, Ickes believed that expanded production could best be achieved if the U.S. government became an actual partner in the oil industry, much as the British government was a stockholder in APOC, and that such government-industry cooperation could be continued into the postwar period.[8] Nevertheless, no formal agreement was made to ensure U.S. government participation in overseas oil development, and American oil companies remained independent.

PAW was successful in overseeing a rapidly expanding oil industry. Between December 1941 and August 1945 the United States supplied 80 per-

---

*They were named the Trucial States because of their adherence in 1853 to a maritime truce to be enforced by the British.

Second World War

SC 197017 U.S. Army

Allied ships off-load war supplies in the Iranian port of Khorramshar for delivery overland to the Soviet Union in early September 1945.

cent of the oil for the Allied war effort. Petroleum products constituted more than half the total tonnage of war material shipped from the United States.[9]

Ickes's bureaucrats assigned the Middle East both production and refining increases under the 1941 Foreign Production Program. Military concerns about the security of the region, voiced early in the war, retarded the execution of plans to expand gulf refining. Nevertheless, Persian Gulf refinery capacity increased by 89 percent between 1938 and 1944. A February 1944 PAW technical report labeled the Persian Gulf "the center of gravity" for future oil development.[10] Moreover, by the end of the war, specialized refined product, such as high octane aviation gas, Navy Diesel, and Navy Specialized Fuel Oil, were being produced in the Persian Gulf at Abadan, Bahrain, and Ras Tanura, Saudi Arabia.[11]

By 1945 the Middle East had assumed a special prominence in American eyes. The United States, anxious to avoid a second postwar clash with Britain over the region's oil, sought to reach an agreement to govern postwar development and to ensure an "open door."

Under Ickes the official government involvement sought by the oil industry unfortunately became tied to plans for joint government-industry participation. The American oil industry's fears of government regulation and intervention led the industry to reject a preliminary accord struck by Brit-

13

ish and American negotiators in August 1944. Industry representatives accepted a revised 24 September 1945 agreement, but peace ended the sense of wartime urgency and the treaty lay before Congress unratified.[12]

Nevertheless, the very course of the Second World War and the growth of American diplomatic, economic, and military involvement in the region ensured that American oil companies would play a leading role in the Persian Gulf. The Lend-Lease programs, for example, that were extended not only to Britain and the Soviet Union, but ultimately also to Iran and Saudi Arabia, brought the American military into the region. Throughout the gulf, the United States constructed pipelines; built and improved airfields, roads, railroads, port and storage facilities; and bolstered communications. The war also strengthened the newly established American positions in Bahrain and Saudi Arabia, and provided the United States ingress to Iran, Britain's major oil supplier.

Iranians were understandably concerned about their national future; their country had been invaded and occupied and their previous monarch forced to abdicate. Not long after the Americans reached the gulf as part of an Anglo-American team planning improvements to the Iranian State Railway, many Iranians started to look to the United States for support against Britain and the Soviet Union, much as the hard-pressed Persian monarchy had done in the 1850s.[13] Now, looking to the postwar period, the Iranians once again offered American companies oil concessions in the north as a lure to involve the United States in the postwar security of Iran. Reluctant to do anything that might upset the Grand Alliance, the United States put off any such negotiations until the end of the war.[14]

In the interim there were some limited actions that the Americans could take to help Iran. Although the Anglo-Russian-Persian Treaty of January 1942 had prevented Iran from entering the war on the side of the Allies, the United States declared Iran eligible for Lend-Lease support. In late 1942 and early 1943 the United States established American military advisory missions in Iran to build up the nation's gendarmerie and army to ensure internal security.[15] Such support was indispensible if the young Shah was to reassert governmental authority when and if the Soviets and the British withdrew. In addition to this advisory presence, the American Persian Gulf Service Command grew by the end of the war to a force of 30,000 men, most of whom were in Iran.[16]

In late 1943 the Iranians formally directed their national concerns to Allied leaders during the Teheran Conference. In response, the Declaration of the Three Powers Regarding Iran, signed on 1 December 1943 by Churchill, Stalin, and Roosevelt, regularized the presence of American forces in Iran. It also noted the special hardships imposed by the wartime occupation and guaranteed Iranian postwar territorial integrity and independence.[17] Thus, as payment for tolerating the Anglo-Soviet occupation and an extensive American presence, Iran received a formal commitment of support from the United States.

In the Arabian Peninsula, ibn-Saud, much like the young Shah, increasingly looked to the United States for assistance, although initially to little avail. The war had lowered oil revenues and depressed the usually lucrative pilgrimage traffic to Mecca. Ibn-Saud's financial problems were evident to British and American observers concerned about the possible pro-German sympathies of the monarch.[18] At first, ibn-Saud viewed Britain as the more important power in the region and considered the United States to be a nation with but a passing interest in the affairs of the gulf region.[19] Thus Britain initially bore the financial costs of supporting ibn-Saud's rule when the California-Arabian Standard Oil Company proved unable, and the U.S. government proved unwilling, to supply the advances and loans demanded by the king. The British quickly increased aid to ibn-Saud after the Iraqi revolt in the spring of 1941. Roosevelt, despite the position of the American oil companies, still considered the peninsula to be a British sphere of interest.[20]

President Roosevelt's unscheduled visit with King ibn-Saud of Saudi Arabia on the Great Bitter Lake symbolized America's interest in the Middle East.

An English Lake

King ibn-Saud's entourage waits on the carpeted deck of the destroyer *Murphy* during the king's post-Yalta meeting with President Roosevelt on board the heavy cruiser *Quincy*.

Although the American oil industry was concerned by the increasing British wartime presence in Riyadh, the main worry was the potential internal collapse of the Saudi monarchy.[21] Not until early 1943, with British economic power waning and British skepticism about ibn-Saud's ability to govern growing, did American aid become significant. The extension of Lend-Lease to Saudi Arabia and increased oil production ended the immediate threat that the monarchy would collapse.[22]

The symbol of American interest in Saudi Arabia was, of course, President Roosevelt's February 1945 unscheduled, face-to-face, post-Yalta meeting with ibn-Saud on the Great Bitter Lake in the Suez Canal. At the President's orders, the American destroyer *Murphy* (DD–603) carried ibn-Saud and his retinue from Jidda to the meeting. Although the discussion focused on Palestine rather than on finances or the future of Saudi oil, the meeting confirmed the growing importance of Saudi Arabia to the United States and demonstrated to ibn-Saud that the United States might well play a more permanent postwar role in the region.[23]

Just what kind of role the American government would play in the Persian Gulf after the war remained a subject of debate in the United States; debate initially focused on the construction of an air base in Dhahran,

Second World War

Saudi Arabia, on the western shore of the gulf. The base had originally been intended to provide a link between Cairo and Karachi for the "redeployment of U.S. forces to the Far East and to increase the efficiency of present and contemplated military air transport operations through the Middle East."[24] After the end of the European war, proponents of the base argued that construction should be completed.

> The oil resources of Saudi Arabia, among the greatest in the world, must remain under American control for the dual purpose of supplementing and replacing our dwindling resources, and of preventing this power potential from falling into unfriendly hands.... The U.S. should have preferred nation status in Saudi Arabia in the event that the construction of military and naval bases in the Persian Gulf area becomes necessary.[25]

Even the impending end of the Pacific war failed to shake the resolve of those advocating the construction of the air base.[26] The Near and Middle East Subcommittee* of the State-War-Navy Coordinating Committee (SWNCC) concluded:

> Thus the world oil center of gravity is shifting to the Middle East where American enterprise has been entrusted with the exploitation of one of the greatest oil fields. It is in our national interest to see that this vital resource remains in American hands, where it is most likely to be developed on a scale which will cause a considerable lessening of the drain upon the Western Hemisphere reserves.... Evaluation of the airfield project cannot be based wholly on questions of utility as an airfield. There are ramifications in the realm of U.S.-Saudi relations that make this issue complex.[27]

As Acting Secretary of State Joseph C. Drew had earlier made clear in a memo to Truman, once the United States had secured ibn-Saud's permission to build the airfield after considerable diplomatic effort, it could not easily change course and drop the project. The Saudi monarch would likely "gain the impression" that American policy toward Saudi Arabia was "of a wavering character," and such action "would contribute to his existing uncertainty as to the extent to which he may rely upon the United States."[28]

On 28 September 1945 President Harry S. Truman approved the continued construction of the air base at Dhahran.[29] His decision symbolized the fusion of American military and economic interests in the Persian Gulf and demonstrated an intent to expand the U.S. role in the region after the war.

---

*Near East refers to Greece, Iran, and Turkey, as well as those Arab countries to the south such as the Levant states, those of the Arabian peninsula, Iraq, and Egypt.

PART TWO

Establishing a U.S. Military Presence in the Persian Gulf, 1946–1950

At the end of the Second World War the United States, unconcerned about possible threats to its commercial and petroleum interests in the Middle East, initiated the rapid withdrawal of American forces from the region.

This optimistic outlook on the prospects for global harmony was quickly challenged. In late 1945 and early 1946 the Soviet Union tested American resolve in the Near East, leading to crises in Turkey and, even more alarmingly, in Iran. The Truman administration also became increasingly aware of what has since become known as "interdependence." Persian Gulf oil supplies were crucial to the recovery of war-torn Europe. That recovery was critical to the economic and political stability of a Western Europe threatened not so much by Soviet military power as by the political specter of communism. European economic health, in turn, was indispensible to the sustained expansion of the American economy. Moreover, although the United States had imported virtually no oil from the Middle East in the 1940s, the American military continued to draw heavily, as it had during the war, on Middle East oil supplies.

By the eve of the Korean War, the United States had become a major diplomatic power in the region and had established a limited naval presence—the Middle East Force—in the Persian Gulf.

3

The Iran Crisis of 1946

During the Second World War strategic planners envisioned a world in which U.S. military power would be exercised in the Western Hemisphere and the Western Pacific. In December 1943, Secretary of the Navy Frank Knox spoke of a postwar "working agreement between the British and the American navies which assigns to the British fleets control of the Eastern Atlantic, the Mediterranean and the Indian Ocean. The U.S. Navy guards the Western Atlantic and the entire Pacific.... There is the backbone of the postwar naval police force, already organized and functioning."[1] As a result, while American naval officers were aware that great-power troubles were brewing and knew that the British wanted and expected American postwar assistance, the U.S. Navy planned and began to execute a complete withdrawal from European waters.[2]

Aggressive Soviet behavior in the immediate aftermath of the war, especially pressures applied against Great Britain in the Near East, caused U.S. policymakers to reassess their assumptions but failed to bring about any immediate shifts in policy.[3] For example, despite evidence of Soviet machinations in the Near East, a Joint Intelligence Committee report of 31 January 1946 virtually wrote off northern Iran.

> Current Soviet moves with respect to Iran and Turkey appear to include the establishment of governments "friendly" to the U.S.S.R., and to bring these areas within the limits of the Soviet security zone. The recent *fait accompli* in Iranian Azerbaijan has virtually achieved Soviet aims in northern Iran.[4]

Three weeks later the Joint Chiefs of Staff (JCS) approved a memorandum recommending that the United States avoid military commitments in the Near East.[5]

The Soviet military moves in northern Iran marked the culmination of an extended campaign of intimidation that had been going on since July 1945. At the Potsdam Conference the Soviets had resisted American and British efforts to force a withdrawal of Russian troops from Iran before the deadline (set for six months after the end of the war) agreed to in Article Five of the Anglo-Soviet-Iranian Treaty of January 1942. When the Japanese surrendered on 2 September 1945, the deadline became automatic, and the Soviets would have to withdraw by 2 March 1946.[6] Concerns over Soviet intentions in Iran heightened when, not long after the Potsdam meeting in July 1945, Soviet-sponsored separatists in Azerbaijan and Kurdistan, under the political leadership of the Democratic Party of Azerbaijan, began seizing control

Establishing a Military Presence

of these areas. When the Iranian government sent troops north to reassert central authority, Soviet troops blocked the way and "threatened to fire if [the] stop order [was] not obeyed."[7]

American diplomats in Teheran and Washington understood that governmental authority in Iran was tenuous. Many elements in Iran were less than enthusiastic about the increasing authority of the monarchy begun under Reza Shah and that would continue under his son.[8] There were also legitimate nationalist sentiments in Iran, especially among the non-Iranian Turkic, Armenian, and Kurdish peoples of the northern and western provinces.

The Russians themselves had several real grievances with the Iranians.[9] But it was clear that the Soviets had both exacerbated and manipulated these tensions to create a puppet regime in the area under their control. From Moscow the American chargé George F. Kennan warned that "nationality" tactics had been used before "in Bessarabia, Ruthenia and Eastern Poland and [were] currently evident with respect to Sinkiang and Turkish Armenia."[10]

The Iranian crisis came to a head in the first days of March 1946. Moscow simultaneously pressured Turkey for control of Kars and Ardahan in eastern Anatolia. Soviet ground and air forces concentrated in Bulgaria and began to prepare for offensive operations in Turkey. The movement of Russian forces through northern Iran towards eastern Anatolia also appeared to be part of a concerted effort to attack or, at the minimum, to unnerve the Soviet Union's two southern neighbors.[11] As Truman later wrote, "Iran would be required to negotiate with Russia while a gun was at her head."[12]

In late winter Stalin cocked the trigger. On 4 March American Vice Consul Robert Rossow, Jr., observed Soviet mechanized troops moving through Tabriz in the northern Iranian province of Azerbaijan. These forces were headed south, "Teheranward," and not north towards the Soviet border. Despite the 2 March deadline for the withdrawal of Soviet troops from Iran agreed to at the Potsdam Conference, Stalin had decided to reinforce his army in northern Iran.[13] Rossow later wrote, "One may fairly say that the Cold War began on March 4, 1946."[14]

So too did acute American concern for the security of the Near East. Over the next few days Soviet-American relations deteriorated rapidly and an atmosphere of crisis and near-war hysteria swept through the United States. On 5 March in Fulton, Missouri, Winston Churchill delivered his famous Iron Curtain speech. Churchill spoke of the "shadow" that had fallen "upon the scenes so lately lighted by the Allied victory." Iran, the former British prime minister noted, was "both profoundly alarmed and disturbed" by Soviet "claims" and "pressure."[15] From Washington that very evening, Secretary of State James Byrnes sent a telegram to Moscow for George Kennan to deliver to Soviet Foreign Minister Vyacheslav Molotov, asking the Soviets to clarify their intentions with regard to Iran.[16] On 6

Iran Crisis of 1946

Loy Henderson, Director of the State Department's Near Eastern and African Affairs office during the 1946 Iranian crisis.

National Archives 59JB383

March the State Department announced that the battleship *Missouri* (BB–63) would carry the remains of the late Turkish ambassador Mehmet Münir Ertegün to Istanbul. Although State had rejected the Navy's proposal to send Vice Admiral Marc A. Mitscher's Eighth Fleet, including an aircraft carrier, to the Mediterranean, the dispatch of *Missouri* was still a significant show of American interest in the region.[17]

Throughout the day of 7 March the State Department's Office of Near Eastern and African Affairs (NEA) monitored the deteriorating situation in Iran. NEA Director Loy Henderson ordered his Special Assistant, Edwin M. Wright, to prepare a large map of Azerbaijan on which to plot Soviet moves. Wright showed the map, covered with arrows indicating the depth of the Russian penetrations, to Secretary Byrnes at 1800 that evening. Byrnes remarked "Now we'll give it to them with both barrels."

The following morning, an updated map was used to brief other State Department officials. Undersecretary of State Dean Acheson, alarmed by the Soviets' failure to respond to Byrnes's telegram and by continued reports from Rossow in Tabriz of Russian moves towards Teheran, eastern Turkey, and Kurdistan, decided that the United States should make certain that the Soviet Union understood that Washington was aware of what was going on in Iran.[18] At Acheson's direction Alger Hiss "scribbled" a draft statement for

Establishing a Military Presence

Byrnes's signature that would convey American concerns to Moscow but leave the Kremlin "a graceful way out" of what was becoming a major crisis. That afternoon the department forwarded a second telegram for Kennan to deliver to the Peoples' Commissar for Foreign Affairs.[19]

> The Govt of the US has the honor to inform the Govt of the Soviet Union that it is receiving reports to the effect that there are considerable movements of Soviet combat forces and materials of war from the direction of the Soviet frontier towards Tabriz and outward from Tabriz in the direction of Tehran, Mahabad and various points in Northwestern Iran.
>
> The Govt of the US desires to learn whether the Soviet Govt, instead of withdrawing Soviet troops from Iran as urged in the Embassy's note of Mar 6, is bringing additional forces into Iran. In case Soviet forces in Iran are being increased, this Govt would welcome information at once regarding the purposes therefor.[20]

From Moscow George Kennan cautioned the United States that no attack was imminent. Stalin had not prepared the Russian people for any such undertaking. Kennan reported that the Soviet moves were part of a coordinated plan meant to succeed "by sheer force of intimidation." He believed that the Soviets would remain "just this side of the line" to avoid "a complete diplomatic break with [the] British." The American chargé and the Soviets apparently saw the British as the major bulwark against Russian expansion towards the Mediterranean and the Persian Gulf. Acknowledging that the Russian war of nerves was fraught with danger, Kennan reminded Byrnes that the Kremlin did not "blunder casually into situations, implications of which it has not thought through."[21]

In his famous "Long Telegram" of 22 February, Kennan had advised what course the United States should follow:

> Soviet power, unlike that of Hitlerite Germany, is neither schematic nor adventuristic. It does not work by fixed plans. It does not take unnecessary risks. [It is] impervious to logic of reason, and it is highly sensitive to logic of force. For this reason it can easily withdraw—and usually does—when strong resistance is encountered at any point. Thus, if the adversary has sufficient force and makes clear his readiness to use it, he rarely has to do so. If situations are properly handled there need be no prestige-engaging showdowns.[22]

As Kennan predicted, Stalin, faced by a resolute response from the Iranians, Americans, and British, ordered Soviet forces to withdraw from Iran on 24 March.[23] By the end of May Russian troops had recrossed the border, leaving the Azerbaijani regime on its own. Nevertheless, the crisis continued as the Iranian government tentatively attempted to reestablish its control over the northern provinces. No one could be sure how Stalin would respond as the Soviet-sponsored Tabriz regime—gradually, ingloriously, and ultimately bloodily—collapsed at the approach of the Iranian army.

Iran Crisis of 1946

Despite the apparent diplomatic victory in Iran, an Office of Naval Intelligence report of September 1946 pessimistically concluded:

> Russian political exploitation of Iranian Azerbaijan, widespread clandestine penetration of rest of Iran, equivocal attitude of Premier Ghvam, wholly amorphous politico-economic situation, degeneracy all aspects of Iranian national life suggest inevitability of eventual Russian suzerainty whole country.[24]

The Iranian crisis of 1946 marked major departures in postwar American policy. The United States adopted a more confrontational approach to its relations with the Soviet Union and also began to rethink its policy towards the Middle East.

Truman decided the time had come to stop playing "compromise." Truman did not base his decision on any determination of the strategic importance of either the Persian Gulf or its oil to American national security. A frustrated President had simply grown "tired of babying the Soviets." The crisis over Iran was the proverbial "straw that broke the camel's back."[25] Truman's new hard-line approach towards the Soviets was applicable not just to the Middle East but to other points of contention in Europe and Asia as well.[26]

Although Iran had been the diplomatic focus of the March 1946 crisis, American diplomats and strategists in general were far more concerned about Turkey. By the end of the year the United States had reversed its military withdrawal from the European waters and become an eastern Mediterranean naval power. The Turks became the chief recipients in the Near East of American military aid. Iran received far less military and economic assistance than this western neighbor. Two years passed before the U.S. Navy established a permanent presence in the Persian Gulf.

On 6 March 1946, in the midst of the Iranian crisis, Secretary of State Byrnes asked the Joint Chiefs of Staff for "an appraisal from the military point of view" of Soviet demands on Turkey, "bearing in mind the possible effect on the security interests of the United States of any undue threat to the security interests of the British Commonwealth of Nations in that area."[27] The JCS responded that the Soviets sought to dominate the Middle East and the Mediterranean as a way to defend their own southern resource regions, to secure control of additional areas, and to undermine the prestige of Britain and the United States in "the Moslem world." Turkish concession to Soviet control of Kars and Ardahan in eastern Anatolia would weaken Turkey and provide a springboard for further moves into Turkey or Iraq or towards the Persian Gulf. With regard to the Turkish Straits, the JCS concluded "a demand for additional bases in or near the Dardanelles cannot be based on a purely defensive attitude since the Soviets now possess and undoubtedly will retain the military capability of closing the Straits at will."

Establishing a Military Presence

National Archives 80–G–702557

The presence of battleship *Missouri* off Istanbul, Turkey, in 1946 showed American interest in the region and was aimed at deterring Soviet intervention in the Middle East.

Britain's fate in the Middle East particularly troubled the JCS: "The defeat or disintegration of the British Empire would eliminate from Eurasia the last bulwark of resistance between the United States and Soviet expansion." Soviet success against Turkey would also undermine the effectiveness of the United Nations Organization. The Joint Chiefs recommended that the United States not acquiesce in meeting any of the Soviet demands.[28]

Unfortunately the immediate military prospects for the United States in the event of a war with the Soviet Union were dismal. A 13 March estimate by the JCS of the "Availability of Land, Sea and Air Forces in the Event of Emergency" pessimistically concluded that even if the Truman administration halted demobilization on 1 April and cancelled or postponed Operation Crossroads (the atomic test scheduled for the Pacific, which required commitment of Navy and Air Force assets), little could be done to defend the Middle East.[29] An April 1946 outline of the course an "unlikely" Soviet-American war might take was particularly bleak. The JCS concluded that the Soviet Union had "the capability of overrunning Iran, Iraq and possibly the Suez Canal area, European Turkey, and making major inroads into Asiatic Turkey."[30] Not surprisingly, the Joint Chiefs were concerned about the inadequacy of the American military if the Near East crisis led to war.[31]

Not until September did the State Department ask the JCS for an analysis of American "strategic interests in Iran" comparable to the one requested by Byrnes on Turkey in March. The initial report prepared by the Joint Strategic Survey Committee (JSSC) focused on petroleum. The JSSC estimated that the United States could wage war for two years without Middle East oil, in the event of a Soviet-American conflict, but thereafter shortages would handicap operations. "If, during a major war, the United States and her allies are deprived of the oil resources of the Iran-Near and Middle East area it is highly improbable that other sources can supply the United States military and economic requirements together with those of her possible allies."

The Soviets too, the JSSC concluded, needed Middle East oil. "In a major war the USSR would at present require oil from the Iran-Near and Middle East area to meet her military and economic requirements." A sound American strategy would seek "*a*. To deny the oil resources of the Iran-Near and Middle East area to the USSR as long as possible, and *b*. Ultimately to regain the use of these resources for herself and her allies." The JSSC recommended that the JCS forward to SWNCC an enclosed memorandum, which considered Iran "of vital strategic interest to the United States" and recommended that the United States provide Iran with "nonaggression" military assistance and advice as a "token" measure of goodwill and support.[32]

At the direction of Fleet Admiral William D. Leahy, Chairman of the JCS, the Joint Chiefs toned down the draft memorandum. The JCS's 11 October response to SWNCC termed Iran "an area of major strategic interest," a defensive "cushion" that offered opportunities to delay any Soviet drive towards the Persian Gulf and provided "one of the few favorable areas for counteroffensive action." The JCS stressed the need to support Iran if the United States was to maintain its reputation in the Middle East and throughout the world.

To secure Iranian central authority and to prevent Soviet moves into the area, "nonaggression" military equipment could be provided to the Iranians. Nevertheless, the 11 October memorandum was restrained in its call for assistance and ended with the reminder that "the military implications in the existing international situation concerning Iran are closely related to the military implications of the current Turkish situation, on which the Joint Chiefs of Staff furnished their views to the Secretaries of War and the Navy on 24 [sic] August 1946."[33]

In mid-October the State Department issued revised policy positions on Iran and Turkey.[34] As the crisis in Iran dragged on and Britain appeared to weaken in its support of Iranian territorial integrity, the Near Eastern and African Affairs Office completed a memorandum on the "Implementation of

Establishing a Military Presence

United States Policy Toward Iran."[35] The State Department's policy went somewhat further than the JCS recommendations regarding the provision of "nonaggression" military equipment to the Iranians. Three days later a draft memorandum on Turkey was ready.[36] Like the Iran statement it was "partially based upon the JCS memorandum." Recognizing that the Soviet's "unrelenting war of nerves" forced Turkey to keep large military forces in the field and posed "a dangerous drain on the nation's economic strength," NEA proposed diplomatic, moral, economic, and military support for the Turks. The memorandum suggested that the military support come from the British, "because the world in general has become accustomed to the fact that Turkey receives arms from Britain." If Britain proved unable to supply such assistance, NEA suggested that American military aid be channeled through the British.

Nevertheless, in Iran and Turkey as elsewhere in the region, the United States accelerated the once-gradual process by which it supplanted positions previously held by Great Britain. By 1947 the United States was clearly the most important foreign power in the gulf. For example, the Iranian policy elite had determined that the United States was central to any effort to maintain the integrity of Iran. The "century-old strategy of *movazaneh* (equilibrium)," wrote Stephen L. McFarland, "endeavored to attract the United States to act as a buffer and counter-balance the Anglo-Soviet threat."[37]

In the spring of 1946 the United States demonstrated its willingness to act as a "buffer" in Iran, at least diplomatically, but remained reluctant to pick up the military burden of the region's defense. For the next three decades the United States sought to avoid military commitment to the defense of the Persian Gulf, with mixed success.

4

The Oil Scare of 1947–1948

In the initial postwar period (1946–1947), strategic factors other than oil shaped American policy towards the Persian Gulf region. Although many historians have been quick to point out American oil concerns in the Persian Gulf, Loy Henderson wrote in 1946:[1]

> The most important interest of the United States in the Near East is not based, as a fairly large section of the American public appears to believe, upon American participation in petroleum extraction or in profits to be derived from trade, but upon preventing developments from taking place in that area which might make a mockery of the principles on which the United Nations Organization rests, which might lead to the impairment, if not the wrecking, of that organization, and which might eventually give birth to a third World War.[2]

The Iranian crisis had been sparked not by any perceived menace to Western oil supplies but by what the Truman administration viewed as a Soviet threat to the postwar world order. NEA's memorandum of October 1946 on U.S. policy towards Iran never once mentioned oil.[3] Of the three Northern Tier states—Greece, Turkey, and Iran—only Iran possessed petroleum; nevertheless, between 1946 and 1953 it received the least American diplomatic, economic, and military support. And despite the supposed criticality of oil, American strategists continually resisted efforts to make any kind of major military commitment to the Persian Gulf.[4]

Although it is difficult to separate Western concerns about the security of Middle East oil supplies from broader strategic interests in the post-World War II period, those interests did exist. The British, after all, had been confronting the Russians in the Near East for a century, well before the discovery of oil. Threats to Britain's imperial lifelines, epitomized by British control of the Suez Canal, and the maintenance of bases in the Middle East from which the West could strike at the southern Soviet Union, remained factors in British policy considerations, and by connection, American policy considerations as well.

Nonetheless, between 1943 and 1950 several remarkable changes occurred in the world oil situation that advanced the strategic importance of oil and altered the focus of American policy in the Persian Gulf. The United States saw its share of world oil production fall from 70 percent to 51 percent, while that of the Persian Gulf states rose from 7 percent to 16 percent. Moreover, the United States, long the world's premier oil exporter, proved unable to maintain this position in the postwar world. In 1946 American petroleum exports were more than twice the barrels imported;

Establishing a Military Presence

by 1950 imports were almost twice as high as exports, and the latter had fallen back to prewar levels.

TABLE 1

World, U.S., and Persian Gulf Petroleum Production
(in 000 metric tons)

	World	U.S.	%	Gulf	%
1930	177,200	123,117	70	7,157	4
1935	200,800	134,675	67	11,445	5
1940	262,000	182,867	70	12,950	5
1945	333,000	231,575	70	25,590	7
1946	356,000	237,526	68	34,276	9
1947	390,000	254,382	65	41,012	10
1948	441,000	276,738	62	55,853	12
1949	465,000	248,919	53	68,542	15
1950	522,900	266,708	51	85,925	16
1955	772,800	335,744	43	159,779	20

SOURCE: United Nations, *Statistical Yearbook, 1949–1950* (New York, 1950), table 41; and 1956 and 1957 editions.

Concern about the drain on the petroleum resources of the New World had begun during the Second World War. In April 1944 the State Department's "Foreign Petroleum Policy of the United States" had called for the "curtailment, in so far as practicable, of the flow of petroleum and its products from Western Hemisphere sources to Eastern Hemisphere Markets, ... [and the facilitation] by international agreement and otherwise, of substantial and orderly expansion of production in Eastern Hemisphere sources of supply, principally in the Middle East, to meet increasing requirements of postwar markets."[5]

Anxiety about dwindling American oil reserves became serious during 1947 and 1948.[6] American concerns were rooted not in the availability of domestic petroleum supplies but in the inability of the United States to resume its pre-1939 role as the major oil exporter to the world. At a 2 May 1947 lunch Navy secretary James Forrestal and Senator Owen Brewster discussed oil.

> I [Forrestal] said that Middle East oil was going to be necessary for this country not merely in wartime but in peacetime, because if we are going to make the contribution that it seems we have to make to the rest of the world in manufactured good, we shall probably need very greatly increased supplies of fuel.
>
> Brewster said that ... Europe in the next ten years may shift from coal to an oil economy and therefore whoever sits on the valve of Middle East oil may control the destiny of Europe. He expressed considerable misgivings about the capacity of American forces to keep Russia out of Arabia if they decided to move there.[7]

Forrestal had recognized the value of Middle East oil supplies during the war. In December 1944 he wrote the Secretary of State about "the strategic interest of the Navy" in Saudi Arabia.[8] Forrestal agreed with those State Department officials who believed that it would be in the long-term interest of the United States to draw upon Middle East reserves, then considered the largest outside the Western Hemisphere, as much as possible so that the nation could conserve its petroleum for the future. Soviet moves in Iran, as well as his belief that support for Zionism would threaten the American position in the Arab world, increased Forrestal's apprehension.

During the Iran crisis, the Navy's Political-Military Policy Division began a study of the world oil situation and presented Forrestal with a report in October 1946. During the Second World War Persian Gulf oil had been critically important, supplying "the British 8th, 9th, 10th, and 14th Armies, the Mediterranean and Indian fleets, as well as India, Africa and the Middle East, and the U.S. Persian Gulf command, the 9th U.S. Air Force, the Eastern Bomber Command, the China-India-Burma A.T.C., the Flying Tigers, the 20th Air Force and the African Middle Eastern Service Command." Although the report dismissed many of the fears of an impending domestic oil shortage, it stressed the long-term need for secure reserves and the growing importance of Middle East supplies. Like Forrestal had two years before, the report recommended drawing on Middle East supplies to preserve American reserves and called for the development of a national oil policy.[9] Forrestal and other American policymakers hoped to increase American reliance on foreign suppliers to exhaust those reserves while American petroleum reserves remained in the ground. But despite such policy recommendations, the United States continued to export massive quantities of oil.

In 1947 domestic shortages developed. On 17 January 1948, President Truman announced stringent governmentwide standards meant to conserve fuel in the midst of an energy-short winter.[10] Truman acted in response to a growing national perception that the United States was in the midst of an energy crisis. Four days before, Secretary of the Interior Julius Krug had warned that the nation faced a critical petroleum situation in twenty-four of the forty-eight states, especially in the Northeast. Rationing was a possibility. Moreover, American oil reserves could be exhausted within ten years. Krug recommended government support for programs to extract oil from shale and to find alternate supplies of energy.

At a 16 January cabinet meeting, Krug had indicated that postwar American domestic demand for oil was 50 percent higher than the prewar level. While the United States was importing 450,000 barrels of oil a day to meet the demand, exports had risen almost 100 percent over the prewar levels, and 450,000 barrels a day were being exported. Secretary of Defense Forrestal remarked "that the Marshall Plan for Europe could not succeed without access to the Middle East oil, that we could not fight a war without access to it and that even in peacetime our economy would be unable to maintain its present tempo without it."[11]

On 19 January Forrestal warned Congress that the oil shortage threatened American national security. The United States would find itself short 2 million barrels of oil a day if a third world war broke out. Forrestal also publicly voiced his concerns about the administration's decision to support the partition of Palestine; in his view this position threatened not only American supplies, especially those on which the U.S. military was increasingly relying, but also the oil that would have to fuel the planned European Recovery Program, or the Marshall Plan. Forrestal hoped that increased American production, especially from newly discovered fields in Alaska, would help ease the situation, but he expected that the United States would have to rely on Persian Gulf suppliers. He suggested that it would be a "good approach" for President Truman to establish a special commission to draw up a national energy policy.[12]

TABLE 2

U.S. Petroleum Exports and Imports

(in 000 barrels)

	Imports	Exports
1930	43,489	132,794
1935	20,396	74,343
1940	41,089	78,970
1945	39,282	149,985
1946	51,610	119,687
1947	61,857	118,122
1948	59,051	94,938
1949	81,873	86,307
1950	132,547	76,483
1955	170,143	122,617

SOURCE: Ben J. Wattenberg, ed., *The Statistical History of the United States: From Colonial Times to the Present* (New York: Basic Books, Inc., 1976), pp. 596–97.

The oil scare of 1948 was less a harbinger of a dramatic oil shortage than a result of a short-term imbalance between production and demand. The booming postwar U.S. economy had begun to expand faster than the output of the world's oil companies as the industry adjusted from wartime to peacetime production.

By mid-1947, restrictions on the use of domestic oil led the U.S. Navy to purchase oil overseas from the refineries constructed to supply military-quality naval fuel during the Second World War. In the fall Forrestal told

Oil Scare of 1947–1948

National Archives 80-G-K-6842

The oil shortage of 1948 led Secretary of the Navy James Forrestal to suggest a national energy policy.

Congress that further development of Saudi oil fields and the construction of a pipeline from those fields to the eastern Mediterranean was "essential."

> I took the position that because of the rapid depletion of American oil reserves and an equally rapidly rising curve of consumption we would have to develop resources outside the country. The greatest field of untapped oil in the world is in the Middle East. . . . We should not be shipping a barrel of oil out of the United States to Europe. From 1939 to 1946 world oil reserves . . . went up about 60 per cent while American discoveries added only about 6 per cent to ours.[13]

Despite the growing shortage in the United States throughout 1947 and into 1948, the administration continued to permit the export of oil, even to the Soviet Union. Not until February 1948, after initial opposition by the Truman administration, did the Commerce Department respond to congressional calls for a halt to petroleum exports. The situation had become so critical that the Navy was forced to turn over one million barrels of oil for domestic use in East Coast cities.[14] Eleven states and the District of Columbia borrowed fuel oil from the Navy. According to a 14 September Navy press release, "the Navy reduced its stock to a bare minimum to meet

33

Establishing a Military Presence

the emergency." Not surprisingly, the Navy turned increasingly to overseas suppliers, contracting with the international oil company Caltex to purchase nearly 100 million barrels of refined product over five years at rates lower than that available domestically.[15]

By early 1949 the oil shortage had evaporated. In January Truman ended federal conservation measures. Even Forrestal began to sound less pessimistic, noting "that we could, by the application of strict rationing in the United States, fight a war for a considerable period of time without access to the Middle East."[16] Some people in Congress began to ask whether there had ever really been a shortage and blamed the oil companies for the previous year's problems. In June, Texas state regulators restricted production, fearing a glut.

Nevertheless, the oil fright of 1948 forged the connection between American energy needs, containment of the Soviet Union, and the Middle East. By 1948 the two strains of American interest in the region—concern over the "Great Game" being played by Britain and Russia, exemplified at the end of the nineteenth century by Shufeldt and Mahan, and the American desire early in the twentieth century to participate in the development of the region's oil—had come together and firmly established the importance of the Middle East and its oil to American national security. To these were added petrostrategic concerns, awareness that the reconstruction of war-torn Western Europe, the continued economic prosperity of the United States, and the fundamental imperative to contain Soviet expansionism depended upon the oil supplies of the Persian Gulf.

By 1948 the U.S. postwar military withdrawal from the Persian Gulf had been reversed. The oil scare of the late 1940s propelled the United States into deeper diplomatic and military involvement in the Persian Gulf, epitomized by the establishment in 1949 of the U.S. Navy's Middle East Force (MEF).[17]

5

Establishment of the Middle East Force

The pressing need for fuel for the fleet brought the ships of the U.S. Navy to the Persian Gulf in the post–World War II era. That dependence began with the expansion of refinery capacity in the region during the final years of the Second World War. Subsequently, domestic shortages, lower prices, and geographic propinquity to naval operating areas increasingly led the Navy to look to the gulf for fuel produced in the refineries built or expanded by the British and the Americans during the Second World War.

From 1946 to 1950, between 30 and 42 percent of the petroleum products moved by the U.S. Navy came from the Persian Gulf.[1] American men-of-war in the Mediterranean and the Pacific relied almost exclusively on Persian Gulf fuels. Moreover, the majority of some critical petroleum products came from the gulf. Between July 1946 and June 1947, 55 percent of the Navy's Special Fuel and 52 percent of its diesel fuel came from Bahraini and Saudi refineries.[2]

Each month the Navy transported between 1.5 million and 5 million barrels of product from the Persian Gulf to the Mediterranean or the Pacific in its oilers and in chartered tankers. The movement of as many as two dozen ships through the Persian Gulf necessitated the establishment of facilities to monitor and control such a large-scale logistical effort.[3] The possibility that the United States might have to fight in the region in wartime also led the Navy to conduct extensive surveys of this new area of operations.

Admiral Richard L. Conolly, Commander in Chief, Northeastern Atlantic and Mediterranean (CINCNELM), based in London, controlled all American naval forces in European and Indian Ocean waters, including those of the Persian Gulf.[4] Conolly believed it was imperative that the U.S. Navy assure the nations of the Old World that the United States would not revert to its "policy of isolationism, as we had after World War I, but would continue to maintain a potent interest, an interest that we would back up with force, if necessary—by the show of force, the presence of force—in that area, and thereby hearten them in their opposition to the spread of Communism."[5]

Conolly formalized and improved the Navy's command structure in the Persian Gulf. CINCNELM Operation Plan 1–48 of 20 January 1948 established Task Force 126, U.S. Naval Force, Persian Gulf. The task force consisted solely of tankers in the gulf to load oil and was commanded by the Senior Officer Present Afloat (SOPA). Conolly reported that "the formation

Establishing a Military Presence

of this new command reflected the Navy's increasing interest in this area as evidenced by additional oilers operating from the Bahrain-Ras Tanura area and the scheduled visits of one or more carrier task forces later in the year."[6] On 29 October Conolly reorganized and subdivided TF 126–TF 126.1, MEF Administration (ashore); 126.2, Survey Group; 126.3, Tanker Group. CINCNELM also established a permanent command position for the force, initially held by Commander Robert C. Woolverton, who was relieved in December 1948 by Captain William V. O'Regan.[7] On 26 June 1949 Conolly turned over operational command of American naval forces in the gulf to the commander of the renamed Persian Gulf Forces.[8] On 16 August 1949 the command was renamed yet again—Middle East Force.[9]

Conolly struggled to place the small command on as firm a basis as possible. In both London and Washington there was a growing sense that the U.S. Navy's role in the Persian Gulf area should be "an operation similar to that now enjoyed in the Mediterranean," where the Sixth Task Fleet, a large force meant to deter Soviet aggression and stiffen the resolve of pro-Western states, had been formed under the command of a vice admiral.[10] At a conference held in Washington in June 1948, Conolly had recommended the appointment of a flag officer and the stationing of a permanent command vessel in the Persian Gulf-Indian Ocean area.[11] But despite the growth of Middle East Force in size and significance and the deployment of a flag ship to the gulf, three years passed before a rear admiral assumed command. Nevertheless, under Conolly's direction MEF was established, and the United States has since maintained a permanent naval presence in the Persian Gulf.

Central to the control and smooth functioning of the American effort in the Persian Gulf-Indian Ocean area was the extension of naval support and logistics facilities to the region. In the summer of 1947 the Navy established a plan for its oilers "to facilitate communications between ships and INSMAT (Inspector of Naval Material) Bahrein and to expedite loading these oilers."[12] By mid-1948 the Navy had established stations in Ethiopia at Asmara and in Saudi Arabia at Dhahran, and had leased facilities for fuel storage at Massawa, Ethiopia; Aden; and Trincomalee, Ceylon.[13]

Recognizing that the U.S. Navy would operate in the Persian Gulf for the foreseeable future, and that the region could become an area of operations in a Soviet-American confrontation, the Office of the Chief of Naval Operations (OPNAV) in October 1947 planned a Persian Gulf cruise for August 1948. The Navy wanted to test its equipment and personnel under the extreme conditions of the gulf, conduct visits to suitable ports, and gather amphibious data and other intelligence.[14] The initial plan called for a force of ten ships, including an aircraft carrier, to conduct hydrographic, photographic, and other reconnaissance of the area stretching from the Suez Canal to the Persian Gulf.[15]

Middle East Force

Carrier *Valley Forge* and F–8F Bearcat fighters during the 1948 spring cruise to the Persian Gulf.

Although commitments elsewhere forced the Navy to alter its plans, a task force that included the carrier *Valley Forge* (CV–45) and other naval units did visit the Persian Gulf during the year. The results of extensive reconnaissance and scientific surveys indicated that environmental conditions in the gulf posed significant, though not insurmountable, problems. Because of the "unbearable heat," most work was best performed early in the day and only essential watches were stood in the afternoon. One captain wrote that the heat was so intense that he did not believe that his crew "could think straight."[16] Another report concluded:

> It was found that all berthing and messing spaces for the crew were untenable with temperatures up to 115°F and high humidity. The officers and crew slept topside on cots or on the deck. Sick Bay was moved topside. The crew was fed on the fantail with mess gear set up, and chow lines passing through the galley. Officers and CPOs ate in their messes, but meals were short and the Wardroom and CPO messes were deserted except for fifteen minutes at meal hours. The uniform aboard, except when rendering honors, was shorts and undershirts.... The shower water was too hot to use except for short periods. The alterations submitted to BuShips were based on those incorporated in HMS Wild Goose and HMS Wren, of the British Persian Gulf Squadron. These ships were fairly comfortable.[17]

Establishing a Military Presence

Captain Harry D. Felt (right) relieves the Middle East Force commander, Captain Ernest M. Eller, in the spring of 1951

Conditions were somewhat better ashore. The Navy operated from Bahrain, the major British base in the Persian Gulf. American sailors played softball with oil company personnel and had access to the British recreation facilities for both officers and men at Jufair, outside Manama. Despite short supplies the Royal Navy even shared its beer, but U.S. Navy commanders reported that American sailors were less than enthusiastic about the "poor quality" of the two bottles of "Scotch beer" allowed each man; they recommended that "Navy tankers destined for the Persian Gulf load a supply of American beer for use by recreation parties."[18] Irregular mail service, another source of complaint, was often a cause of poor morale.

Americans found the Arabs of the gulf hospitable and impressed by displays of U.S. Navy might. When the carrier *Valley Forge* visited Ras Tanura in the spring of 1948, bad weather unfortunately forced the cancellation of most of the planned fight operations, including a flyover by the carrier's aircraft—in a formation that spelled S-A-U-D. Nevertheless, the tour of *Valley Forge*, a limited air demonstration, and a showing of the film *Fighting Lady* greatly impressed Crown Prince Saud of Saudi Arabia and his retinue.[19]

The visit of the escort carrier *Rendova* (CVE–114) to Bahrain was similarly well received. About twenty members of the Bahraini royal family came on board *Rendova* for a demonstration that included several catapult launchings and a Navy film about carrier operations. But a more prosaic piece of technology most interested the Bahrainis; apparently drinking ice water from the ship's water-coolers was the prize indulgence for the royal retinue. The congenial mood continued ashore when the sheik threw a massive dinner for the Americans that was marked by inordinate amounts of food (including Sunkist oranges) served in splendid Arab fashion.

By 21 April 1951, when Rear Admiral Harry D. Felt relieved Captain Ernest M. Eller as commander, Middle East Force had become a symbol of the U.S. military and diplomatic interest in the region. A flagship, a pair of destroyers, command aircraft based at Bahrain or Dhahran, tankers, and, occasionally, additional combat, support, and survey vessels cruised the strategic shipping lanes of the gulf and the Indian Ocean. They "supplied much needed intelligence, maintained liaison with all allied military and diplomatic forces present, conducted both informal and official calls on civilian and military dignitaries in all countries and pursued an active type people-to-people program." [20]

The search for fuel for its fleet had brought the U.S. Navy to the Persian Gulf and led to the establishment of a small but permanent force in the heart of the Middle East after the Second World War. The economic requirements of the United States and the West gave an added importance to the American naval force as its mission evolved. Captain Eller, Commander Middle East Force (CMEF), wrote Chief of Naval Operations Forrest P. Sherman early in 1951: "Great nations are stirring and great events are shaping up in this part of the world. I hope the United States will comprehend them and will be equal to the opportunity." [21]

PART THREE

Assuring Access to Adequate Oil Supplies, 1950–1981

Between 1950 and 1980 the United States faced innumerable challenges in the Middle East: the never-ending Arab-Israeli dispute, rising Arab nationalism, internal discord in Iran, and the growing economic and strategic importance of a region too important to surrender but too distant to defend. The situation tested American resolve, complicated American policy, threatened regional stability and American interests, and led to ever-deepening political involvement in the region.

As Britain's inability to carry the military burden of defending the Persian Gulf became increasingly evident, planners in Washington continually reassessed the situation but, just as consistently, they rejected calls for a significantly increased American military commitment. When the British announced in the late 1960s that they would no longer bear the burden of defense "East of Suez," the United States chose to rely on the regional powers.

The major American military involvement in Indochina, which began in 1964 and lasted until 1973, further impaired development of an American policy in the Middle East, a region of far greater economic and strategic importance than Southeast Asia. The U.S. policy of relying on regional powers in the Middle East collapsed in January 1979 when the Shah of Iran fled Teheran. Ultimately, the United States had little choice but to shoulder a conventional military commitment in defense of the region.

6

Arab Nationalism and the Defense of the Middle East

In the immediate aftermath of the Second World War, American policymakers confronted the realities of Arab nationalism. The war had accelerated and strengthened the forces of nationalism and anticolonialism already at work in the Islamic world. The newly independent and quasi-independent Middle East states struggled to assert themselves nationally and often collectively as Arabs, to protect their Islamic way of life, and survive in a dangerous, rapidly changing environment.

The United States entered the post-World War II era without any imperialist baggage in the Middle East. Unlike the British, French, and Russians, Americans had no history of territorial aggrandizement in the region, and the anticolonial tenor of American wartime policy appealed to the Arabs. The United States supported Arab governments in Beirut and Damascus during the Levant crisis of 1945 when the French attempted to reimpose colonial control in Lebanon and Syria.[1] As a result, much like the Iranians and the Turks who benefitted from similar American support in 1946, the Arabs initially viewed the United States as a counterweight to those powers intent on asserting or reasserting colonial influence and control.

Nevertheless, as the United States became more involved in the region, attempts to achieve American policy aims were bound to lead to occasional conflicts with Arab governments. In the highly volatile and unstable Middle East, the United States could not forever escape the opprobrium that often comes with international leadership.

The most pressing problem facing the United States in the Middle East was what Dean Acheson termed the "Puzzle of Palestine."[2] The debate over Palestine was highly charged. In the Middle East, Jews imbued with Zionist aspirations and post-Holocaust determination to secure a homeland confronted Arab nationalists who violently opposed such settlement. In the United States the politics of the debate frequently overshadowed the more pragmatic concerns of American foreign policy.

The extent to which domestic political concerns shaped American policy towards Palestine has been and will continue to be debated. President Truman's motivations may well have represented "a deep conviction," as Acheson believed, or "the disastrous and regrettable fact that the foreign policy of this country was determined by the contributions a particular bloc of special interests might make to party funds," as Secretary Forrestal presumed.[3] What is certain is that American political leaders controlled the debate and overruled the political-military bureaucracy. Dean Acheson later wrote that "it was clear that the President himself was directing policy on Palestine."[4]

The American military had expressed anxiety about the possible impact of the Palestine question on American policy in the Middle East in early 1946.[5] The Joint Chiefs of Staff were concerned that a pro-Zionist policy might force an already overstretched American military establishment to commit forces in Palestine, drive the Arabs into the Soviet camp, complicate American Middle East policy, threaten the West's strategic position in the region, and lead the Arabs to deny the United States access to Middle East oil.[6] As the crisis continued, JCS apprehensions increased. An October 1947 paper concluded:

> The Joint Chiefs of Staff are of the opinion that implementation of a decision to partition Palestine, if the decision were supported by the United States, would prejudice United States strategic interests in the Near and Middle East and that United States influence in the area would be curtailed to that which could be maintained by force. Further, there is grave danger that such a decision would result in such serious disturbances throughout the Near and Middle East area as to dwarf any local Palestine disturbances resulting from the decision. As a consequence the USSR might replace the United States and Great Britain in influence and power throughout the area.[7]

As the Joint Chiefs considered the potential problems of evacuating Americans from the volatile region, they reiterated a June 1946 recommendation that the United States not make any decision that would lead to the commitment of American forces into Palestine or turn the Middle East away from the United States, since the United States had a vital security interest in the area.

American military leaders grew even more alarmed when the diplomatic debate at the United Nations appeared likely to lead to a proposed United States-Soviet Union trusteeship and occupation of Palestine. To the prospect of American military intervention in a region torn by violence and terrorism was added the possibility of Soviet diplomatic involvement in the Middle East.[8] In early February 1948 Chief of Naval Operations Admiral Louis E. Denfeld argued that such an outcome would lead to all kinds of problems and the continued "deterioration" of the American position in the Arab world.[9] Nevertheless, the JCS dutifully prepared contingency plans that projected extensive force requirements for Palestine (100,000 troops) as well as a plan to secure Jerusalem.[10]

The surprising, if not shocking, victory of the newly established Israeli state over its Arab neighbors in the 1948 war dramatically altered the character of U.S. Middle East policy. The American military establishment performed a rather dramatic volte-face. The JCS, which no longer had to

Arab Nationalism

concern itself with the possible dispatch of American forces to Palestine, stopped producing papers that argued against American support for a Jewish state and began studying the "U.S. Strategic Interest in Israel."[11] These American military assessments early in 1949 were as overly optimistic as previous appraisals had been alarmist. JCS reports began to tout the advantages of a strategically located base in Palestine. A May 1949 report concluded that U.S. policy ought to endeavor to assure Israel's Western orientation, seek to reconcile the differences between Israel and its Arab neighbors, and work to include Israel in any regional defense pact.[12]

In September and October 1949, the National Security Council (NSC) formalized more sober and realistic assessments that established the basic outlines of American Middle East policy for the next four decades. NSC 47/2 concluded that the "Eastern Mediterranean and the Near East" were critically important to American security. The United States had to engage in "impartial" but "constructive leadership" to promote pro-Western ties, prevent Soviet penetration of the region, and ensure that disputes internal to the region did not prevent Middle East states from acting "in concert to oppose Soviet aggression." With regard to the Palestine problem the NSC argued that although Israel and her Arab neighbors had to reach an accord on their own, such an agreement ought to include the resettlement of all refugees, either within Israel or in neighboring Arab states.[13]

National Archives 80–G–453225

Rendova in Bahrain.

Assuring Oil Supplies

Israel's 1948 victory made the interposition of American troops between Arabs and Jews unnecessary, but the crises in the region continued. The Arabs, stung by their defeat at the hands of the Israelis, vented much of their anger and frustration at the West, especially the United States.

Nevertheless, despite the worst fears of many in the political-military bureaucracy in the 1940s, American policymakers managed (and continue to manage) to juggle the interests of "the competing nationalisms" in the Middle East. Combined with a perceived Soviet menace, the realities of American political, economic, and military might ensured that the United States remained a recognized and respected, if not admired, power throughout the Middle East. But those same realities themselves took on menacing aspects. The United States, as a world power and as a purveyor of materialist mass culture, threatened traditionalist, rapidly modernizing Islamic states. American support for Israel placed the United States in direct conflict with the dreams of Arab nationalists. These dual realities gave the postwar Arab-American relationship a schizophrenic character.

For the U.S. Navy in the Persian Gulf the paradoxical nature of this relationship became apparent during *Rendova*'s 1948 visit to Bahrain.[14] After the sumptuous banquet thrown by the Bahrainis for the Americans, the latter reciprocated, but only sixteen of the more than sixty Arabs invited attended the American reception. The *Rendova*'s commander received an explanatory note.

> To the Commanding Officer and Officers of the U.S.S. RENDOVA:
>
> We thank you for your kind invitation to your ship but regret that owing to the present policy of the United States towards the Palestine affair and Arabs, we can not accept your invitation.
>
> Bahrein   20/5/48 With best respect,
>   Yours
>
>   [signed in Arabic by 54 Arabs][15]

The Bahraini refusal to attend the American dinner shortly after feasting *Rendova*'s crew symbolizes the U.S. experience in the Persian Gulf. Parallel interests, combined with underlying tensions generally have led the Arab states to welcome only a circumscribed American presence in the region. In times of crises a threatened state might well set aside its pan-Arab concerns and allow, or even request, an expanded American presence. But if the crisis in question involves Israel, the Arab reaction could easily expand beyond mere symbolism.

Nationalist ferment in the Middle East further complicated Western efforts to develop a framework for the defense of the region. Despite growing concern

Arab Nationalism

George McGhee, Assistant Secretary of State for Near Eastern, South Asian, and African Affairs, favored U.S. involvement in a Middle East defense organization.

National Archives 306–PS–49–4690

about the security of the Middle East, between 1946 and 1950 the United States not only refrained from direct military commitment to regional defense, but also resisted British suggestions for the establishment of a Middle East command.[16] At the March 1950 Cairo conference American representatives continued to argue that "it would be impractical and undesirable for the United States to encourage any Near Eastern regional defense pact."[17]

But by late 1950, with the situation in the Middle East becoming increasingly unstable, American thinking about Britain's proposed Middle East Command had begun to change. With its adherence to the North Atlantic Treaty Organization (NATO) the United States had broken with its historic tradition of avoiding peacetime "entangling" alliances. The war that began in Korea in June 1950 and the subsequent Chinese Communist intervention had raised the specter of a possible Soviet attack against the Middle East. Tension over Palestine, which had complicated Arab-American relations, seemed to be lessening. George C. McGhee, Assistant Secretary of State for Near Eastern, South Asian, and African Affairs and a leading proponent of a Middle East defense structure, noted that "the UK, which has the primary responsibility for the defense of the area, lacks both manpower and resources successfully to defend the area and has no plans for defense of Saudi Arabian oil fields and the Dhahran Air Base." McGhee proposed:

47

Assuring Oil Supplies

> To establish (for political as well as military reasons) a combined US-UK command structure in the Middle East which would stimulate basic cooperation among the states of the area not now possible through indigenous organizations or groupings such as the Arab League. This structure would not alter the fact that the UK and Commonwealth have primary responsibility for the defense of the area.[18]

By the summer of 1951 the American military, although still unwilling to commit forces to the region, had fallen into step with the State Department and had come to support the establishment of a Middle East defense organization.[19] American and British political and military representatives quickly worked out satisfactory preliminary agreements on the nature of a regional command structure to be headed by Great Britain.

But Britain, which as the power "responsible" for the Middle East took the diplomatic initiative within the region, found few Middle East countries eager to align themselves with the West. The Turks were an exception. As the only Near East power with a sizable, effective military, they were indispensible to the Middle East Defense Organization (MEDO). Unfortunately, they were reluctant to join a Middle East security framework until they had been accepted within the European defense community—NATO. In Iran, because of disputes over oil, and in Egypt, because of disputes over the Suez Canal, the British faced strong nationalist challenges. Rising Arab and Iranian nationalisms, the still-fresh legacy of colonial rule, and the somewhat antagonistic attitude of British diplomats handicapped efforts to reach settlements with Teheran and Cairo.

Egypt and the Suez Canal were the strategic keys to the Middle East for Great Britain. Egypt was a historic bastion of imperial strength, a complex that in the event of another world war would witness a buildup of United Kingdom and Commonwealth forces and serve as a base for a strategic bombing campaign against the Soviet Union. But far from leading to an agreement over the Suez Canal and British basing rights, a necessary precursor to any regional alliance, Anglo-Egyptian negotiations led to disorder and outright military action in early 1952. The outbreak of violence not only dashed hopes for an accord but aggravated existing nationalist sentiments, bringing down the heretofore relatively pro-Western Egyptian government and ultimately leading to the July 1952 overthrow of King Farouk by army officers, among them Gamal Abdel Nasser. Subsequent efforts to interest the new Egyptian government in MEDO were destined to fail.

7

The United States and Iran

The British and Americans also faced challenges in Teheran, for the Arabs held no monopoly on nationalist and anticolonial sentiment. Iranian nationalism manifested itself in a variety of forms, at times conducive and at times harmful to Western interests in the Persian Gulf. Nationalist Iranians had withstood Soviet threats in March 1946. In March 1951 those same nationalists pushed their government to nationalize the oil industry in Iran, principally the wholly British-owned Anglo-Iranian Oil Company (AIOC).

Several factors led to the ensuing crisis. Most Iranians viewed the long-standing agreements with the AIOC as symbols of British imperial political and economic domination. During the early stages of the negotiations, which began in 1948, the British were understandably unwilling to weaken their control of strategically important concessions. However, after the December 1950 American settlement with the Saudis, in which the Arab-American Oil Company (Aramco) agreed to a fifty-fifty split of net operating revenue (retroactive to 1 January 1950), there should have been little hope that the Iranians would agree to anything less. Continued AIOC recalcitrance toward nationalization fed Iranian intransigence and generated increased popular support for nationalization.[1]

The United States did not favor nationalization, although it recognized the right of sovereign states to do so, provided "just compensation" was made. Moreover, with regard to Iran the State Department did not oppose AIOC nationalization because to do so would "jeopardize politically US and West in Iran and might result in loss of Iran to Sovs."[2]

American concern over the situation was genuine, for Iran was no longer considered strategically expendable. "Strictly from the United States military point of view," a 1951 JCS memorandum noted,

> Iran's orientation towards the United States in peacetime and the maintenance of the British position in the Middle East now transcend in importance the desirability of supporting British oil interests in Iran. The Joint Chiefs of Staff would be forced immediately to reexamine their global strategy in the event that the USSR breached the Truman Doctrine in regard to Iran by measures short of war.[3]

A mid-March 1951 draft report prepared by the National Security Council reiterated points made in earlier assessments: Iran was a "key strategic position" and a screen for Middle East oil-producing areas. "Iranian oil resources are of great importance to the economies of the United Kingdom and Western European countries," the report argued, and the "loss of these

Assuring Oil Supplies

The Arab-American Oil Company refinery in Saudi Arabia, 1952.

resources would affect adversely those economies in peacetime." Moreover, if Iran "fell," neighboring countries, with the exception of Turkey, would probably also succumb to Soviet pressure. The draft concluded that "for these reasons, the United States should continue its basic policy to take all feasible steps to assure that Iran does not fall victim to communist control," strengthen the Iranian government, and, in the event of Communist internal subversion, consider options such as "correlated political action by the United States and United Kingdom." [4]

It is significant that the final version of the report approved by President Truman equated the Iranian government with the person of the Shah. NSC 107/2 of June 1951 appraised the Shah as the "only present source of continuity of leadership," and spoke of the need to "strengthen the leadership of the Shah and through him the central government." [5]

Despite the language of NSC 107/2, not all U.S. policymakers considered the Shah to be a strong leader or the prospects good for a stable Iran. Few Americans viewed Iran as a national and governmental entity comparable to Turkey or Greece.[6] At best, Iran was a country in transition from absolute monarchy to a constitutional form of government. In the interim, unfortunately, it possessed neither the attractions of a democracy nor those redeeming attributes of stability and strength often associated with a despotically ruled state. The Iranian Majlis (parliament) was seen as the bastion of the landowning class, not the voice of the people; the military, as corrupt and incompetent, incapable of providing either effective internal security or even slowing a Soviet attack; and the Shah, as a weak and indecisive ruler, not the Shah-of-Shahs familiar to Americans in the 1960s and 1970s. In January 1951 CINCNELM Admiral Robert B. Carney offered a dismal "appraisal of Persian capabilities."

> The key to Persian intentions and capabilities is to be found in the character of the Persians; there is nothing in the analysis of Persian character which gives rise to any reason for placing dependence of Persian intentions nor confidence in Persian ability to resist major Russian armed aggression.[7]

Not all the reports coming from Iran and the Persian Gulf were negative. Captain Ernest Eller, Commander Middle East Force in 1950, provided a rather optimistic picture of the situation in Iran and advised the Navy's senior leadership to reject the views of those who warned that the Iranians were useless and incapable of improvement. Eller recommended that the United States provide Iran with aid and loans on the same scale as Turkey.[8]

Eller's recommendations paralleled those of the Shah, who blamed the unstable internal political situation in Iran partly on the lack of American aid.[9] The Shah believed that only the provision of an aid package similar to that provided Greece and Turkey would give Iran "something dependable to rely on." [10]

> American support for Greece and Turkey would extend even to armed hostilities if either of those countries were the victims of open Soviet aggression. [The Iranians] are not certain with regard to Iran and feel that their greatest danger lies in this uncertainty. If the Soviet Govt knew definitely that an attack on Iran would mean armed hostilities with the United States, they feel that the Soviet Union would not attack. They are afraid, however, that if any doubt on the subject is allowed to continue in the Kremlin, Iran may become the victim of aggression.[11]

The Shah and many Iranians also felt that American military assistance ought to be provided free, rather than as part of a loan package.[12] The Shah and pro-Western Iranians saw the extension of the Truman Doctrine, the Economic Cooperation Administration, and extensive economic and military aid packages to Greece and Turkey but not Iran as an expression of an unwillingness on the part of the United States to commit itself to Iran's defense.

The American military was, in fact, reluctant to obligate itself to the defense of Iran or any other Middle East country. As they had between 1946 and 1949, JCS studies conducted in the early 1950s routinely outlined the strategic importance of the Middle East but habitually rejected proposals for any formal American commitment to the region's defense. A Joint Strategic Survey Committee report of October 1950 concluded that

> the loss of Western Europe would represent a most serious blow to the Western Powers. The loss of the Middle East in the early stages of a global war

Assuring Oil Supplies

President Truman and the young Reza Shah Pahlavi of Iran.

would not in itself be fatal, although the recapture of the Middle East would be essential for victory. The strategic defense contemplated for the Far and Middle East indicates that those areas are, for planning purposes, now considered to be in a lower category than Western Europe.[13]

The Persian Gulf was geographically remote. Estimates of the resources necessary to conduct an effective defense far exceeded the capability of the American military, which was already fully committed elsewhere in Europe and the Pacific, including the stalemated war in the Korean Peninsula until mid-1953. The JCS supported the much talked-about establishment of the multinational MEDO. However, they refused to commit American forces to it and recommended that the obligation for the defense of the Middle East "should be accepted by the British as a British responsibility, and that they should develop, organize, and as necessary provide forces for an effective defense thereof."[14]

When the Iranian internal situation deteriorated rapidly in 1952, Truman's National Security Council adopted a more forceful policy. NSC 136/1 of 20 November concluded that present trends in Iran were unfavorable for the long-term survival of a non-Communist regime. Soon the only alternative to the National Front led by Prime Minister Mohammed Mossadegh, which was systematically wresting political power from the Shah, the landlords, and other traditional power centers, would be the Communist Tudeh party. Moreover, the ability of the National Front to maintain control of the situation indefinitely appeared uncertain. The political upheaval that brought the nationalists to power had heightened popular desire for economic and political improvements and reforms, but the failure to restore the oil industry to operation had led to the progressive deterioration of the economy. Although a Communist takeover seemed unlikely during 1953, the NSC concluded:

> [T]he Iranian situation contains very great elements of instability.... It is clear that the United Kingdom no longer possesses the capability unilaterally to assure stability in the area. If present trends continue unchecked, Iran could be effectively lost to the free world in advance of an actual communist takeover of the Iranian Government. Failure to arrest present trends in Iran involves a serious risk to the national security of the United States.

To "check" these "trends" in Iran, the NSC proposed that the United States expand ongoing economic and military assistance, prepare to offer technical help to the Iranians when they chose to resume oil production, assist them in marketing their oil, plan to include Iran in any regional defense pact, and in

> the event of either an attempted or an actual communist seizure of power in one or more of the provinces of Iran or in Tehran, the United States should support a non-communist Iranian Government, including participation in the military support of such a government if necessary and useful. Preparations for such an eventuality should include:
> a. Plans for specific military, economic, diplomatic, and psychological measures which could be taken to support a non-communist Iranian Government or to prevent all or part of Iran or adjacent areas from falling under communist domination....[15]

The NSC decision placed the American military in a difficult position. As the debate over NSC 136 continued during the fall of 1952, the Joint Chiefs demonstrated increased concern over the situation in Iran but stressed the difficulties inherent in military action in the region and the low priority accorded the Middle East in American war plans. The latter was an important consideration since the Joint Chiefs were concerned that any overt American move into Iran could provoke Soviet intervention under the terms of their 1921 treaty with Iran.[16]

Assuring Oil Supplies

Ultimately the JCS supported an NSC draft that envisioned possible American military intervention if, as the result of external invasion or internal subversion, Iran went Communist.[17] In the interim the JCS called for the services and the Strategic Air Command and CINCNELM to draw up plans for air demonstrations and for the movement of Air Force units to southern Turkey and of ground forces to Basra, Iraq. They emphasized that no decision had been made to deploy forces.[18]

For its part the U.S. Navy suggested a modest buildup of naval forces—a destroyer division, a minesweeper division, a reduced small boat group, three medium landing ships (LSMs), and a seaplane tender (AVP).[19] The Navy rejected proposals that it move a carrier into the gulf to participate in possible air demonstrations over Iranian cities.[20]

While the American military debated the possibilities of intervention, the Truman administration began a final diplomatic effort to resolve the crisis. Paul H. Nitze, Director of the State Department's Policy Planning Staff, wrote:

> As a result, by the end of 1952, it appeared that a solution was at last in sight. Early in January 1953, Mossadegh gave his final approval and we thought everything was settled. A few days later, however, Mossadegh changed his mind, probably in the mistaken belief that he could cut a better deal with the incoming Eisenhower administration.[21]

The negotiations appeared to be nearing a settlement in January 1953, but when presented with a formal draft agreement, Mossadegh continually altered and reinterpreted his demands.[22] In early February the frustrated British recommended breaking off talks and leaving the next move to Mossadegh.[23] The new American Secretary of State, John Foster Dulles, also grew pessimistic about the chances of an ultimate solution.[24]

The Iranian prime minister himself suddenly changed course, set the negotiations aside, and began a vociferous campaign against the Shah, the royal family, and the institution of the monarchy.[25] In late February American diplomats in Teheran reported that the Shah was about to abdicate. Only appeals by the British, Americans, members of the Iranian general staff, Mossadegh's enemies in the Majlis, and, most important, popular demonstrations in support of the monarchy (the fervor of which surprised both Iranian and American observers) convinced the Shah to remain in Teheran.[26]

Mossadegh's decision to embark on an anti-Shah campaign came at a critical moment in U.S. decisionmaking. If Mossadegh believed that Iran could get a better deal from the Eisenhower administration and that increased pressure on the Shah would move the Americans to push the British to make further concessions, he was mistaken.[27] Attacks on the monarchy and threats to sell oil to the Communist bloc convinced the Eisenhower administration that Mossadegh's leadership posed dangers to the United States and the West.

Iranian Prime Minister Mohammed Mossadegh.

Moreover, Washington policymakers saw Mossadegh's late February failure to force the Shah's abdication as a sign of the prime minister's weakening power. Americans were surprised to find Iranians taking to the streets in strength in support of the Shah.[28] A 1 March CIA report concluded, "The institution of the Crown may have more popular backing than was expected," presenting the monarch with an opportunity to act, although "his past record does not suggest that he will act."[29]

At a 4 March 1953 NSC meeting, John Foster Dulles lamented that the Shah had, in fact, missed his chance and that the monarchy would continue to be a target for attack. Dulles also expressed concern about Mossadegh's future. Mossadegh's political strength was obviously waning. Soviet broadcasts into Iran had become disturbingly anti-Shah and anti-Mossadegh. According to the minutes of the NSC meeting:

> The probable consequences of the events of the last few days, concluded Mr. Dulles, would be a dictatorship in Iran under Mossadegh. As long as the latter lives there was but little danger, but if he were to be assassinated or otherwise to disappear from power, a political vacuum would occur in Iran and the communists might easily take over.

Assuring Oil Supplies

When Treasury Secretary George M. Humphrey asked Dulles if he felt "that we are going to lose that country," the Secretary of State "replied in the affirmative." President Eisenhower interjected that a military option, namely the movement of American troops into Iran, would probably provoke Soviet intervention under the terms of the 1921 treaty.[30] But with the situation in Iran clearly deteriorating, what options remained?

The possibility of taking "political action" in Iran had been raised within the Truman administration as early as March 1951.[31] C. M. "Monty" Woodhouse, a British intelligence officer, discussed the coup with CIA and State Department representatives in Washington in October and November 1952 at the time that the NSC was developing NSC 136.[32] The CIA responded favorably to Woodhouse's proposal; the State Department responded coolly. At a subsequent meeting in December, also held in Washington, the American representatives refused to rule out a coup, although they intended to wait to see how Mossadegh responded to the proposal for a settlement painstakingly worked out by Truman administration negotiators.[33] Mossadegh's rejection of the American proposal and his mounting attacks against the monarchy thus came at a critical moment—as the Eisenhower administration in the late winter and early spring of 1953 weighed its options in Iran.[34]

Throughout the spring and summer of 1953 Mossadegh's popularity declined as the failure of his policies became increasingly evident. The prime minister's brand of nationalism had led Iran to economic and political ruin. Faced with the failure of his policies, the Iranian premier lashed out at the monarchy, the Majlis (which would ultimately be dissolved in August 1953), and the British. In an earlier assessment, Ambassador Henderson had warned, "If coop [coup] of kind desired not forthcoming he may give Americans same treatment as that given British."[35]

In early March the possibilities of a coup were being weighed in Washington, London, and Teheran. On 6 March Ambassador Henderson wrote from Iran: "Difficult for us believe Shah really would have courage or resolution to take part in movement to effect either by force or peacefully downfall Mossadeq government. He would undoubtedly be frightened at thought of military coup being attempted in his name and if given the opportunity would probably try discourage it."[36] Nevertheless, planning and preparation for a coup continued. Barring some change in the situation in Iran, the United States and Britain were committed to political action.[37]

In the summer of 1953 the Eisenhower adminstration feared an Iranian internal collapse. Americans saw Mossadegh not as a Communist sympathizer but as an incompetent politician and administrator whose policies had so undermined Iranian stability that ultimately the only remaining organized force in the country would be the Tudeh party. Mossadegh himself foolishly played up the Communist threat, warning Henderson that the United States had best realize that "drastic measures must be adopted if Iran not

The United States and Iran

Carrier *Lake Champlain* (CVA–39) in Aden in May 1953 before her entry into the Korean conflict.

fall Commie hands."[38] To the Eisenhower administration in the spring and summer of 1953, the time seemed ripe for an effort to "save" Iran.

Nevertheless, although the decision to act in Iran was taken by Eisenhower, the critical policy premises on which the President acted had been shaped by the Truman administration. In the spring of 1951 the NSC had identified the Shah as the focus for American support and the hope for a stable Iran. NSC 107/2 and 136/1 ruled out the "loss" of Iran and envisioned military or political operations if diplomatic efforts failed. By the spring of 1953 it was clear that all such efforts had failed and that the situation in Iran would continue to deteriorate.

The Eisenhower administration thus had few options in Iran. A diplomatic solution appeared impossible since Mossadegh was either unwilling or unable to reach any agreement on nationalization that the Americans or British were likely to consider reasonable. Given the existence of the 1921 Soviet-Iranian treaty, American military intervention posed the risk of world war. Eisenhower feared, as had Truman, that continued inaction would allow conditions to deteriorate to the point where the government in Teheran lost control, either as the result of a domestic coup or through the breakdown of central authority. Centrifugal forces would lead to the breakup of Iran and possibly civil war. Both the United States and the Soviet Union would most likely receive calls for assistance. The United States would then be forced to sit back and watch the Soviet Union move into Iran, or to intervene itself

Assuring Oil Supplies

and risk a third world war.[39] To the administration a coup appeared to be the cheapest and safest course to pursue.[40]

Another factor central to the Eisenhower administration's decision to undertake political action in Iran was the conviction that Mossadegh was losing support; had the Shah been more forceful, they held, the prime minister might well have been removed from power in the late winter. The Anglo-American coup rested on the assumption that the Shah had widespread support in Iran, but that he would refuse to act without the United States holding his hand.[41] As Kermit Roosevelt later wrote, "If our analysis had been wrong, we'd have fallen flat on our, er, faces."[42]

Operation Ajax—the American code name for the coup—owed its success in no small measure to the extent of the Shah's popularity and Mossadegh's unpopularity.[43] On the evening of 15 August the initial stage of the planned coup failed when Mossadegh loyalists arrested the commander of the Imperial Guard after he had delivered the Shah's decree (*firman*) removing the prime minister from power.[44] In the meantime the Shah had fled the country "as planned," going to Iraq and subsequently to Rome. The situation in Teheran looked rather bleak. On the seventeenth, Mossadegh's supporters took to the streets in displays of antimonarchical fervor. But Mossadegh hesitated, fearing overreliance on his most fervent supporters in the Tudeh party. Throughout the day pro-Shah forces reorganized and published copies of the royal *firman* removing Mossadegh from power and naming General Zahedi as prime minister. On the morning of 19 August the pro-Shah demonstrators took to the streets and routed both the Mossadegh and Tudeh mobs.[45] An official British postcoup assessment concluded:

> It is widely believed that the success of the coup was due to the fact that it was well planned, that it was kept secret, and that plenty of money was made available to carry it out. . . .
> The general feeling in Tehran among influential people was one of jubilation that the U.S.A. should have come to the country's rescue when Dr. Musaddiq was about to deliver it to the Tudeh Party. There was general agreement that, were it not for America's assistance and guidance, its financial contribution, and its encouragement to the Shah to withstand further humiliation, the plan for the overthrowing of Musaddiq's government could not have succeeded. Unfortunately it appeared that these influential persons regarded American support as something obligatory and continuous, which would enable them always to shelter behind it and continue, as in the past, without paying any real attention to the basic needs of the country.[46]

The Iran coup was a watershed in Iranian-American affairs. Some Iranians immediately accused the United States of complicity in the coup, and American involvement caused deep resentment on the part of those who opposed the Shah in 1953 and would come to oppose him over the following decades.[47]

As a result the desire to eliminate the American presence, both commercial and diplomatic, from Iran following the revolution of 1979 would be rooted, in part, in a desire to make a second American-sponsored coup impossible.

Nevertheless, as Iran expert James Bill writes:

> [T]he American intervention of 1951–1953 did not determine the revolutionary events of 1978–79. Although the American image was tarnished severely by its actions against Musaddiq, the United States had numerous opportunities to rethink and revise its policy towards the shah's Iran in the quarter-century before the revolution.[48]

One might also add that the Shah had twenty-five years and ample opportunity to prove himself a capable ruler.

But the most important aspect of Operation Ajax was that it signaled the adoption by the United States of a new policy towards Iran that involved not only "political action" to rescue the Shah but also a decision to provide greater political, economic, and military support to Iran. Secretary of State John Foster Dulles wrote:

> We believe that if the present opportunity is seized we can capitalize on the existing favorable situation in Iran and make a significant advance toward bringing Iran into closer cooperation with its neighbors in a free world and changing it from a liability to a positive asset in the Middle Eastern area.[49]

The decision to use political action in Iran also saved the American military from having to confront the difficulties of operations in the Persian Gulf region. U.S. military forces, most noticeably the Navy's Middle East Force in the gulf, played no role in the coup.[50] The United States did not even reinforce MEF in the months before Ajax. CINCNELM's involvement consisted of preparing contingency plans should the coup fail and intervention become necessary either to support the Shah or as a response to a Soviet move into Iran.

Nevertheless, as the events of mid-August unfolded in Teheran, the Eisenhower administration pushed the military to consider greater involvement in the region. On 19 August as the second stage of the coup began, the NSC directed the chairman of the JCS to consider possible military responses beyond those outlined in JCS 1714/50 to support the Shah in the event of the failure of the coup or a countercoup. Since the final months of the Truman administration the NSC, unlike the JCS, had been prepared to risk Soviet intervention in Iran. But now with the Korean War ended and with new leadership on the JCS, the military was also more willing to consider such contingencies.[51]

By end of the year, the JCS had developed a plan for a multiservice operation that, over the course of several months, would draw on forces deployed all over the world to build up substantial American military strength in the Persian Gulf region.[52] Fortunately, the success of the coup made intervention unnecessary.

8

War, Intervention, Crisis, and War

The Eisenhower administration, as it demonstrated in Iran, brought a more forceful and active brand of American diplomacy to the Middle East as well as a somewhat different conception of MEDO. The United States now took the diplomatic lead (although not the military lead) from Great Britain in an effort to strengthen the West's position in the region. Secretary of State John Foster Dulles acknowledged that many "of the Arab League countries are so engrossed with their quarrels with Israel or with Great Britain or France that they pay little heed to the menace of Soviet communism." But Dulles, who had just returned from a tour of the region, reported that he had found "more concern where the Soviet Union is near. In general, the northern tier of nations shows awareness of the danger."[1] American policy henceforth focused on Turkey, Iran, and Pakistan in an effort to foster the development of an indigenous Middle East security arrangement.[2]

Eisenhower administration policies in the Middle East were less expressions of a major shift in direction than indications of the more dynamic leadership of the United States both in the region and within the context of the Anglo-American relationship.[3] Long before 1953 the United States had focused on an "outer ring" for the defense of the Middle East—for example, Turkey and Iran in 1946—but had deferred to Britain because Americans were unwilling to supply the forces necessary to defend such a line.[4] But the British fixation on Egypt, on what Americans considered an "inner ring" concept, had become a dead issue by 1953. A fiercely nationalist Arab government in Cairo refused to become a party to an agreement that by definition served Western interests and, moreover, involved non-Arab states such as Britain, the United States, Iran, and Turkey. In Egypt, and in Iran as well, British policies had done little but fan the flames of nationalist fires. Thus by late 1953 the Eisenhower administration had little choice but to adopt a more assertive stance in the Middle East. With the Shah seemingly secure on his throne and the American military freed from the albatross of the war in Korea, the United States pursued an "outer ring" concept for the defense of the Middle East.[5]

The more aggressive U.S. policy quickly bore fruit. On 24 February 1954 Turkey and Iraq signed a bilateral security agreement—the Baghdad Pact. Great Britain joined the pact in April 1954, Pakistan in September 1955, and Iran in October 1955. The United States never signed the accord but

Assuring Oil Supplies

did provide the requisite military assistance, sat on various alliance committees, and performed crucial diplomatic tasks in the region.

The Baghdad Pact has often been viewed as a cheap imitation of NATO, whose political and military strength the Middle East alliance never attained. Instead it remained a loose alignment of mostly unstable states primarily interested in acquiring Western arms to insure internal security and enhance their power within the Near and Middle East. In the view of some critics of American policy, the Western-aligned defense organization on the whole weakened American interests in the Middle East in return for a marginally improved capability to defend the region. The pact intensified regional discord, increased domestic political pressure from nationalist and anti-Western groups against the governments of the signatory states, and facilitated and accelerated Soviet penetration of the Middle East. For example, the July 1958 nationalist coup in Iraq—the only Arab member state of the pact—took the "Baghdad" out of the pact and opened the Middle East to the Soviets.

But the United States considered the possibility of a direct Soviet invasion remote, never expected the Baghdad Pact to improve regional defense substantially, and most certainly did not expect the pact to become a Middle East version of NATO. An NSC statement of policy concluded:

> In the Near East the current danger to the security of the free world arises not so much from the threat of direct Soviet military attack as from a continuation of the present unfavorable trends. Unless those trends are reversed, the Near East may well be lost to the West within the next few years.[6]

American policymakers hoped to reverse the anti-Western bent of Arab and Iranian nationalism by strengthening the morale of Middle East states and by reinforcing whatever pro-Western sentiments existed. An April 1952 State-Defense Working Group paper noted:

> The United States supports the establishment of a Middle East Command Organization in the belief that such an organization may make an early contribution to the political stabilization of the vitally important Middle East area, and in the long run increase the capacity of the area to resist Soviet aggression.[7]

Paul Nitze admitted quite frankly that MEDO would be "in its initial phases merely a paper organization."[8] A 22 June 1954 National Intelligence Estimate noted that "the immediate effects of a loose regional defense grouping based on the Turk-Pakistani agreement and backed by U.S. military aid programs would be primarily political and psychological rather than military."[9] The Shah once remarked that the pact "has never been really serious you know."[10]

Perhaps the most important effect of the Baghdad Pact was the indirect link of NATO, through the participation of Turkey in the pact, to the defense of the Middle East. American diplomats in Western Europe made a conscious effort to play down such a connection.[11] But the possibility that a Middle East war might lead to hostilities with three NATO members—Britain, the United States, and Turkey—certainly complicated planning for the Soviets and to some extent probably served as a deterrent.

Because American policy sought political, not military, benefit from MEDO and because the United States had despaired of enticing Arab states into a pro-Western defensive alignment, the Baghdad Pact survived the Iraq coup of 1958. Renamed the Central Treaty Organization (CENTO) on 5 March 1959, the pact—now comprising the Islamic, non-Arab states of Turkey, Iran, and Pakistan—survived for another twenty years thanks to British membership and American political, economic, and military assistance.

Although American military expectations for CENTO were low, the alliance, such as it was, remained a framework within which the United States sought to improve the defensive capabilities of the Northern Tier states. Coordinated aid programs, much like those accorded to Greece and Turkey under the Truman Doctrine, sought to strengthen the internal, regional, and external security of Turkey, Iran, and Pakistan.

The principal Soviet threat in the Middle East during the 1950s and 1960s was the Red Army. Hence American military aid to the CENTO countries placed paramount importance on the expansion of their ground and air, not naval, forces. Nevertheless, in cooperation with Great Britain's Royal Navy, the U.S. Navy (already committed to the buildup of the Turkish navy in the eastern Mediterranean and the Black Sea) now undertook the modernization and expansion of the Iranian and Pakistani navies. Modest naval assistance programs provided funding; equipment; surplus British frigates, destroyers, and corvettes; and American minesweepers, patrol boats, and training.[12]

American, British, Pakistani, and Iranian ships and aircraft also participated in regular bilateral and multilateral exercises. In 1956 Middle East Force and Iranian navy warships conducted the first of what became an annual, combined exercise. The MEF command history noted that "His Imperial Majesty Shah Reza witnessed the first exercise from Commander Middle East flagship."[13] Larger, multinational—American, British, Pakistani, and Iranian—annual exercises (MIDLINK) began in 1958 and continued until 1978, just before the fall of the Shah.[14]

Although the Baghdad Pact may have improved the prospects for the defense of the Middle East marginally, it did not, as its Western proponents had hoped, enhance regional political stability. In fact the pact further exacerbated many of the existing tensions within the region. Egyptian President Nasser viewed the agreement as the first step in a Western scheme to isolate his country and denounced the agreement, in the words of George

Assuring Oil Supplies

V. Allen, Assistant Secretary of State for Near Eastern, South Asian, and African Affairs, as "a new form of imperialism . . . designed to imprison all of the Arab people."[15]

Nasser's attacks on the Baghdad Pact reached a crescendo in 1956 as the crisis over the Suez Canal came to a head. Desperate for economic and military assistance denied by the West, the pan-Arab Nasser turned to the Communist bloc for support and became increasingly anti-Western in his rhetoric. On 26 July 1956 he announced the nationalization of the Universal Company of the Suez Maritime Canal, "an edifice of humiliation."[16] Negotiations to resolve the dispute made little headway.[17]

In collusion with Great Britain and France, Israel broke the subsequent diplomatic deadlock on 29 October when its forces attacked the Egyptians in the Sinai and drove westward toward the canal. The British and French, who since August had been planning and preparing to intervene and had agreed beforehand to cooperate with the Israelis, promptly issued a cease-fire ultimatum that called for both Israeli and Egyptian withdrawal and temporary Anglo-French occupation of Port Said, Ismailia, and Suez. On 30 October, following the expected and desired Egyptian rejection of the ultimatum, France and Great Britain began operations against Egypt, bombing military installations and seizing about 40 percent of the canal area.

American policymakers, who had been closely monitoring the situation, responded quickly to the Anglo-French aggression. In August the Joint Chiefs had argued that the United States ought to support Great Britain and France politically and logistically if they attacked Egypt.[18] Chairman Admiral Arthur W. Radford had suggested that such a course would prevent the spread of war. Failure to do so might lead to conflagration in the Persian Gulf, a region critical to the support of U.S. operations in the Far East.[19] But both President Eisenhower and Secretary of State Dulles, while they expressed an understanding of the dilemma in which British and French leaders found themselves, demonstrated no inclination to take sides against Egypt in the event of a showdown. The administration was eager to lessen Nasser's influence in the Arab world but believed that the dispute over the Suez Canal was not the issue on which to confront the Egyptian president.[20] The administration took its even-handedness seriously, so much so that in June it had initiated Operation Whiplash, the prepositioning in the eastern Mediterranean of ships loaded with arms that would be delivered to the victim of aggression, be it Israel or a neighboring Arab state.[21] Accordingly, when hostilities began, the United States, working through the United Nations, forced a cease-fire and, with the Israeli pullout from the Gaza strip in early March 1957, a complete withdrawal from Egyptian territory.

The Anglo-French-Israeli operation was immediately considered to be a debacle and history has sustained this opinion. In his history of the Royal Air Force in the Mediterranean in the postwar period, retired Air Chief

War, Intervention, Crisis

Sailors and Marines begin to load the six thousand pieces of luggage that arrived at the docks for the Suez evacuation.

Marshal Sir David Lee wrote, "It is impossible to look back upon the Anglo-French intervention in Egypt without coming to the conclusion that it was a fiasco."[22] Nasser survived; the canal, far from being secured, remained closed for months after the war and, of course, in Egyptian hands. British prestige plummeted throughout the Middle East. In his diary David Ben-Gurion, the Israeli Prime Minister, wrote, "60,000 British and 30,000 French troops participated in the Anglo-French campaign, as well as 1,200 jet planes and two-thirds of the active British navy. If they had only appointed a commander of ours over this force—Nasser would have been destroyed in two days."[23] Even Secretary Dulles, recovering from cancer surgery at Walter Reed Hospital, remarked to Eisenhower that

> the British having gone in should not have stopped until they had toppled Nasser. As it was they now had the worst of both possible worlds. They had received all the onus of making the move and at the same time had not accomplished their major purpose.[24]

Assuring Oil Supplies

As American policymakers had expected and feared, the Anglo-French-Israeli attack also provoked violent reactions throughout the Arab world. Because the United States supported United Nations calls for cease-fire and withdrawal and refused to support "the use of force as a wise and proper instrument for the settlement of international disputes," it avoided Arab wrath, for the most part.[25]

Nevertheless, the reaction against Britain in the Middle East demonstrated the depth of Arab emotions. The Saudis mobilized their armed forces, began training volunteers, broke off diplomatic relations with Britain and France, banned the refueling of their ships in Saudi ports, and embargoed oil shipments to both countries. Rioting and demonstrations broke out in Kuwait and Bahrain, both still British protectorates. For nine days Bahrainis rioted in Manama and Muharraq, attacking British nationals as well as a few unfortunate Americans and destroying property. A work stoppage by Bahrain Petroleum Company (Bapco) workers quickly became a general strike. As the situation deteriorated, Britain airlifted troops into Bahrain.[26] The demonstrations were somewhat less violent in Kuwait, but the repercussions of the Suez affair in Kuwait were longer lasting. Arabs sabotaged British-owned and controlled oil fields and facilities and subjected British firms to a boycott that lasted two months.[27]

The Suez affair led to a deeper crisis in the Middle East. The failure of the Anglo-French assault increased the legitimacy and strength of Nasserite, anti-Western forces and was followed by the formation on 21 February 1958 of the United Arab Republic (UAR) of Egypt and Syria, headed by Nasser. Those Arab leaders who continued to resist Nasser's brand of pan-Arabism—most notably in Iraq, Saudi Arabia, Jordan, and Lebanon—quickly found themselves threatened by internal and external forces.

The situation was most critical in Iraq, which suffered major economic losses as a result of the Suez crisis. Nasserite forces in Syria blew up the pipelines that carried oil from Iraq to the Mediterranean and the West. With the Suez Canal also closed, Iraqi oil revenues fell and King Feisal of Iraq, a moderate, pro-Western leader, found himself isolated and weakened. Feisal's efforts to develop a counteralignment of Arab nations met limited success in the form of the short-lived Iraqi-Jordanian Arab Federation established on 14 February 1958.[28]

Sensing the deteriorating situation in the region, the United States responded by reevaluating its policy. As ultimately adopted by a joint resolution of the House and Senate on 5 March 1957, the Eisenhower Doctrine provided for increased economic and military assistance:

> Furthermore, the United States regards as vital to the national interests and world peace the preservation of the independence and integrity of the nations

War, Intervention, Crisis

of the Middle East. To this end, if the President determines the necessity thereof, the United States is prepared to use armed forces to assist any such nation or group of such nations requesting assistance against armed aggression from any country controlled by international communism: Provided that such employment shall be consonant with the treaty obligations of the United States and with the Constitution of the United States.[29]

The United States also began to reevaluate its military plans for the region. The Joint Middle East Defense Plan 1–57 of May 1957 sought to meet a possible Soviet move into the region within the existing force structure of the United States. An American "strategic defense" of the Middle East would shield "the NATO right flank, airbase sites, the Turkish Straits, the Eastern Mediterranean, the Cairo-Suez-Aden area, and the Persian Gulf and contiguous oil-bearing area." Depending on the course of events elsewhere, significant ground, air, and naval forces would move to the Persian Gulf and Indian Ocean areas where they would be directed by a Commander in Chief, Middle East (CINCME), to be designated by the Joint Chiefs.[30]

During the Suez crisis the JCS had drawn up plans to move ground forces from Germany to the Persian Gulf in the event of escalation.[31] But following the crisis the Army began to develop a reserve force in the United States capable of deployment overseas. In 1958 the service established the U.S. Strategic Army Corps (STRAC), a corps headquarters for the control of forces such as the 82nd Airborne Division which were not already committed under existing plans to a specific theater in wartime.

These preparations had not fully matured when in the spring and summer of 1958 the United States observed with growing concern UAR aid going to rebels in Iraq, Lebanon, and Jordan. The situation appeared most threatening in Lebanon, where a virtual civil war erupted in May. As a result, the American military busily prepared contingency plans, Operation Bluebat, for possible intervention.

But the expected Middle East crisis originated in Baghdad, not Beirut. On 14 July midlevel Iraqi Army officers engineered a successful coup d'etat. The rebels executed pro-Western King Feisal and the senior political leadership of Iraq—the linchpin of the Middle East's regional defense organization.

The coup surprised the Eisenhower administration. Faced with another Middle East crisis, American policymakers believed that inaction would lead to the further spread of Nasserism and the erosion of Arab perceptions of American influence and dependability. Some form of action was therefore necessary.

Air Force General Nathan Twining, Chairman of the Joint Chiefs of Staff, favored intervention in Iraq, as did the Saudis, Iranians, and Turks who wished to topple the new regime in Baghdad. But reports from Iraq indicated that little or no royalist resistance had materialized and that the populace, displaying anti-royalist, anti-Western, and pro-Arabist senti-

Assuring Oil Supplies

An assault wave of Marines lands at Red Beach, Beirut, Lebanon, July 1958.

ments, had embraced the revolution. The Iraqis also kept the oil flowing to the West and made no move to nationalize foreign oil companies.

President Eisenhower considered a forceful but limited display of American resolve necessary to forestall additional moves against pro-Western regimes. He was aware that U.S. actions could provoke a broader war in the region or possibly even a third world war.[32] Thus, when only hours after the Iraqi coup, President Camille Chamoun of Lebanon requested American, French, and British military support, President Eisenhower decided to send troops into Lebanon. At 1330 Beirut time on 15 July, amphibious ships from the U.S. Navy's Sixth Fleet landed Marines of the 2/2 Battalion Landing Team on the beach south of the Lebanese capital.[33] On the sixteenth, King Hussein of Jordan requested the assistance of Great Britain, and the following morning British paratroopers began landing at Amman as American carrier aircraft from the Sixth Fleet flew demonstration missions over Jordan's West Bank.[34] Anglo-American military forces remained in Lebanon and Jordan into late October 1958.

Despite the focus on Lebanon and the eastern Mediterranean, the crisis of the summer of 1958 was regional in scope and global in character. The United States placed its military forces throughout the Atlantic, Pacific, and European commands at higher states of readiness and alert. On the afternoon of 14 July the Chief of Naval Operations, Admiral Arleigh Burke, directed that a Middle East Force destroyer remain near Dhahran, Saudi Arabia. On the fifteenth the MEF flagship *Greenwich Bay* (AVP–41) moved into the northern Persian Gulf nearer Kuwait. On the seventeenth, Commander Middle East Force, with CNO approval, ordered the destroyer *Holder* (DD–819), in the Strait of Tiran at the mouth of the Gulf of Aqaba be-

War, Intervention, Crisis

tween Egypt and Saudi Arabia, to operate so that it would be visible from the shore; it was hoped that this move would help stabilize the situation. That same day, at Eisenhower's direction, Admiral Burke directed CINCPAC to load and sail a Marine battalion from Okinawa to the Persian Gulf, a move designed to meet a potential Iraqi threat against Kuwait.[35] On 21 July the British strengthened their garrison in Bahrain, also the major base for the U.S. Navy's Middle East Force, with 1,000 additional troops. Demands on MEF's limited resources led to an 11 August request for the transfer of additional destroyers from the Mediterranean to the Indian Ocean, but the Sixth Fleet was overcommitted and unable to spare any additional ships.[36]

The wisdom of intervening in the Lebanese civil war escaped many Americans at the time, and Eisenhower's decision to send in the Marines has since been the subject of considerable historical debate. There was a comic-opera quality to the affair, with armed Marines hounded by ice cream and soft-drink vendors as they scrambled up a beach crowded with sunbathers. There is no doubt that the administration oversold the nature and extent of the Communist menace throughout the Middle East. And the ultimate settlement in Lebanon between the various factions owed as much to America's cool-headedness and effective diplomacy as it did to the display of U.S. military muscle.

Nevertheless, an assessment of American Middle East policy in the summer of 1958 must acknowledge that the Eisenhower administration based its policy not only on a determination to restore orderly government to Lebanon but also, and most important, on the assumption that the failure of the United States to respond to Chamoun's call for help would have deleterious consequences for American relationships with those countries still friendly to the United States. King Hussein of Jordan waited until American troops were ashore in Lebanon before he requested help from Great Britain to secure his throne. The United States was no more hawkish than its most important regional allies. The Turks, Iranians, and Saudis all supported American moves and also favored intervention in Iraq. The Eisenhower administration's decision to use military force in the Middle East demonstrated—for the first, but not the last, time—the U.S. determination to defend its interests in the region, not just to Arabs be they pro- or anti-Western in their orientation, but also to the Soviet Union. In his memoirs President Eisenhower stated that he believed the landing had a sobering effect on Nasser, making him rethink the reliability of his Soviet patron.[37] And according to Egyptian accounts the Soviets were indeed taken aback by the American response, to the chagrin of Nasser who was in Moscow at the time.[38]

However one chooses to assess the results of the Lebanon operation, the lessons that can be drawn from the crisis are much more obvious. First, de-

Assuring Oil Supplies

spite a plethora of reports about internal problems in Iraq, the 14 July 1958 coup surprised and shocked the American military, diplomatic, and intelligence communities. A country which had been the centerpiece of Anglo-American hopes for regional defense suddenly became anti-Western in outlook and policy, leading a President to use force to protect American interests and to demonstrate resolve. Twenty-one years later the fall of the Shah of Iran, then the linchpin of CENTO, the successor of the Baghdad Pact, would similarly catch the United States by surprise and ultimately lead to the commitment of American military forces into the midst of an intraregional dispute. Second, the use of Marines in Lebanon marked a departure from past U.S. policy, which until 14 July 1958 had resisted the commitment of military force in the Middle East. Moreover, the deployment of conventional forces in a limited war scenario indicated a perceptible shift away from the Eisenhower administration's pronounced doctrine of "Massive Retaliation." Third, the Lebanon experience highlighted the effectiveness of naval forces in the Middle East, both as a crisis management asset and as a force well tailored to meet contingencies in the region. During the operation the absence of modern airfields handicapped efforts both to move land-based combat aircraft and to airlift troops into the region and placed a premium on carrier aircraft and ship-based Marines.

In terms of U.S. interests, the Middle East remained relatively quiescent for nearly a decade after the Lebanon crisis. Regional instability, anti-Westernism, anti-Americanism, Nasserism, and expanding Communist influence continued to threaten U.S. interests, but the American and British position in the Middle East, which appeared to be on the verge of collapse in the mid-1950s, seemed to have weathered the worst of the storm.

For the U.S. Navy's Middle East Force, however, the inherently unstable nature of the region was readily apparent. During 1963, for example, MEF destroyers deployed to the Red Sea when friction developed between Saudi Arabia and the UAR over "civil strife in Yemen." Egyptian fighters and bombers with open bomb bays overflew the carrier *Essex* (CV–9) during a transit of the Suez Canal in an "extremely provocative gesture." And because of "political considerations," the commander of the Middle East Force was unable to visit Iraq, Yemen, or Afghanistan.[39]

Despite these problems the Navy's MEF continued its work. An early 1967 assessment concluded that "1966 was a most successful year for Middle East Force." The ships assigned to the command at one time or another conducted 128 visits to 34 ports located in 12 countries and 6 protectorates or possessions.[40] The flag aircraft logged 77,328 miles, carrying CMEF to forty different cities. In 1966 the Navy designated Bahrain as the homeport for a permanent flagship—*Valcour* (AGF–1). Overall, the report noted, "attitudes

War, Intervention, Crisis

Official U.S. Navy Photograph

The command ship *Valcour* became the flagship, living facility, and communications center for Commander Middle East Force and his staff.

towards the U.S. Navy were friendly and cordial everywhere. The political climate in Somalia was somewhat disturbing because of Soviet penetration of the economy and the Army." Nevertheless, the command experienced several difficulties, including severe personnel shortages related to the manpower drain imposed by the Vietnam War, as well as concern about possible refueling problems for the MEF's fuel-hungry destroyers if, following a planned British pullout, Aden denied the United States access to the port's strategically located facilities.[41]

If 1966 had been Middle East Force's most successful year, 1967 proved to be one of its most trying. In April and May, MEF ships helped evacuate Americans from Yemen and patroled off troubled Aden. Simultaneously, tensions between Israel and the UAR grew. On 16 May, Nasser called for a partial withdrawal of United Nations peacekeeping forces from the Sinai peninsula. UN Secretary General U Thant rejected the idea of a partial pullout but then surprisingly acceded to Nasser's subsequent demand for a complete withdrawal. On 22 May, Nasser announced the closing of the Tiran Strait to Israeli shipping, a move Israel had heretofore considered a casus belli.

The United States, politically, militarily, and emotionally trapped in the quagmire of Indochina, unfortunately failed to respond promptly and unambiguously to the increasingly deteriorating situation in the Middle East. Not until the crisis was virtually out of control did President Lyndon B. Johnson begin to seek a multilateral approach to avoid another Arab-Israeli confrontation.

Assuring Oil Supplies

Because of earlier tensions in the Yemens many Middle East Force assets were already concentrated near the Red Sea, well positioned to respond to the new Arab-Israeli crisis. By 28 May, according to MEF assessments, when the Egyptians had completed their buildup, including the establishment of a surface and submarine barrier at the mouth of the Gulf of Aqaba, the Commander Middle East Force had completed his concentration as well. The American destroyer *Dyess* (DD–880) raced to reinforce MEF and, jeered by anti-American crowds during its passage, inchopped through the Suez Canal on 4 June, "just in time." That very day Israel decided to strike, and on 5 June simultaneously attacked Egypt and Syria.[42]

The lightning Israeli victory, since known as the Six Day War, was a complete debacle for the front-line Arab states. Israeli forces overran the Gaza Strip, the Sinai, the West Bank (following Jordanian intervention), and the Golan Heights, and decimated Arab air and ground forces. Although the Israelis had chosen to preempt, the United States did not call for an immediate withdrawal as it had in 1956, but instead sought a negotiated settlement—land for peace. The United States chose to be heavily involved in the diplomatic struggle to end the Arab-Israeli conflict.

The United States now was drawn dangerously towards the vortex of the new Middle East war. The hotline connecting Washington and Moscow came alive for the first time since its installation after the Cuban missile crisis of October 1962. MEF forces were among those that went to a heightened alert status on 5 June 1967. In the eastern Mediterranean Israeli planes attacked the U.S. Navy's intelligence ship *Liberty* (AGTR–45). Fabricated tales of American aircraft supporting the Israelis sparked anti-American demonstrations throughout the region. The Middle East Force historian noted:

> On the 6th numerous anti-American demonstrations erupted throughout the Middle East but of immediate concern to Middle East Force were those in Bahrain and Dhahran. The Ruler of Bahrain demonstrated genuine leadership capabilities by allowing carefully controlled demonstrations for several days and then ordering them to cease. But he was careful to offer an alternative to the demonstrators. He offered free transportation to the battle zone for those who wished to fight and accepted donations from those who couldn't or wouldn't fight but wished to contribute. In contrast, uncontrolled mob violence in the Dhahran area resulted in several hundred thousand dollars worth of damage to U.S. property, and many dependents there were forced to evacuate.[43]

Despite these anti-American outbursts the impact of the crushing Israeli victory on the Arab nationalist mood led to a relatively rapid resumption of routine in the Middle East. On 12 June MEF returned to its regular operating status. By the end of the summer the situation in the Indian Ocean basin had slowly returned to normal.

Nevertheless, the immediate aftermath of the 1967 war clearly demonstrated that anti-Western and anti-American sentiments, the latter exacer-

War, Intervention, Crisis

Following the Israeli attack on her, *Liberty* awaits assistance from other Sixth Fleet units.

Damage to the bridge of U.S. Navy intelligence ship *Liberty* inflicted by an Israeli rocket attack off the Sinai Peninsula in June 1967.

Assuring Oil Supplies

bated by U.S. support of Israel, were growing stronger in the Arab world. Americans had tasted Arab wrath, both political and economic, as had the British after the Suez crisis of 1956. Despite the apparent rapid return to business as usual, the United States and the U.S. Navy's Middle East Force faced difficult times ahead. While American policymakers remained focused on the struggle in Indochina, they also struggled to prevent another Arab-Israeli conflict and to limit Soviet diplomatic, economic, and military penetration into the Middle East. MEF found itself becoming increasingly important in the region as the British began their pullout east of Suez and Soviet naval forces appeared in the Indian Ocean. In addition, the entire Indian Ocean basin seemed ready to explode into conflict from the borders of India and Pakistan to the Horn of Africa. By the early 1970s one-third of the countries of the Indian Ocean basin suffered from internal or external crises manifesting themselves in anti-American policies.

But an unaugmented three-to-five-ship Middle East Force continued its work as it had for over twenty years despite the new demands it faced: the continued shutdown of the Suez Canal; the closure of many Indian Ocean, Persian Gulf, and Red Sea ports to American ships; and the manpower drain imposed by the war in Vietnam that reduced manning levels by as much as 50 percent.[44] The role of the Middle East Force remained unchanged.

> The mission of COMIDEASTFOR [Commander Middle East Force] is to plan for and conduct operations within assigned area to manifest the continuing strong interest of the United States in the Persian Gulf and to visit friendly countries there and in the Arabian and Red Seas and Indian Ocean areas.[45]

9

The Nixon Doctrine and the Twin Pillars

In the wake of the 1967 Arab-Israeli war American political leaders and diplomats once again found themselves reassessing a Middle East policy that had sought to avoid a substantial buildup of regional forces or the commitment of American units to the defense of the Middle East. Three factors forced this reappraisal: the British pullout from east of Suez announced in January 1968 and completed in 1971; the deployment of Soviet navy warships to the Indian Ocean in March 1968; and the physical and psychological effects of the Vietnam War on the U.S. government and the American people.

Great Britain's determination to relinquish its already diminishing position east of Suez marked the end of what C. J. Bartlett has termed "The Long Retreat." Historians continue to debate whether the absence of will on the part of both Labour and Conservative politicians or inadequate financial resources precipitated the withdrawal.[1] Whatever the cause the decision undermined existing concepts of Middle East defense because Britain had been the principal Western power responsible for the security of the Middle East, and its military power was still the major source of stability within the volatile Persian Gulf.[2] British forces had intervened in Kuwait in July 1961 to deter an Iraqi invasion and were engaged actively against radical forces in Aden and the Yemens.[3] The concern of several of the smaller Persian Gulf states was evident when they offered to finance a continued British presence.[4]

Worse yet, the British announcement was almost immediately followed by the appearance of the Soviet navy in the Indian Ocean, another indication of the expanding Soviet and Communist interest in a region torn by nationalist and anti-Western sentiments.[5] By the end of the year Soviet warships had spent more time in the Indian Ocean than had U.S. Navy men-of-war. During 1973 the Soviet presence was four times as great as that of the Americans.

President Lyndon B. Johnson had little opportunity to digest the full implications of the British withdrawal from east of Suez. The war in Vietnam held center stage in Washington, especially after 31 January 1968 and the start of the Communists' Tet offensive. On 31 March Johnson announced that he would not seek reelection; the United States was being led by a lame duck president. To the extent that the Johnson administration focused on Middle East policy questions, the search for a diplomatic solution to the Arab-Israeli conflict was considered the most pressing problem. The question of who would replace Britain in the Middle East remained unanswered.

Assuring Oil Supplies

TABLE 3

U.S. and Soviet Ship-Days in the Indian Ocean, 1968–1973

(surface combatants and auxiliaries)

	1968	1969	1970	1971	1972	1973
U.S	1,688	1,315	1,246	1,337	1,435	2,154
Soviet	1,760	3,668	3,579	3,804	8,007	8,543

SOURCE: "Means of Measuring Naval Power with Special Reference to U.S. and Soviet Activities in the Indian Ocean," prepared for the Subcommittee on the Near East and South Asia of the Committee on Foreign Relations by the Foreign Affairs Division, Congressional Research Service, Library of Congress, 12 May 1974, Washington, 1974, 93rd Cong., 2d sess., pp. 4–7.

President Richard M. Nixon assumed office at a difficult moment in American history. The new President recognized that the American people were deeply divided by the Vietnam War and were no longer willing to "bear any burden." At a 25 July 1969 discussion with the press at Guam, the President remarked that henceforth Asian nations would have to accept greater responsibility for their own defense.[6] Nixon eventually globalized this concept, in what became known as the Nixon Doctrine, during his State of the Union Address of 22 January 1970:

> Neither the defense nor the development of other nations can be exclusively or primarily an American undertaking.
> The nations of each part of the world should assume the primary responsibility for their own well-being; and they themselves should determine the terms of that well-being.
> We shall be faithful to our treaty commitments, but we shall reduce our involvement and our presence in other nations' affairs.[7]

The Nixon Doctrine had a profound impact on American policy in the Middle East. The United States increasingly looked to a regional power—Iran—to replace the British in the gulf. Henry Kissinger, then Nixon's National Security Adviser, later wrote:

> It was imperative for our interests and those of the Western world that the regional balance of power be maintained so that moderate forces would not be engulfed nor Europe's and Japan's (and as it later turned out, our) economic lifeline fall into hostile hands. We could either provide the balancing force ourselves or enable a regional power to do so. There was no possibility of assigning any American military forces to the Indian Ocean in the midst of the Vietnam war and its attendant trauma. Congress would have tolerated no such commitment; the public would not have supported it. Fortunately, Iran was willing to play this role. The vacuum left by British withdrawal, now menaced by Soviet intrusion and radical momentum, would be filled by a local power friendly to us.[8]

TABLE 4

U.S. and Soviet Port-Calls in the Indian Ocean, 1968–1973

	U.S.	Soviet
1968	71	42
1969	71	68
1970	65	65
1971	97	47
1972	74	110
1973	115	153

SOURCE: "Means of Measuring Naval Power with Special Reference to U.S. and Soviet Activities in the Indian Ocean," prepared for the Subcommittee on the Near East and South Asia of the Committee on Foreign Relations by the Foreign Affairs Division, Congressional Research Service, Library of Congress, 12 May 1974, Washington, 1974, 93rd Cong., 2d sess., pp. 4–7.

To further strengthen its position in the region and provide a balance between Iranian and Arab interests the Persian Gulf, American policy soon fixed on Saudi Arabia as a second, and somewhat junior, regional power in a policy known as the Twin Pillars.[9]

The Nixon Doctrine and the Twin Pillars were reasonable and understandable options for a United States that, as Henry Kissinger understood, was unable and unwilling to play a larger role in the Persian Gulf. Iran and Saudi Arabia were important oil producing, pro-Western, strategically located states whose friendship and security were critical to the United States.

Nevertheless, the Nixon Doctrine as applied to the Persian Gulf, along with the Twin Pillars, were not only policy directions shaped by Washington but also Iranian initiatives accepted and embraced by the United States. Immediately following Great Britain's announced pullout from east of Suez, the Shah began a diplomatic offensive designed to ensure Iran a leading role in the Persian Gulf and the Indian Ocean; his offensive was meant to preclude the possibility that the United States would replace Great Britain in the gulf.[10] By the end of 1968, before Nixon had even taken office, the Shah had settled several, though not all, outstanding issues with the Saudis and during a November visit to Riyadh issued a joint communiqué that spoke of Arab-Iranian friendship and cooperation in the gulf.[11] In late December 1967 a joint Iranian-Turkish-Pakistani communiqué "affirmed that the responsibility for the preservation of peace and stability in the Persian Gulf rested only with the littoral states."[12] Similar sentiments were echoed during the Shah's January 1969 trip to India.

Nor were the policies of the Nixon administration entirely consistent with those of previous American administrations (despite Kissinger's claims to the contrary). The Nixon-Kissinger policies reversed an American approach

Assuring Oil Supplies

to Middle East security in place for nearly a quarter century. That approach had rejected as destabilizing and possibly counterproductive any attempt to create a strong military bulwark or to risk an arms race within the region. Statistics for arms expenditures and imports between 1969, when the Nixon administration took office, and 1978, the last complete year of the Shah's rule, support the view that the buildup of the Iranian military did prompt a regional arms race (table 5). Since the late 1940s the United States had repeatedly rejected the Shah's schemes to build up the Iranian military. CENTO had been primarily a political, not a military pact.

TABLE 5

Iranian and Iraqi Arms Expenditures and Imports, 1969–1978

(million/dollars)

	Expenditures		Imports	
	Iran	Iraq	Iran	Iraq
1969	1,828	826	220	70
1970	2,045	822	160	50
1971	2,505	857	320	40
1972	3,093	977	525	140
1973	3,729	1,304	525	625
1974	6,303	1,686	1,000	625
1975	8,646	1,738	1,200	675
1976	9,521	1,837	2,100	1,000
1977	8,747	2,007	2,400	1,500
1978	10,598	2,136	2,100	1,500

SOURCE: Derived from Anthony H. Cordesman, *The Gulf and the Search for Strategic Stability* (Boulder, CO, and London: Westview Press/Mansell Publishing, 1984), p. 160.

Many critics noted the policy change and emphasized the dangers inherent in such policies. Senator Edward M. Kennedy argued that the United States was encouraging an arms race in the Persian Gulf thereby increasing the risk of internal instability.[13] Many observers, both official and unofficial, expressed strong concern about the situation in Iran.[14] During Anglo-American talks held in Washington in October 1974, a British official warned his American counterparts that they had "better watch out," because "the Shah may have overreached himself."[15]

There were also obvious and myriad problems in bringing Iran and Saudi Arabia into a smoothly working partnership. An otherwise upbeat Department of State report on the Iranian-Saudi relationship, appropriately entitled "The Odd Couple," noted that the two countries' concerns about Arab radicalism and an increasing Soviet presence in the Middle

East had yet to be translated into effective cooperation.[16] Traditional problems, such as religious discord between the predominantly Shia Iranians and the Sunni Saudis, territorial disputes over several small islands in the gulf, and the differences in scale and internal development, continued to divide the Twin Pillars.

> The Iranians, who tend to look down on the Arabs anyway, consider the Saudi regime's approach to its problems simplistic and ultraconservative. The Saudis have their own doubts about the stability of the Iranian regime, which they consider dangerously dependent on the survival of the Shah.[17]

Within months, the State Department issued a second report that ended on an even less optimistic note. "The upshot of all these cross-currents is that the logic of Iranian-Saudi cooperation is being undercut by psychological, nationalistic, and prestige factors, which are likely to persist for a long time."[18]

There were also doubts about the reliability of the Shah. Dependent as he was on foreign military and economic support, he had little choice, at least in the short term, but to accept "that aspect of the Nixon Doctrine dealing with the responsibility for regional powers to provide the primary protection for their own areas as tacit agreement by the United States to help provide Iran the wherewithal to do so."[19] The Shah did not want the United States to replace the British in the region; in fact he did not wish to see the Middle East Force remain based in the gulf. When asked about the American presence in Bahrain at a 29 January 1972 press conference, he responded: "Well, you know what we declared long ago that we should not like to see a foreign power in the Persian Gulf. Whether that power be Britain, the United States, the Soviet Union or China our policy has not changed."[20]

Following Indira Gandhi's call for a "zone of peace" in the Indian Ocean, the Shah announced his own, similar plan in 1974.[21] In October 1974 a British foreign ministry official warned the United States that "in the long run the Shah may be more audacious than shrewd and may not even be an ally" and that he suffered from "delusions of grandeur." A 1973 Defense Intelligence Agency estimate raised the possibility that the Shah "might himself embark on adventures" after he completed his military buildup in 1980.[22] A 1974 State Department assessment cited the Shah's leading role in hiking up oil prices to the detriment of the West, noting "heretofore his ambitions, though grandiose, have been limited to his own region, but he now seems to envision a global reallocation of capital resources and industry."[23] According to 1975 press reports a CIA psychological profile of the Shah termed him "a dangerous megalomaniac, who is likely to pursue his own aims in disregard of U.S. interests."[24] Senator Kennedy, who visited Iran in 1975, later wrote, "As I was told during my visit to Iran in May, leaders of that country now see it as part of both the Gulf and West Asia, with wider interests and ambitions, extending even to the Indian Ocean."[25] Such concerns led the U.S.

Assuring Oil Supplies

Navy in 1974 to argue against allowing the Shah to purchase three *Sturgeon*-class, nuclear-powered attack submarines.[26] What course Iranian policy might have taken had the Shah survived and completed the transition of Iran into a modern, well-armed state must remain a subject of debate.

As for the Iranian military buildup itself, the Shah had pretensions of his country becoming a Middle East and a Southwest Asian power as well as the dominant naval force in the Persian Gulf and the Indian Ocean. But a 1973 Department of Defense assessment termed the Iranian effort "superficial," falling as it did "outside and far in advance of the Iranian industrial base." The report concluded that "by 1978, Iran's military machine may actually turn out to be a 'parade ground army,'—physically impressive but incapable of prolonged military action."[27]

The Saudi military buildup differed markedly from the Iranian. Between 1969 and 1978 both Saudi Arabia and Iran dramatically increased defense spending. In fact the Saudis outspent the Iraqis and nearly kept abreast with the Shah's defense expenditures.[28] But the Saudi military buildup involved heavy investment in infrastructure—roads, port expansion, training facilities, and air bases. As a result the actual size and armament of the Saudi armed forces increased at a much lower rate than either Iran or Iraq.[29] Whereas the Saudis imported $3 billion worth of arms between 1986 and 1978, the Iraqis imported $6.2 billion, and the Iranians $10.5 billion.[30]

Like the Iranians the Saudis turned to the United States for weapons, advice, and support. The air defense of Saudi Arabia became the top priority of the buildup. The effort to improve the Saudi air force and air defense system—the Peace Hawk program—met with great success and would continue into the 1980s. The Saudi army also underwent both qualitative and quantitative expansion.

The Saudi navy had, understandably, been the stepchild of the kingdom's armed forces. When Great Britain's navy was cruising the waters of the Persian Gulf, there was little need for a Saudi naval force beyond what was necessary for coastal patrols. But the British withdrawal, the U.S. decision to maintain but not expand its naval forces in the gulf, and the expansion of the Iranian navy led the Saudis to begin a massive naval buildup of their own with the advice and support of the U.S. Navy.

The plan developed by a Saudi-American study team proved to be overambitious.[31] Moreover, the low priority accorded the plan by the Saudis, rising prices, a shortage of skilled Saudi personnel, the U.S. provision to the Saudis of equipment unsuitable for the gulf, and the U.S. Navy's reported unwillingness to commit high quality personnel to the effort left the program in shambles by 1980. Dissatisfied with the American-sponsored program, the Saudis turned increasingly to Europeans for equipment and advice after 1980.[32]

The Saudis were genuinely and understandably concerned about their security but, unlike the Shah, they had no ambitions to dominate the gulf

The Nixon Doctrine

President Nixon and Commander Sixth Fleet Vice Admiral Isaac C. Kidd (right) visit the attack aircraft carrier *Saratoga* (CVA–60) during its deployment to the eastern Mediterranean in 1970.

or southwest Asia. As a result the Saudi effort was balanced, well designed, and led to a significant increase in the kingdom's military capabilities, especially in the air. The strains on the social fabric of Saudi Arabia were minimized. Saudi military expansion seemed less threatening to the other gulf states and, unlike the Iranian effort, did little to destabilize the region. Nevertheless, as the events of August 1990 were to demonstrate, more than twenty years after the programs began Saudi Arabia still lacked an effective defensive force.

The Nixon Doctrine proclaimed U.S. unwillingness to replace the British in the Middle East and willingness to accede to the Shah's self-proclaimed status as a regional power. But despite the war in Vietnam the Nixon administration had no intention of reducing the limited American presence in

Assuring Oil Supplies

the Persian Gulf and Indian Ocean. Between 1969 and 1977 the American influence in the region expanded, although that expansion reflected the Nixon administration's predilection to avoid the use or commitment of ground forces. Given the absence of American bases in the Indian Ocean basin, that policy implied an increased reliance on U.S. naval forces.[33]

When the British began withdrawing from the region, however, the United States had to decide if the Middle East Force should remain in the Persian Gulf, and if so, where it should or could be based. The Johnson administration initiated an interagency review of this issue that lasted for more than two years.

Several complicating factors in both domestic and international politics slowed the review process. (The change in administrations did nothing to accelerate the procedure.) A continued U.S. presence in the gulf after the British withdrawal might imply, for example, a heightened U.S. presence in the Middle East; this position might not sit well with an American citizenry to whom international commitments had become anathema. The forceful policy that emanated from Teheran after the British announcement further complicated the issue. The Iranians restated their long-standing claim that Bahrain was part of Iran; in Washington there was a clear understanding that "no assertion of influence in the area by the Americans or others was desired or acceptable" by the Shah.[34] Thus an increased reliance on Iran in the region appeared to rule out a continued American presence in the Persian Gulf, certainly one based in Bahrain.

Despite the Shah's policies, however, the U.S. Navy intended not only to keep the Middle East Force in the gulf at Bahrain but also to enhance American naval capabilities in the Indian Ocean. Pending final administration approval and the Shah's reactions to such American initiatives, the Navy refrained from formally opening the necessary negotiations, although MEF officials in Bahrain were permitted to begin "informal discussions with the British." "However," Admiral Thomas H. Moorer, Chief of Naval Operations, emphasized, "you are still cautioned to avoid any action or commitment that could lead the British to believe that we intend to pick up their commitments in the area."[35]

By early 1969 the Joint Chiefs and the commanders in chief (CINCs) of the major military commands responsible for the Middle East had gone on record in support of the Navy's effort to keep the Middle East Force at Bahrain and to maintain the American presence in the region.[36] More than a year later on 5 June 1970 the National Security Council recommended that MEF remain "at about its present strength [four ships], homeported in Bahrain."[37] Final presidential approval did not come until December 1970.[38]

On 24 December 1970 the Commander Middle East Force received permission to hold a formal discussion with the British and the Bahrainis about the facilities necessary for a continued American presence. A plan already prepared by the MEF staff called for the United States to take over

10 of the 100 acres of the existing British base at Jufair. The required facilities included a receiving antenna, priority use of Berth No. 1 on the Mina Sulman jetty, a small waterfront area for work and recreation boats, landing rights for aircraft with suitable hangar and office space at the Muharraq airfield, and a radio building with a transmitting antenna.[39] The staff had also developed plans for various withdrawal contingencies if the negotiations with the Bahrainis failed. By the time the Americans learned on 19 August 1971 that the British expected to complete their withdrawal by December, the negotiations were well under way. On 23 December, a week after it became independent and assumed full control over both its administration and international affairs, Bahrain signed a lease-basing agreement with the United States. Both countries reserved the right to end the agreement one year after serving an official notice of intent.

Opposition in both the United States and the Arab world greeted the accord. The U.S. Senate approved the arrangement on 29 June 1972 after a tough and spirited debate, with the Navy emphasizing that the lease implied no political or military commitment to Bahrain.[40] Arab nationalists throughout the Middle East attacked the Bahrainis for allowing a vestige of colonialism to remain after the British withdrawal. But the Bahrainis, concerned about Iranian designs on the archipelago, weathered the attacks and early in 1972 "stated that there would be no objection to an increase in the US presence provided it could be done quietly, at a politically realistic time and in such a way not to force the Government of Bahrain to make a choice between the US and the Arab world." [41]

In the United States, the 1972 political mini-debate over the basing of Middle East Force at Bahrain paled in comparison to the decade-long struggle to develop an American base at Diego Garcia, the chief island in the Chagos Archipelago. The U.S. Navy's interest in such an Indian Ocean base had originated during long-range planning conducted in the late 1950s under the direction of Chief of Naval Operations Admiral Arleigh Burke. The Navy needed a politically secure base to support operations in the Indian Ocean basin, which included the Arabian and Red Seas and the Persian Gulf. As a result of these studies the Navy proposed in 1959 that the British separate Diego Garcia from the Seychelles and develop it as a distinct political entity.[42] In the early 1960s, with strong support from Paul Nitze, Assistant Secretary of Defense for International Security Affairs, the Indian Ocean base concept progressed slowly. Finally, in November 1965 the British split off the Chagos Islands, including the Diego Garcia atoll, and established the British Indian Ocean Territory. On 30 December 1966 the United States and the United Kingdom signed an executive agreement that authorized the United States to construct a communications facility. Again Paul Nitze played a

Assuring Oil Supplies

Aerial view of the U.S. Naval Support Activity, Diego Garcia, British Indian Ocean Territory.

leading role in this accord, first as Secretary of the Navy (1967) and then as Assistant Secretary of Defense (1968), and the pace of development quickened. After Congress approved funding for a modest base in June 1968, base development continued slowly, marked by constant political battles tied to a debate over the nature of the American role in the region.

The development of a base on Diego Garcia was, and still is, central to a continued U.S. role in the Indian Ocean. Given the historic international and domestic difficulties inherent in an American effort to establish a base in one of the littoral states, the development of the virtually unpopulated atoll was a politically acceptable and attractive alternative. Diego Garcia is about 2300 nautical miles from the Persian Gulf and a long way from everywhere else (or, as some have said, a long way from nowhere); nevertheless, it is centrally placed to support Indian Ocean operations and has proved its worth during regional crises such as the latter stages of the Iran-Iraq war and Operations Desert Shield and Desert Storm.

The U.S. Navy's long-standing desire to strengthen its strategic position in the Indian Ocean was enhanced by "the unprecedented entrance into the Indian Ocean of Soviet naval units."[43] The Soviets' sudden and unexpected appearance, the impending withdrawal of the British on whom the

The Nixon Doctrine

USN 711597

A Soviet F-class submarine en route to the Indian Ocean.

Americans had relied for thirty years, and the awareness that MEF strength was not likely to be increased left Americans in the Persian Gulf and Indian Ocean feeling somewhat exposed. The 1971 Middle East Force command history noted:

> Current year 1971 was marked by the phased withdrawal of British forces from East of Suez. The withdrawal resulted in the loss of a huge reservoir of historical knowledge, political expertise and analytic ability on events in the Persian Gulf and Arabian Peninsula that previously had been available to COMIDEASTFOR. Additionally, the withdrawal of Royal Navy ships and the Royal Air Force removed the only available assets for maritime reconnaissance in the Persian Gulf and Gulf of Oman. Prior to withdrawal, U.K. sources and analysts had contributed about 80% of the political intelligence on the Persian Gulf area available to COMIDEASTFOR.[44]

The Soviet presence in the Indian Ocean represented a political and a potential military challenge to the U.S. Navy, but the more immediate problem facing Middle East Force was the mundane but critically important task of collecting intelligence about this Soviet presence. During the 1960s and early 1970s the Soviet military presence grew around the basin in countries such as India, Iraq, the Yemens, Somalia, and Ethiopia. Soviet ships in the Persian Gulf, the Red Sea, the Arabian Sea, and elsewhere in the Indian Ocean had to be tracked and their activities monitored. The intelligence tasks confronting the small Middle East Force were daunting. For example, in late 1971 the Soviet squadron in the Indian Ocean included two cruisers, two de-

85

Assuring Oil Supplies

stroyers, an LST, a minesweeper, seven submarines, nine support vessels, an intelligence collector, and four space and research ships. MEF assets had to monitor the Soviet anchorages off Socotra, Cape Guardafui, Coetivy Island in the Seychelles, and Speakers Bank in the Chagos.[45]

With the British withdrawing, the Americans began to cooperate with the French. By 1972 the French and Americans were informally exchanging information. On 15 February 1973 the two countries reached a formal agreement and established improved communications and a direct link between the Commander Middle East Force and the French Indian Ocean commander (ALINDIEN) on the island of Reunion.[46]

Franco-American cooperation eased the burden of intelligence collection and made possible improvement in the MEF efforts during the critical years of the mid-1970s. The October 1973 war between Israel and its Arab neighbors, during which the two superpowers placed some of their respective forces on alert, stretched American capabilities to the limit. So too did the April 1975 global exercise, OKEAN, during which twenty-three Soviet ships of various types operated in the Indian Ocean. About the same time Soviet long-range aircraft began flying reconnaissance missions from Indian Ocean bases. These surface and air operations demonstrated a growing Soviet presence and increased capability in a volatile region, critically important to the United States and the West.[47]

That volatility became evident on 6 October 1973 with the Yom Kippur War. This fourth Arab-Israeli conflict began when Syria and Egypt attacked Israeli positions in the Golan and the Sinai. Once again Middle East events took Americans by surprise and plunged the United States into crises that had both regional and global implications.

Expecting a quick Israeli victory, the United States initially adopted a low profile. American policymakers hoped to avoid Arab wrath and to maintain a position as "honest broker." But on 9 October reports from the Golan and Sinai fronts indicated that the Israelis were in trouble, and rumors abounded that they were readying their secret atomic arsenal. The United States responded with a sizable resupply effort that, in combination with the fighting power of the Israeli Defense Forces, allowed Israel to regain the initiative. The Arab nations, led by Saudi Arabia, responded with an oil embargo of the United States. The Soviet Union began its own aerial resupply of Syrian forces and placed several airborne divisions on alert.

A fortnight into the war, Secretary of State Kissinger commenced an active diplomatic campaign to end the conflict before it escalated further. Kissinger directed his efforts at the belligerents themselves, the several Arab states not directly involved in the fighting, and the Soviet Union. His exertions led to a 22 October U.N. resolution calling for an in-place cease-fire that was accepted by all

The Nixon Doctrine

parties that same day. But continued Israeli efforts to destroy the Egyptian Third Corps, isolated in the Sinai, threatened the agreement. By the twenty-fourth, the United States was concerned enough about Soviet military moves that Washington, early on 25 October, placed American military forces on a higher state of alert—DEFCON THREE. Fortunately, the situation deteriorated no further, the cease-fire held, and difficult negotiating led to disengagement on all fronts.

The Yom Kippur War forced the United States to confront a new reality in the Middle East. After the successful resolution of the 1970 Jordanian crisis, the United States had increased military and economic aid to Israel in the belief that a secure Jewish state, freed from the specter of Arab attack, would become a force for stability in the region. Nixon and Kissinger would then be able to focus on the truly important foreign policy problems of the day, for example, the on-going struggle in Indochina, the Soviet-American detente, and the U.S. relationship with Communist China.[48] But reliance on Israeli military superiority had secured neither peace nor stability. The improved fighting capability of Egyptian and Syrian forces did much to obliterate the memory of the Arabs' 1967 defeat and rekindle their pride and nationalism. The Arabs had also demonstrated their willingness to use oil as an effective political weapon and witnessed the shock inflicted on dependent Western economies by an embargo that continued into March 1974. Soviet influence in the region, which had been expanding since the mid-1950s, not only challenged American interests but also threatened to turn a regional crisis into superpower confrontation.

The 1973 war and its aftermath also tested the U.S. Navy's Middle East Force. The MEF's command historian noted:

> The 1973 Arab-Israeli war, commencing 6 October, had significant impact on MIDEASTFOR operations. The destroyer units were directed to wartime readiness and involved in escort duty of merchant shipping, anti-submarine surveillance, and increased intelligence collection. The subsequent oil boycott of the United States closed numerous ports of visit due to fuel constraints during the remainder of the year.[49]

The war threatened American access to Persian Gulf and Indian Ocean ports at a time when the U.S. Navy needed to expand its presence in the basin. On 20 October the Bahrainis announced that they were terminating their lease with the Americans. The United States once again had to review the pros and cons of a naval presence in the Persian Gulf. The Navy examined the possibility of basing the Middle East Force at Diego Garcia or at an Iranian port inside or outside the gulf. But it was not long after the announcement that the Navy began to sense that it might not have to relocate MEF, noting the "absence of any immediate pressure" from the Bahrainis.[50] Commander Middle East Force, Rear Admiral Robert J. Hanks, advised his superiors that he believed the Bahraini decision was reversible.[51] In fact, they did quietly drop their demand for immediate withdrawal.

Assuring Oil Supplies

In July 1975 the United States agreed to amend certain provisions of the 1971 agreement, and on 12 August 1975 the Bahrainis extended the provisional agreement to 30 June 1977.[52] Continued negotiations resulted in a further exchange of notes (28 June 1977) in which both parties agreed to abide by the amended terms of the 1971 agreement. According to the 1977 accord, the United States no longer retained the right to base its MEF in Bahrain, although American civilian and military personnel could be assigned to an Administrative Support Unit in Bahrain which would support American ships in the gulf.[53] Officially, U.S. Navy warships were no longer to be homeported in Bahrain, and most of the staff was considered to be on temporary duty.

Although the Navy was able to hold on at Bahrain, a June 1974 review of the situation revealed that twenty-eight ports in eleven countries were closed to American warships. Only Manama (Bahrain), Port Louis (Mauritius), Karachi (Pakistan), Colombo (Sri Lanka), and Bandar Abbas and Bandar-e Shahpur (Iran) (and only the Iranian ports were considered "dependable") continued to supply U.S. Navy ships. The report concluded: "The fuel tail has long 'wagged the dog' in MIDEASTFOR [Middle East Force] scheduling. It now firmly dictates scheduling and, unless a solution to the recent conflict can be found which is acceptable to the Arabs, the fuel outlook is likely to worsen."[54] Ironically, the U.S. Navy's small four-destroyer force was hard-pressed to find fuel while patroling the waters adjoining the world's largest oil preserve.

In fact, the oil embargo threatened to disrupt the overseas operations of the U.S. Navy as a whole.[55] Arab efforts to limit the movement of oil products not only to American refineries but also to those that supplied the U.S. Navy with fuel threatened American operations in the Mediterranean, the Indian Ocean, and the Western Pacific. In congressional testimony the Navy admitted that about 95 percent of the fuel for the Pacific Fleet came from foreign sources.[56] The Navy found itself relying increasingly on Iranian sources of supply, a move seen as a vindication of the Nixon administration's policy of reliance on the Shah.[57]

10

The Carter Administration and the Gulf

The Arab reaction to the October 1973 war—that is, the Bahraini decision to evict the Middle East Force and the efforts of other littoral states to close their ports to American ships—further strengthened and accelerated American efforts to develop a secure basing infrastructure to support a U.S. presence in the Indian Ocean. In addition, the impact on Western and Third World countries of the oil embargo, combined with the higher oil prices driven by the Organization of Petroleum Exporting Countries, was becoming apparent. Between September 1973 and January 1974, for example, the embargo pushed the cost of a barrel of crude from $3 to $11. These developments forced the United States to reassess its strategy for an unstable region of increasing global significance. American policymakers sought some chimerical formula that would allow a solution of the Arab-Israeli dispute, permit the United States to strengthen its ties with "moderate" Arab countries, secure the flow of oil to the West and Japan, and limit Soviet power and influence in the region.

One of many options American policymakers considered was a new correlation between military policy and diplomacy. In late 1974 and early 1975 the Western press and many senior American officials speculated openly about a possible U.S. military operation to secure critical oil-producing areas in the event of an embargo. In a January 1975 interview with *Business Week*, Secretary of State Kissinger responded to a question about such an option:

> A very dangerous course. We should have learned from Vietnam that it is easier to get into a war than to get out of it. I am not saying that there's no circumstance where we would not use force. But it is one thing to use it in the case of a dispute over price, it's another where there's some actual strangulation of the industrial world.[1]

In fact, American officials were engaged in more than mere speculation. Planners conducted preliminary studies examining possible military responses to an Arab cutoff of oil to the United States, Western Europe, and Japan. Navy planners considered the impact of an increased naval presence in the Indian Ocean, a blockade of Arab ports, the diversion or sinking of tankers headed to nonembargoed countries, air strikes against non-oil-related facilities, and direct amphibious assault. None of the proposals appeared practical. Chief of Naval Operations Admiral James L. Holloway III wrote on the cover letter of one such study, "It becomes evident that there is little we can effectively accomplish in M.E."[2]

Assuring Oil Supplies

Recognizing the strategic importance of the Persian Gulf, President Jimmy Carter authorized reinforcement of the Middle East Force.

Nevertheless, despite the practical difficulties of projecting American military power into the Middle East, a new factor had been added to the strategic equation, one that could not be ignored by the Arabs and Iranians. Since the end of the Second World War the United States had sought to avoid the commitment of American military forces to defend the Middle East against external aggression. Now, in the mid-1970s, the United States began to contemplate the use of military force to ensure the flow of oil to the West, as well as to shield the region from the Soviet Union.

Concerns about the stability of the Middle East, the growing reliance of the West on Persian Gulf oil, the British pullout from east of Suez, and the Soviet navy's entry into the Indian Ocean contributed to a growing American realization of the importance of the gulf and continued emphasis on strengthening the American position in the region. Encumbered as they were both physically and psychologically by the war in Vietnam, the Nixon and Ford administrations sought only marginal improvements in infrastructure in the gulf and, given the turmoil in the region, meager increases in naval presence by making occasional carrier forays into the Indian Ocean rather than reinforcing the MEF in the Persian Gulf.

The Carter administration accelerated this process. In mid-1977 Presidential Review Memorandum 10 identified "the Persian Gulf as a vulnerable and vital region, to which greater military concern ought to be given."[3] Pres-

The Carter Administration

idential Directive (PD) 18, signed by Carter on 24 August 1977, called for the establishment of a "deployment force of light divisions with strategic mobility for global contingencies, particularly in the Persian Gulf region and Korea."[4] In a December 1977 address Secretary of Defense Harold Brown stressed the importance of naval and tactical air forces and improved strategic mobility. Such assets would give the United States the capability "to respond effectively and simultaneously to a relatively minor as well as a major military contingency."[5] These Carter administration decisions mark the immediate origin of the Rapid Deployment Force (RDF), what later became United States Central Command, and laid the groundwork that made Operations Desert Shield and Desert Storm possible.

The RDF concept had deep roots in American military thinking. The Army had established the Strategic Army Corps in 1958.[6] About the same time the Navy had begun considering use of Diego Garcia as a base. The debate with regard to a command structure began after the Suez crisis when the Joint Chiefs contemplated the establishment of a temporary specified command to handle contingencies in the Middle East. Such a command—Commander in Chief, Specified Command, Middle East (CINCSPECOMME)—did control Operation Bluebat in Lebanon in 1958. In July 1960 during the Congo crisis, when American intervention seemed a possibility, the services argued once again over who should plan for such contingencies that fell outside the normal bounds of the existing Atlantic, European, and Pacific command structures. The Navy and Marine Corps believed that responsibility for Africa and the Middle East ought to belong to the Commander in Chief, Atlantic (CINCLANT); the Army and Air Force favored Strategic Air Command, Europe (SACEUR), or the establishment of a separate joint task force reporting directly to the JCS. In the interim the Joint Chiefs agreed to an unsatisfactory compromise with continued divided responsibilities.[7]

The following year the Kennedy administration brought many new ideas to Washington, among them a renewed emphasis on conventional forces embodied in the term "flexible response." This was a departure in tone, if not in substance, from the Eisenhower administration's reliance on nuclear weaponry and "massive retaliation." On 1 January 1962 the Joint Chiefs established Strike Command (STRIKCOM) to direct possible contingency operations. Headquartered at MacDill Air Force Base, it was STRIKCOM under which Middle East Force subsequently operated during times of crisis. There were also improvements in special operations and plans for the expansion of strategic air and sealift assets. Unfortunately, American involvement in Vietnam slowed many of these developments.[8] When the JCS disestablished STRIKCOM on 31 December 1971, the responsibilities of the newly established Readiness Command did not include the Middle East. Preparations and planning for contingency operations in the region reverted to SACEUR and his naval component command and successor to CINCNELM—Com-

Assuring Oil Supplies

mander in Chief, U.S. Naval Forces Europe (CINCUSNAVEUR). It was not until 1983 that the dispute over the command structure for the Persian Gulf subsided, at least temporarily, with the establishment of Central Command at MacDill Air Force Base in Tampa (see appendix B).

The Carter administration's search for a new defense framework for the gulf was thus evolutionary rather than revolutionary, and a realistic grappling with difficult strategic questions too long left unanswered. In response to PD 18 the Joint Chiefs oversaw a slow, methodical review of American strategy for the Middle East. On 7 September 1978 the JCS approved the "Review of US Strategy Related to the Middle East and the Persian Gulf" and that same day forwarded it to Secretary of Defense Brown.

The review focused on three major U.S. interests in the region.[9]

1. To assure continuous access to petroleum resources.
2. To prevent an inimical power or combination of powers from establishing hegemony.
3. To assure the survival of Israel as an independent state in a stable relationship with contiguous Arab states.

The review recommended expanded basing—especially for land-based aircraft—at Diego Garcia, as well as in Oman, Saudi Arabia, and Djibouti. Projected naval force increases would include an increase both in carrier battle group (CVBG) strength, from four to six combatants and one or two auxiliaries, and in deployment, from the previous one to three months to three to four months of the year. During other months a battle group built around large, amphibious assault ships with AV–8A Harriers and an embarked Marine Air-Ground Task Force (MAGTF) would cruise the Indian Ocean.

> These forces will be capable of supporting US and allied interests in contingency situations by conducting a variety of tasks (not necessarily simultaneously) at several levels of intensity. These tasks would include: a range of conventional air operations; amphibious operations; SLOC [sea line of communication] protection; naval gunfire support; protection and evacuation of US and designated third-country nationals from crisis/conflict areas; surveillance of Soviet and other maritime operations; operations and exercises with allied forces; and port visits.

Given the strain on American resources, especially on the naval assets of the Seventh and Sixth Fleets, and because the security of the area was vital to the United States and its allies, the report recommended that the British, Dutch, Germans, and Australians be encouraged to increase their naval deployments to the Indian Ocean. The French, the report noted, already had deployed a sizable force to the region.

The Joint Chiefs' Middle East strategy review also suggested the possibility of establishing a numbered fleet in the Indian Ocean, the Fifth Fleet. The

The Carter Administration

A Soviet guided missile frigate observes Carrier Battle Group Eight off the coast of Lebanon, February 1979.

Army, the Air Force, and the European Command (EUCOM) were unenthusiastic about the establishment of the fleet as an extension of the Pacific Command (PACOM), which was already responsible for the Indian Ocean. Even within the Navy there was little support for the formation of another numbered fleet. Many in the Navy, whose officers knew that operating in the Indian Ocean was "a bitch," saw a Fifth Fleet as a device for Secretary of Defense Brown to create a "Lite Fleet" as a showpiece for his small carrier concepts.[10] An April 1979 OPNAV memo advised that "designating an increased presence force as a 'Fifth Fleet' would be 'political gamesmanship' and 'cosmetic,' since no additional forces are being generated. The force should be kept as a Task Force or Task Group, and subordinate to the U.S. Navy's Seventh Fleet."[11] Ultimately, Chief of Naval Operations Thomas B. Hayward reasoned that the Fifth Fleet concept was "no good deal."[12]

The JCS review predated the Iranian revolution and the near collapse of the American position in the gulf by only a few months. For the United States 1979 was a year of crisis. In January the Shah abdicated. The centrist government that replaced the monarchy quickly demonstrated its ineffectiveness and the radical mullahs, or clerics, increasingly dominated Iranian politics. In November the Iranians seized the American embassy and its occupants in the capital city of Teheran and the interminable

Assuring Oil Supplies

hostage crisis began. Then, in December, the Soviet Union began moving troops into Kabul, Afghanistan. Some observers interpreted the Soviet decision as a defensive move to aid a threatened socialist state under the terms of the Brezhnev Doctrine. Others saw the Soviet invasion as the first step in a Communist master plan to drive towards the warm waters of the Indian Ocean and secure the oil of the Persian Gulf. Whatever the cause of the decision taken by the "drunken" Soviet leadership,[13] for the first time since the end of the Second World War the Soviet Union used force beyond its own borders or those of eastern European countries "liberated" by the Red Army at the end of the Second World War.

For the United States the fall of the Shah in early 1979 undermined the American position in the Persian Gulf, the Indian Ocean, and the entire Middle East. In the aftermath of the Iranian revolution contemporary criticism of U.S. policies during the 1970s appear rather prescient. Indeed, since the fall of the Shah there has been no dearth of "I told you so" analysis. For example, in a recent history of Iranian-American relations, Professor James Bill, who had long held a pessimistic view of the Shah's prospects for survival, quotes from a paper he delivered to the State Department in early 1978; in this paper he painted a rather "grim" but realistic assessment of the state of affairs in Teheran.[14]

In his memoirs Henry Kissinger attempted to refute the ex post facto attacks on the policy on which he had been the chief architect. He stressed the continuity of U.S. policy on Iran and noted the Shah's often-demonstrated cooperation with and friendship for the United States, for example, his sale of oil to Americans during the 1973–1974 Arab embargo.[15] Kissinger rejected the idea that extensive American arms sales imposed a "guns or butter" dilemma for Iran, writing, "nor can it be said that the Shah's arms purchases diverted resources from economic development, the conventional criticism of arms sales to developing countries. The Shah did both."[16] In Kissinger's view, the Shah fell not because his reforms were proceeding too slowly but because they were moving too fast. The Shah was a victim of a modernization crisis.

But the Shah's American-supported modernization drive—the rapid military buildup, and just-as-rapid attempt to drag his country into the twentieth century—exacerbated internal tensions and hastened or perhaps even precipitated his downfall. In an article written shortly before the revolution, Theodore H. Moran noted that "in the first years of euphoria following the fourfold oil price increase in 1973–1974, Iranian planners felt that they had the financial resources needed for all aspects of development. This proved not to be the case."[17] Controlled food prices, meant to keep urban supplies cheap, were not matched by controls in the countryside and led to a drop in agricultural production and a multibillion-dollar food-import bill. The Shah's defense expenditures totaled about a third of his budget and, despite

The Carter Administration

the country's oil wealth, Iran actually ran a budget deficit in 1976.[18] Perhaps the most obvious example of Iran's internal problems was that by 1977 Teheran was enduring six-hour-long blackouts because of lack of fuel and inadequate generating capacity. Moreover, the Shah's evident willingness to support American policy heightened internal xenophobic pressures, as did the ever-expanding American presence in Iran.

The Iranian religious leader Ayatollah Ruhollah Khomeini had first gained national notoriety as a vociferous critic of the Shah's acceptance of a 1964 Status of Forces Agreement, which gave American military personnel in Iran virtual extraterritoriality. Khomeini had denounced this agreement that "reduced the Iranian people to a level lower than that of an American dog," and was shortly thereafter exiled.[19] Although the Nixon Doctrine called for a reduced American involvement in the gulf, the extensive assistance needed to oversee military and economic aid programs necessitated an expanded presence. A mid-1970s Department of Defense estimate projected that about 150,000 Americans would be in the Middle East by 1980.[20] When President Carter visited Iran in December 1977, there were 30,000 Americans in the country, as many as had been in Iran during the Second World War.[21]

In retrospect it is obvious that the modernization process in Iran reached a crisis stage during the mid-1970s. Inflation, rapid internal development, and the expansion of the Iranian military beyond realistic security needs (and beyond what it could usefully absorb) exacerbated the crisis. Moreover, as the modernization process accelerated and internal pressures mounted, the Shah himself was increasingly preoccupied with oversight of the military buildup and the direction of Iranian foreign policy.[22]

The Iranian situation resembled that of a train, hurtling downhill along old track. The Shah was the engineer, obsessed with the train's speed but oblivious to the deteriorating state of the roadbed. The Americans were the stokers and brakemen; in the past they had provided only measured amounts of fuel and had applied the brakes when necessary to avoid disaster, but during the 1970s they eagerly answered the Shah's calls for more coal by shoveling as fast as they could as they simultaneously released the brakes. It is not surprising that the train derailed.

Nevertheless, the Shah, far from being an American puppet, bore the ultimate responsibility for his own fate.[23] If the Iranian government was unresponsive to the needs of its people, it was because that government had been fashioned by the Shah to ensure his own security by preventing the development of any rival center of political power. If the Iranian military was unwilling or incapable of rescuing or replacing their monarch, it was because the Shah had made certain that the military was divided and led by men unlikely to seize power for themselves in a military coup. The system placed all authority in the hands of a man who in 1978–1979 was too sick (he was al-

Assuring Oil Supplies

USN 1176332

Midway, fitted with an air-defense missile system, is underway in the Indian Ocean during the Iranian Crisis.

ready dying of cancer and under chemotherapy) to direct the government.[24] As he had many times before, the Shah fled the country. James Bill wrote, "He in the end understood better than disgruntled Western critics and his own hard-line military generals that such a national uprising could not be put down by force indefinitely."[25] Even Kissinger later admitted:

> Wise is the ruler who understands that economic development, far from strengthening his position, carries with it the imperative of building new political institutions to accommodate the growing complexity of his society. It cannot be said that either the Shah or his friends possessed this wisdom; but, it must be remarked, neither did his enemies.[26]

Shortly after the Shah fell, the Carter administration, in an effort to quickly strengthen the U.S. position in the region, began shifting additional forces to the Middle East. Unarmed U.S. Air Force F–15s and Airborne Warning and Control System (AWACS) aircraft deployed to Saudi Arabia in January and March 1979 respectively.[27] A CVBG built around *Midway* (CVB–41) steamed from the Western Pacific. Following the seizure of the hostages in November, *Kitty Hawk* (CVA–63) left Subic Bay for the Arabian Sea.[28]

Coming on the heels of the revolution in Iran, the Soviet invasion of Afghanistan provoked a sharp response from the West. The Carter administration embargoed grain shipments to the Soviet Union and withdrew

The Carter Administration

TABLE 6

Growth of Middle East Force, 1978–1988

	No. of Ships
1978–79	5
1980	7
1981–86	5
1987	13
1988	17

SOURCE: Derived from a variety of sources. The strength of Middle East Force varied as ships came and went, frequently with overlapping reliefs. The figures for a given year represent an average strength for that year.

TABLE 7

Increases in U.S. Navy Strength in the Indian Ocean, 1976–1988

	Surface Ship Days	Carrier Ship Days	Percent of Deployed Carriers	Average Yearly Carrier Strength
1976	1,279	19	3	0.1
1977	1,439	100	7	0.3
1978	1,207	35	3	0.1
1979	2,612	153	9	0.4
1980	6,993	836	51	2.3
1981	5,651	646	39	1.7
1982	5,361	443	27	1.2
1983	4,704	406	24	1.0
1984	5,335	410	28	1.1
1985	5,136	475	36	1.3
1986	3,580	185	13	0.5
1987	6,760	412	30	1.1
1988	7,991	412	30	1.1

SOURCE: Derived from Adam Siegel, Karen Domabyl, and Barbara Lingberg, *Deployment of U.S. Navy Aircraft Carriers and Other Surface Ships, 1976–1988* (Alexandria, VA, 1989), pp. 13, 15, 21, 26–27.

Assuring Oil Supplies

the U.S. team from the forthcoming Moscow Olympics. Carter decided that forceful action was necessary to deter further Soviet moves to the south. In his 23 January 1980 State of the Union address, the President announced what became known as the "Carter Doctrine."

> Let our position be absolutely clear: An attempt by any outside force to gain control of the Persian Gulf region will be regarded as an assault on the vital interests of the United States of America, and such as assault will be repelled by any means necessary, including military force.[29]

To back this new policy the administration continued to build up American forces in the region. U.S. Air Force AWACS deployed to Egypt and eight B-52 bombers from Guam overflew the Arabian Sea in a demonstration of American air power. But the principal measure of U.S. military power remained naval. By mid-January, when Carter delivered his address, the Navy had twenty-five ships, including three aircraft carriers, in the Indian Ocean.[30]

In a 6 March 1980 address Secretary of Defense Brown outlined the military aspects implicit in the Carter Doctrine. Brown listed American interests in the region: "to insure access to adequate oil supplies; to resist Soviet expansion; to promote stability in the region; and to advance the Middle East peace process, while insuring—and, indeed, in order to help insure—the continued security of the State of Israel." Regarding oil, the Secretary of Defense emphasized the importance of conservation as an element of national security but also stressed

> that no conceivable combination of measures—conservation, stockpiling, or alternative energy sources—can totally eliminate the near term security problem that is created by threats to the gulf and its oil. The hard fact is that there is nothing the United States—or our industrial world partners or the less developed countries—can do in the coming decade, or probably even the next, that would save us from severe damage if the bulk of the oil supply from the Persian Gulf were cut off for a sustained period.

Accordingly, Brown announced that the United States was developing rapid deployment forces and increasing its strategic sealift and airlift capabilities.[31]

Unfortunately for the United States and the Carter administration, 1980 proved to be almost as difficult a year as 1979. The April attempt to rescue the hostages ended in disaster at Desert One, a rendezvous on the Iranian plateau.[32] The hostage rescue fiasco further weakened the administration's credibility and appeared, at least on the surface, to illustrate American military incapacity in the region. Even though it failed, however, the rescue attempt demonstrated the long reach to the planned rescue that was to be made by American power and the critical contribution of naval forces. Because of the political restrictions that denied the United States access to bases around the periphery of the gulf, and the need for secrecy, the carrier *Nimitz* (CVAN–68) served as the base for the U.S. Navy helicopters meant to carry the hostages to freedom.

The Carter Administration

TRH–53 Sea Stallion helicopters take off from *Nimitz* in the Indian Ocean beginning Operation Evening Light, the mission to rescue American hostages in Iran, 24 April 1980.

In September deteriorating relations between Iran and Iraq led to open warfare. Most Western analysts expected a quick Iraqi victory, something like a World War II-type blitzkrieg; early initial Iraqi successes seemed to support that view.[33]

The United States reacted promptly to the war, continuing the naval buildup that had begun in early 1979. A cruiser and a destroyer reinforced Middle East Force to a strength of seven ships.[34] U.S. Air Force AWACS and tankers returned to Saudi Arabia. A pair of carrier battle groups remained in or near the North Arabian Sea, bringing the U.S. Navy's strength in the region to more than thirty ships. In a pattern that would be followed throughout the decade, other Western men-of-war also deployed to the gulf. By October about sixty American, French, British, and Australian warships were in the Indian Ocean or the gulf, keeping a close eye on the belligerents as well as the nearly thirty Soviet warships in the region.[35]

But to what purpose? In the Iran-Iraq war the Carter administration faced a new dilemma. The Carter Doctrine had addressed the issue of external, that is, Soviet, threats to the Gulf. In his March 1979 speech Secretary of Defense Brown, echoed the conclusions of the 1975 JCS Middle East strategy review by calling "access to adequate oil supplies" the primary American objective in the region. Would the United States respond with force to an internal threat posed by a Middle Eastern state to the West's oil supplies?

Assuring Oil Supplies

Speaking to reporters at the White House on 24 September, President Carter proclaimed the U.S. neutrality in the Persian Gulf war. He remarked that the loss of both Iranian and Iraqi oil would not have a major impact on the world's supply. But the President cautioned:

> Of course, a total suspension of oil exports from the other nations who ship throughout the Persian Gulf region would create a serious threat to the world's oil supply and consequently a threat to the economic health of all nations. Therefore, it's important that I add my own strong support and that of my Nation to the declaration which the nine European Community nations made yesterday. Freedom of navigation in the Persian Gulf is of primary importance to the whole international community. It is imperative that there be no infringement of that freedom of passage of ships to and from the Persian Gulf region.[36]

Three weeks later Secretary of State Edmund Muskie reiterated the President's position: "We have pledged to do what is necessary to protect free shipping in the Strait of Hormuz from any interference."[37] The Carter Doctrine would be applicable to internal as well as external threats to the oil of the Persian Gulf.

PART FOUR

The United States, the Gulf, and the Iran-Iraq War, 1981–1988

Ronald Reagan brought a renewed sense of optimism to the American presidency in January 1981. The incoming administration's promises to end the "malaise" that had gripped the American people, get the economy moving, rebuild the American military, and give new direction to American global policy were meant to reverse what many perceived to be a period of decline for the United States. Reagan's early policy towards the Soviet Union will long be associated with his remark about the "Evil Empire." Reagan also promised a tougher line towards Iran and strong policy in the Middle East. A joke frequently heard in late 1980 was, "What's flat and glows in the dark?" The answer, "Iran the day after Reagan's inauguration."

Historians and political analysts will long debate the extent to which Reagan gave new direction to the nation or simply reflected and capitalized on an existing American mood. But with regard to U.S. policy in the Persian Gulf and Indian Ocean region, Reagan inherited clearly defined and annunciated diplomatic and military policies—the Carter Doctrine and the Rapid Deployment Force—from the previous administration.

The Reagan administration built on and ultimately executed these policies. The continued development of the Rapid Deployment Force led to the establishment in 1983 of a new unified command, United States Central Command; in 1987 President Reagan chose to act on Secretary of State Muskie's 1980 pledge to do what was "necessary" to keep the tanker traffic safe from "interference" in the Persian Gulf.

11

"Not While This President Serves": The Reflagging Decision

Although spokespersons in the Reagan administration generally attempted to disassociate themselves from anything that bore the "Carter" label,[1] the new administration nevertheless embraced some of their predecessor's policies. In a 28 January 1981 appearance before the Senate Armed Services Committee, Secretary of Defense Caspar W. Weinberger called for a Navy "capable of maintaining a 3-ocean commitment," implying a continued, if accelerated buildup of naval forces in the Indian Ocean.[2] In 1981 the administration's first Defense Guidance projection for fiscal years 1983–1987 stressed the need "to assure the continued flow of oil" from the Persian Gulf and to "make a heavier investment in the near term in upgrading our capabilities to project forces to, and operate them in, this region."[3] In an interview with *Time* magazine, Secretary of State Alexander Haig responded to a question about the Carter Doctrine:

> ... Western industrialized societies are largely dependent on the oil resources of the Middle East region and a threat to access of that oil would constitute a grave threat to the vital national interest. That must be dealt with; and that does not exclude the use of force.[4]

During an appearance before the Senate Armed Services Committee on 9 March 1981, Deputy Secretary of Defense Frank C. Carlucci spoke of American concerns for the security of the gulf region. He outlined several responses, such as an increased American naval presence in the Indian Ocean to include one or two carrier battle groups and an afloat Marine Air Ground Task Force, further development of what was now termed the Rapid Deployment Joint Task Force (RDJTF), a diplomatic attempt to improve access to local facilities, expansion of facilities at Diego Garcia, and the prepositioning of equipment and supplies.[5]

The new administration's reluctance to embrace existing policies forthrightly was both philosophical and political. Having assailed the Carter presidency during the campaign, Reagan well understood that his inheritance came with a fair amount of political baggage.[6] From the start both the Carter Doctrine and the Rapid Deployment Force had come under bipartisan attack. Long an opponent of an increased American role in the region, Senator Edward Kennedy had questioned the wisdom of the Carter commitment to the defense of the gulf. Others had expressed doubts about the substance of the policy; some called it a bluff. Analysts had charged

The Iran-Iraq War

The Indian Ocean Battle Group underway in May 1980 includes guided missile cruisers *Virginia* (CGN–38) and *California* (CGN–36) (background) and carriers *Dwight D. Eisenhower* (CVN–69) and *Nimitz* (CVN–68).

that the RDF concept had been hastily thrown together and was unworkable because it was dependent on nonexistent airlift and sealift capability that left it neither rapid, deployable, nor a force.

The most substantive criticisms focused on the logistical problems that would confront any American effort to project military force into the region. Logistical shortcomings led military analyst Jeffrey Record to argue that the RDF was "a standing invitation to military disaster" because "the Rapid Deployment Force currently envisaged by the Department of Defense is a fatally flawed instrument for effective U.S. military intervention in the Persian Gulf."[7]

In a balanced and cogent examination of the Rapid Deployment Force concept, analyst Joshua Epstein attacked what he viewed as the underlying precepts of the Carter strategy, namely, that the RDF was a tripwire backed by the threat of American horizontal or vertical escalation.[8] Successful deterrence, Epstein argued, had to be based on a conventional capability to check a Soviet move into Iran. Unlike most other critics of the RDF concept, Epstein demonstrated that because the Soviets also faced enormous logistic difficulties in the Middle East, the United States could in fact develop a small, deployable force capable of effective action in the Persian Gulf area.[9]

Criticisms of the Carter Doctrine and the Rapid Deployment Force had some merit. The military force necessary to support the stated policies did not yet exist in the early 1980s. The logistical realities inherent in operations halfway around the world were too exacting to make conventional deterrence feasible. Would the United States go to war with the Soviet Union and risk nuclear conflict to save revolutionary Iran?

Nevertheless, as Zbigniew Brzezinski noted in the memoir of his service as Carter's National Security Adviser, in a democracy pronouncements had to be issued in advance of the development of capabilities.[10] Only in this way could an administration garner sufficient public and political backing to support the long-term programs needed to implement the policy. The American military had been no better prepared to defend Greece and Turkey when Truman announced his doctrine in 1947 or to defend Western Europe when the NATO treaty was signed in 1949.

The Rapid Deployment Force concept was the result of a lengthy process of strategic thinking about the Middle East and about the nature of the American military with a long history in the United States. Secretary of Defense Brown remarked in early 1980: "The United States has been in the rapid deployment and power projection business for a long time. If you doubt that, ask the Marines who 5 years ago celebrated their 200th anniversary."[11]

The Carter Doctrine and the RDF were evolving concepts. In 1980 Secretary Brown acknowledged the weakness of available forces but specifically rejected the notion that the RDF was to be no more than a tripwire. The administration's planned improvement of conventional airlift and sealift capabilities was meant to develop the Rapid Deployment Force into a true conventional deterrent over time.[12]

The American military was not blind to the logistical problems connected with projecting power into the Indian Ocean. A 1979 "JCS Strategic Mobility Study on the Persian Gulf" concluded that even "the most productive alternatives" currently available for the support of forces deployed to the Persian Gulf were "inadequate."[13] The Carter administration, the Congress, the Department of Defense, and the services were working diligently to upgrade the assets necessary to deploy and support a sizable force in the Persian Gulf as soon as possible.

When Jeffrey Record suggested in 1981 that the United States establish a unified command for the Persian Gulf region, the Department of Defense already had such proposals under consideration.[14] A 1981 Navy memorandum acknowledged that the "present command arrangements for the RDJTF are cumbersome." Planning was divorced from peacetime control and responsibilities. Among the myriad options under consideration was the creation of a unified command.[15]

The ultimate establishment of the United States Central Command (US-CENTCOM) on 1 January 1983 was, to quote Lieutenant General Robert C.

Kingston, U.S. Army, its first commander, "the product of an evolutionary process which sought the best methods for integrating our nation's military and security interests with those of nations of the region and our allies."[16] From his MacDill Air Force Base, Florida, headquarters, Kingston oversaw the formative period of the new unified command, the first established in twenty-one years.[17]

CENTCOM's marching orders were consistent with the policy objectives in the JCS Middle East review of 1978–1979: to assure Western access to oil, preserve regional stability, deter Soviet aggression, and halt and reverse the spread of Soviet influence. Identified threats included local instability, intraregional conflicts, and outright Soviet aggression. To secure these objectives, Kingston controlled, on paper, substantial, multiservice forces.[18] CENTCOM also managed and coordinated the Security Assistance programs in the nineteen countries located within the command's area of responsibility.

Although the establishment of CENTCOM marked a step forward in the development of a coherent defense policy for the Middle East, the new command just as certainly did not immediately resolve those problems that had hampered American efforts to project military power into the region since 1979. In a January 1984 lecture delivered to the Royal United Service Institute in Great Britain, Kingston noted:

> It would be less than prudent to advise you that in my Command, now one year old, that all the problems confronting us have been solved. Consider for a moment, by comparison with the European and Pacific Commands, some of the challenges facing the US Central Command. There are sizeable US forces in-place in the European and Pacific theatres. The Central Command area has almost none. There are in-place Command and Control Communications systems in both the European and Pacific theatres. In the Central Command area there is none. There is an extensive logistic infra-structure in place in Europe and the Pacific. But in the Central Command area there is none. There are extensive host nation support agreements between the United States and the nations of Europe and the Pacific. In the Central Command area we have none. And we have long-term alliances with Western Europe and many nations of the Pacific. We have none with nations in the Central Command area. In short, if we had to send a combat force in the Central Command area we would start from almost zero in terms of combat power and support structure in the region.[19]

Despite this pessimistic assessment, Central Command demonstrated the U.S. commitment to provide not only diplomatic but also military leadership and a military presence in the Middle East. Other nations—both regional and extraregional—with economic or security interests in the area were invited to cooperate. But reliance on Britain, CENTO, and the Twin Pillars finally gave way to the realization that the United States had to take the lead in securing the West's interests in the Persian Gulf.

TABLE 8

Notional Central Command Forces

Army	Air Force
1 Corps Headquarters	7 Tactical Fighter Wings
1 Airborne Division	2 Strategic Bomber Wings
1 Airmobile/Air Assault Division	
1 Mechanized Infantry Division	**Marine Corps**
1 Infantry Division	⅓ Marine Expeditionary Force
1 Mechanized Brigade	
1 Cavalry Brigade (Air Combat)	**Special Operations Forces**
	1 Special Forces Group
Navy	1 Ranger Regiment
3 Carrier Battle Groups	1 Special Operations Aviation BN
1 Surface Action Group	1 Navy Special Warfare Task Group
5 Maritime Patrol Squadrons	1 Air Force Special Ops Base

As the Reagan administration refined its political-military policy towards the Middle East, the situation in the region steadily deteriorated. In Egypt Moslem fanatics assassinated Anwar Sadat on 6 October 1981. In the Levant the decade-old Lebanese civil war dragged on, and in June 1982 Israel invaded southern Lebanon. In August the United States sent 800 Marines of the 32nd Marine Amphibious Unit into Beirut as part of a multinational peacekeeping force. The following April terrorists struck at the American embassy in Beirut, killing sixteen Americans. In October a terrorist drove an explosives-laden truck into the barracks at Beirut International Airport, killing 241 Marines. President Reagan promised not to be "intimidated by terrorists." But a disastrous naval air strike in December cost the United States two aircraft downed by the Syrians; one American aviator was killed and a second was captured but released.

By late February 1984 the Marines had been withdrawn. The civil war in Lebanon continued unabated. In the Mediterranean U.S. naval forces clashed repeatedly with air and naval forces of Mu'ammar al-Qadhafi's Libya. On 14 April 1986 U.S. Navy and Air Force aircraft struck targets in Tripoli and Benghazi in retaliation for a Libyan-engineered terrorist bombing of a West German disco frequented by Americans. To the east, the Soviets persisted in their efforts to subdue Afghanistan. This stalemated conflict threatened to spill over into neighboring Pakistan, which served as the base for Western aid to the Afghan resistance fighters. And in the Persian Gulf the Iran-Iraq war continued.[20] As the stalemated gulf war dragged on, the Reagan administration became increasingly concerned. In September 1981 Iranian aircraft bombed a Kuwaiti oil facility, demonstrating the possibility of escalation and highlighting the air-defense problem confronting the gulf Arabs.[21]

The Iran-Iraq War

DN-SN-82-02188

A Navy A-7E Corsair II and a Soviet Il-38 May aircraft share the skies over the Arabian Sea, October 1981.

The Iranian attack came at a timely moment for the administration, which was facing stiff congressional opposition as it worked to complete the AWACS sale to Saudi Arabia initiated by President Carter. Opponents of the sale argued that the Saudi monarchy was unstable and might go the way of the Shah of Iran. The Reagan administration recognized the need to send a clear signal of American concern over events in the gulf to the belligerents and the gulf Arabs, and assured Congress that there would be no repetition of the Iranian revolution in Riyadh. At a press conference President Reagan remarked, "there is no way... that we could stand by and see [Saudi Arabia] taken over by anyone that would shut off the oil."[22] Subsequent press conferences and interviews with administration officials made evident the Reagan administration's commitment to the security of Saudi Arabia; this pledge went beyond the bounds of that made by Carter and ultimately became known as the Reagan Corollary to the Carter Doctrine.[23]

In testimony before Congress on 26 September 1983, Deputy Assistant Secretary of State for Near Eastern and South Asian Affairs Robert H. Pelletreau remarked:

> The longer this war of attrition lasts, the greater the risks will be that either Iran or Iraq will risk some desperate military escalation in the gulf that would widen the war. We would regard as especially serious any threat by ei-

"Not While This President Serves"

ther party to interfere with free navigation or act in any way that would restrict oil exports from the gulf.

I wish to emphasize, as we have made clear to both Iran and Iraq, that the unrestricted flow of oil from the gulf is vital to the entire international community. Our commitment to freedom of commerce and navigation in the international waters of the gulf is firm. Even if Iran and Iraq cannot come to grips with the basic issues that divide them and to make peace, we expect them to respect this principle.[24]

As American policymakers had feared, the conflict escalated in 1984. In an attempt to break the stalemate, the Iraqis began using chemical weapons, launched air and missile attacks against Iranian cities, and stepped up attacks against ships bound to or steaming from Iranian ports.[25] The Iranians responded as best they could. Their aircraft raided Baghdad and other Iraqi cities. Although the tanker war initially was a one-sided affair, Teheran struck at the shipping of the gulf Arab states providing financial support for Saddam Hussein's war effort.[26] The "tanker war" had begun in earnest.

The United States responded promptly to the spread of the war to gulf waters, and on 1 June supported United Nations Security Council Resolution 552, which condemned Iranian attacks on ships bound to neutral Kuwaiti and Saudi ports.[27] That same month Richard W. Murphy, Assistant Secretary of State for Near Eastern and South Asian Affairs, warned Congress that the widening war threatened Western oil supplies and the security of the nation's "moderate Arab friends."[28] The United States would seek a negotiated settlement through the United Nations, strengthen the defenses of the gulf states, and weigh the option of using military force. In a July statement Murphy made it clear that although the United States did not seek to become involved in hostilities, it was not prepared to see the gulf's oil traffic threatened.[29] When it became obvious late in the year that the Iraqis had given up any hope of achieving victory and were eager to find a diplomatic solution to the conflict, the United States tilted toward Baghdad, resuming diplomatic relations with Iraq. The United States announced publicly that in its view the war continued primarily "at insistence of Iran."[30]

Unfortunately, although the tempo of the tanker war slowed, 1985 witnessed little movement towards peace. The Iraqis continued their assault against Iranian oil facilities but attacked fewer ships bound to or steaming from Iran. The total number of attacked vessels fell from fifty-three to thirty-three. The Iranians showed similar restraint (from eighteen to fourteen), although they warned that renewed Iraqi attacks would lead to retaliatory strikes against tanker traffic headed to the gulf ports of Arab nations.[31]

The United States expressed continued official concern. In an 11 June 1985 interview President Reagan remarked that "the United States has a vital interest in maintaining freedom of navigation in the gulf and stability

The Iran-Iraq War

NH 102678

The small seaplane tender *Duxbury Bay* (AVP–38), as a flagship to Commander Middle East Force, visits the Shatt-al-Arab during quieter times.

in the region generally."[32] At a 1 October luncheon in New York City in honor of the Gulf Cooperation Council (GCC), Secretary of State George Shultz commented on the effectiveness of the Iraqi attacks and the Iranian policy of stopping and searching ships in the gulf: "The United States stands by its commitment to the right of international access to the gulf and free transit passage of neutral shipping through the Straits of Hormuz. We take seriously any infringement on these rights and are ready to work with the GCC in areas such as joint contingency planning."[33]

For the United States, 1986 proved to be a critical year in the Iran-Iraq War. In a February-March offensive Iranian troops overran the Fao Peninsula, and Iran appeared to be on the threshold of victory. The Arabs were weakening—Iraq, militarily, and the gulf states, economically. As a result of the oil glut of the early and mid-1980s, the oil revenues of Saudi Arabia, Kuwait, and United Arab Emirates fell from $186 billion in 1982 to $57.6 billion in 1985, and were heading further downward.[34] The loss of income, combined with the cost of subsidizing the Iraqi effort and the impact of the war on commercial activity in the gulf, sent economic and political shock waves through the region that increased the risks of internal problems and

"Not While This President Serves"

tensions. With the Iranians threatening to march on Baghdad, the Iraqis stepped up their attacks on tankers carrying Iranian oil. The Iranians, apparently sensing the shift in the war's momentum, responded in kind, as they had warned they would.[35]

For Iran the asymmetry of the tanker war posed special problems. Because of the closing of the Shatt-al-Arab, the Iraqis had no access to the Persian Gulf and virtually no naval forces there. But Iraqi aircraft could strike at vessels bound to or from Iranian ports within a declared war zone in proximity to the Iranian coast. The Iraqis could justify these actions as attacks against belligerent ships or vessels headed to a belligerent port. Fronting the entire Persian Gulf and the Gulf of Oman approaches to the Strait of Hormuz, Iran was geographically far better situated to conduct the tanker war. Although the Iranian navy had not recovered from the turmoil of revolution, it remained the most powerful navy in the gulf.

Unfortunately for Teheran and despite this nation's inherent advantages at sea, there were no Iraqi ships or vessels bound to or from Iraqi ports in the gulf. Iraq exported its oil via pipelines that ran through Turkey,[36] or via transshipment through Kuwait and Saudi Arabia.[37] Imports, including war material, arrived in neutral ships and were unloaded at neutral ports in Kuwait and Saudi Arabia. To strike at the economic underpinnings of the Iraqi war effort, Iran had to attack the pipelines in Turkey; attack neutral ships carrying war material to Kuwaiti ports, including Western and especially Soviet ships; or strike indirectly at Iraq by attacking tankers carrying oil from the gulf states supporting Saddam Hussein.

The Iranians apparently chose this last option and late in 1986 began to strike at Kuwaiti and Kuwaiti-bound ships in the gulf. During 1986 the Iranians attacked three Kuwaiti and ten other tankers headed to or from Kuwaiti ports. The number rose precipitously to forty in 1987.[38]

The Reagan administration, aware of the renewed escalation in the tanker war, was alarmed. In February, Secretary of State Shultz spoke of the need to help the gulf states defend themselves and the importance of improved bilateral relations, noting that the U.S. access agreement with Oman was "a vital element of our Central Command strategy."[39]

Unfortunately, 1986 was a year of political division and debate over Middle East policy, not one of consensus and decision. After completing the AWACS deal with Saudi Arabia in 1984, the subsequent sale of air-defense weaponry foundered as did various planned arms transfers to other gulf states, most notably Kuwait.[40] Concerned about Israeli security and the deepening American involvement in the gulf, Congress remained less than enthusiastic about arms sales to the gulf Arabs.

But the Reagan adminstration had only itself to blame when in early November 1986 details of arms shipments to Iran became public. The subsequent debate and investigations—Irangate or Iran-Contra, as they came to

The Iran-Iraq War

be called—diverted attention from the worsening problem in the Persian Gulf and undermined the administration's policy towards the war.

Whatever one's view of the legal niceties of the Iran-Contra dealings, within the context of American policy in the Persian Gulf the "strategic opening" towards Iran was inconsistent with the existing U.S. policy of embargoing arms shipments to Iran. To quote former Secretary of Defense Weinberger, it was "one of the more absurd proposals" undertaken during the Reagan administration.[41] At a critical moment in the Iran-Iraq war, when the United States, fearing an Iranian victory, was publicly tilting towards Iraq, the National Security Council was secretly shipping arms and providing intelligence to the Iranians.[42] How seriously could the Iranians take the Reagan administration's public warnings against stepping up the tanker war when planeloads of antitank and antiaircraft missiles were being flown into Teheran as late as October 1986, after the Iranians had begun attacks on Kuwaiti ships? And what were the gulf Arabs to think of American declarations of support on their behalf?

Thus the Reagan administration entered the new year struggling to focus the debate on the deteriorating situation in the gulf. On 27 January 1987 Secretary Shultz told Congress that the Persian Gulf was "critical to the economic health of the West" and that Iran had been so warned.[43] Shultz called for international support for Operation Staunch, the embargo of arms transfers to Iran, which continued to reject United Nations calls for a cease-fire. In February President Reagan spoke of the American commitment to the "free flow of oil through the Strait of Hormuz."[44] But behind the scenes the administration debated its response to a Kuwaiti request for more than just another restatement of American policy.

In late 1986 the increasing number of attacks on Kuwaiti-bound ships, evidence of Iranian attempts to foment trouble among Kuwait's Shia minority, and the presence of Iranian troops in the Fao Peninsula alarmed not only the Kuwaitis but also the United States. "By September of 1986," Caspar Weinberger noted, "it had become increasingly clear to U.S. Defense Intelligence officials that Iran had singled out Kuwait as the focal point of the pressure it elected to use against the gulf Arab states."[45] On 10 December 1986 the Kuwaitis asked the U.S. Coast Guard for information regarding reflagging requirements for merchant vessels. Since the beginning of the gulf war the United States had been escorting American flag ships in the gulf and the Kuwaitis obviously viewed reflagging—that is, reregistering in the United States—as a means to protect their most valued tankers.[46]

The Kuwaiti request sparked a series of high-level meetings in Washington as the Reagan administration confronted a rapidly deteriorating situation in the gulf. The administration was aware that the Kuwaitis had also approached the Soviets about reflagging tankers. The Kuwaiti move was in keeping with the traditional unwillingness of this small Arab state to rely

"Not While This President Serves"

President Reagan and Secretary of Defense Caspar Weinberger agreed to reflag Kuwaiti tankers.

exclusively on either East or West for security. Nevertheless, the Kuwaitis no doubt knew that the prospect of deeper Soviet involvement in the Persian Gulf would probably move the United States to react quickly and positively to the reflagging request.

In February it became apparent that the Iranians were installing Chinese-built Silkworm antiship missiles opposite the Strait of Hormuz. Secretary of Defense Weinberger and National Security Adviser Frank Carlucci recommended the reflagging. Secretary of State George Shultz did not.[47] But after considerable debate, during the first week of March President Reagan agreed to protect eleven reflagged Kuwaiti tankers. Weinberger, the "advocate" of the decision, recalled:

> I recognized that the option of American reflagging would be more politically difficult to fulfill, but the basic effect was the same. . . . [A]nd it seemed imma-

113

The Iran-Iraq War

The guided missile frigate *Stark* after being struck by an Iraqi-fired Exocet missile, May 1987.

terial to me whether the Kuwaiti ships were reflagged or not. To my mind the main thing was for us to protect the right of innocent, nonbelligerent and extremely important commerce to move freely in international open waters—and, by our offering protection, to avoid conceding the mission to the Soviets.[48]

After providing classified briefings for key congressional members and staff, Assistant Secretary of State Murphy announced on 21 April 1987 that the United States was "consulting" with Kuwait about the registration of certain Kuwaiti ships under the American flag.[49]

The Iraqi attack on the frigate *Stark* (FFG–31) on 17 May 1987 demonstrated to the administration, Congress, and the American people the dangers inherent in an increased U.S. role in the Persian Gulf. Two French-made Exocet missiles, errantly fired by an Iraqi Mirage F–1, nearly sank *Stark* and left thirty-seven Americans dead. Thus as the administration worked to implement the reflagging decision, it faced a political debate over the concept of an expanded American role and the wisdom of a continued American presence in the war-torn Persian Gulf.

"Not While This President Serves"

A close view of the Stark's damage.

The Iran-Iraq War

Despite the *Stark* incident the Reagan administration was determined to follow through on its 7 March offer to Kuwait to reflag the tankers and issued official notice of intent on 19 May. Assistant Secretary of State Murphy announced:

> Consistent with longstanding U.S. commitment to the flow of oil through the gulf and the importance we attach to the freedom of navigation in international waters, as well as our determination to assist our friends in the gulf, the President decided that the United States would help in the protection of Kuwaiti tankers.[50]

The United States viewed Kuwait as "the weakest link on the Arab side of the gulf." Close to the front lines of the Iran-Iraq war, it had been the focus of internal Iranian-sponsored terrorist attacks, as well as efforts to provoke civil unrest in Kuwait; at sea, ships headed to and from Kuwait had been singled out for attack. Moreover, Murphy emphasized that the administration had no intention of allowing the Soviet Union to increase its role in the region, a development that U.S. policy had long sought to preclude. The prospect of the Soviets safeguarding the West's oil was an unattractive alternative.

The continued flow of Middle East oil remained the focus of the administration's policy. Murphy pointed out that in 1986 the gulf had supplied Western Europe with 46 percent of its oil; Japan, 60 percent; and the United States, 15 percent.[51] In a 19 May White House statement President Reagan reiterated the same points and recalled the dislocations of the 1970s "that shook our economy to its foundations."

> But this will not happen again, not while this President serves. I'm determined that our national economy will never again be held captive, that we will not return to the days of gas lines, shortages, economic dislocation, and international humiliation. Mark this point well: The use of the sea lanes of the Persian Gulf will not be dictated by the Iranians. These lanes will not be allowed to come under the control of the Soviet Union. The Persian Gulf will remain open to navigation by the nations of the world.[52]

The American decision to escort the Kuwaiti ships, later termed by Secretary of Defense Caspar Weinberger as *"very real military action"* taken to meet a *"very real military threat,"* was part of a "two track" policy.[53] The second track was diplomatic. On 30 June 1987 the United States called on the United Nations to take immediate action to pressure the combatants to agree to a cease-fire.[54] On 20 July the U.N. Security Council adopted Resolution 598, which demanded that "Iran and Iraq observe an immediate cease-fire, discontinue all military actions on land, at sea and in the air, and withdraw all forces to the internationally recognized boundaries without delay."[55]

As part of its military and diplomatic efforts, the United States sought the support of its friends and allies. Many of the gulf Arab states responded cautiously but cooperatively, providing crucial assistance while

"Not While This President Serves"

keeping a low profile. At the June European economic summit the United States received firm, public support from its European allies. Ultimately French, British, Italian, Belgian, and Dutch naval forces would play significant roles in the effort to keep the sea lanes open and the oil tankers moving through the gulf.[56]

Nevertheless, in deciding to reflag and escort the tankers in an operation codenamed Earnest Will, the United States risked further escalation and heightened tension with Iran and the Soviet Union. The Soviets, who had built up their own forces in the region to about a dozen ships, responded harshly, attacking the increasing American presence in the gulf as "sinister," "impermissible from the standpoint of contemporary humanitarian international law," and "fraught with far-reaching negative consequences."[57] The somewhat-restrained rhetoric from Iran indicated little desire to provoke the United States, although Ali Akbar Hashemi Rafsanjani, speaker of Iran's parliament, threatened, "If even one single drop of blood is shed by the United States in the Persian Gulf, there will be rivers of blood throughout the world."[58]

Those in the United States who opposed the Reagan administration's policy worried about the possible ramifications of the reflagging decision. A staff report prepared for the Senate Foreign Relations Committee concluded:

> The United States seriously risks being drawn into the war in the Persian Gulf. Although the stated purpose of the huge American fleet in the region is narrowly defined—to escort U.S.-flagged vessels through the gulf—this mission, given the circumstances, is dangerously nebulous.
>
> The U.S. is perceived by Iranians and Arabs alike as having sided with Iraq, and the expanded U.S. naval presence is likely to invite more Iranian attacks of increasing severity. Moreover, the greater the Iraqi assault on Iranian shipping, the greater the likelihood of Iranian retaliation against U.S. forces. Thus, American naval forces in the gulf are now, in effect, hostage to Iraqi war policy.[59]

The report's authors also noted that the world oil glut and the increasing percentage of the region's petroleum output going to the Mediterranean by pipeline made the tanker escort mission superfluous. They also stated that, despite the administration's oft-stated policy of reducing Soviet involvement in the region by siding with Iraq, the United States was increasing the chances that the Iranians would be driven into a closer relationship with the Soviets. In addition, they said, the gulf states needed to upgrade their air defenses, the reflagging decision had been hastily reached, and the U.S. Navy was "ill prepared" to execute its new role in the Persian Gulf. They concluded the report by recommending a diplomatic offensive focused on the United Nations.

The administration was not of one mind with regard to the decision. Caspar Weinberger considered the Kuwaiti request "an opportunity," noting that Secretary of State Shultz "did not share my enthusiasm for this mission."[60] The

The Iran-Iraq War

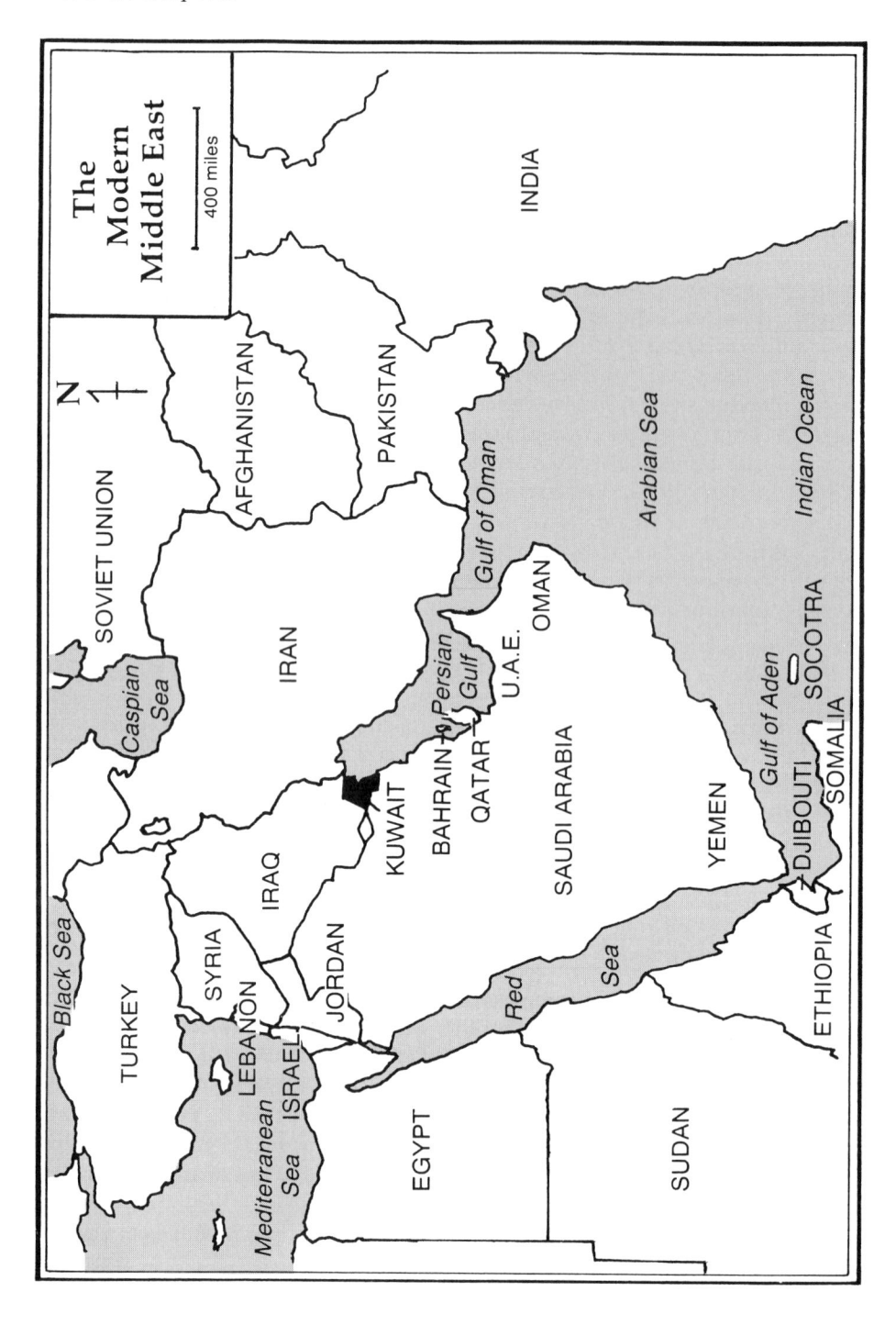

new Secretary of the Navy, James H. Webb, Jr., a veteran of the Indochina war, voiced concerns about the open-ended, Vietnam-like nature of the commitment. The Secretary of Defense viewed the Navy's concern over its prospective gulf role "understandable" given its "direct, immediate responsibility for the safety of the men and the ships," but more than "was warranted." But Weinberger found strong support within the Navy's "operational end, the people who were called on to do the job," saying "there was no lack of eagerness there, and there wasn't much lack of eagerness at the top."[61]

Fears of becoming too involved were well founded, as was some of the critical analysis of the Foreign Relations Committee's staff report. The administration's hope that a strong American response would deter further Iranian escalation was just that—a hope. The tanker war had ebbed and flowed according to decisions made in Baghdad, not in Teheran. And the world's dependence on oil supplies shipped through the gulf was declining.

Nevertheless, even a minor shortfall in oil supplies could have a dramatic impact. During the Arab oil embargo in 1973 and 1974, disruptions totaling no more than 5 percent of world petroleum supplies had led to severe adverse economic consequences.[62] At a time when Soviet freighters regularly delivered war material to Kuwaiti ports for shipment to Iraq, the possibility of the Soviet Union drawing closer to Iran was unlikely. The reflagging decision, made over a period of six months, could hardly be termed impetuous. If the gulf states felt vulnerable in the area of air defense, Congress had increased that sense of vulnerability by routinely killing administration-sponsored arms sales to Arab states. The United States had not "generally ignored" a diplomatic approach and continued to push the United Nations to take a firmer stand. And if, as the report posited, the major threat to American interests in the region was an Iranian victory on land, why chide the Reagan administration for taking action that made such a victory less likely?

The administration recognized the risks it was running in the gulf and readily admitted that it could not "predict with absolute certainty" how the Iranians would respond.[63] Secretary of Defense Weinberger noted:

> There is no risk-free way to safeguard our longstanding vital interests in the Persian Gulf, which today is an increasingly volatile region. We can only do our best to minimize and manage the risks, chart a steady course aimed at our strategic goal of ending the war, and reassure our friends—and our adversaries—of our resolve as we move ahead.[64]

Whether the gulf Arabs piped or shipped their oil to the West, developments in the region, exacerbated by the Irangate fiasco, led to calls for a firm American commitment to the gulf. Admitting the difficulties the administration faced, Weinberger nevertheless remained "convinced that the risks of alternative courses of action or inaction are even greater."[65]

The Iran-Iraq War

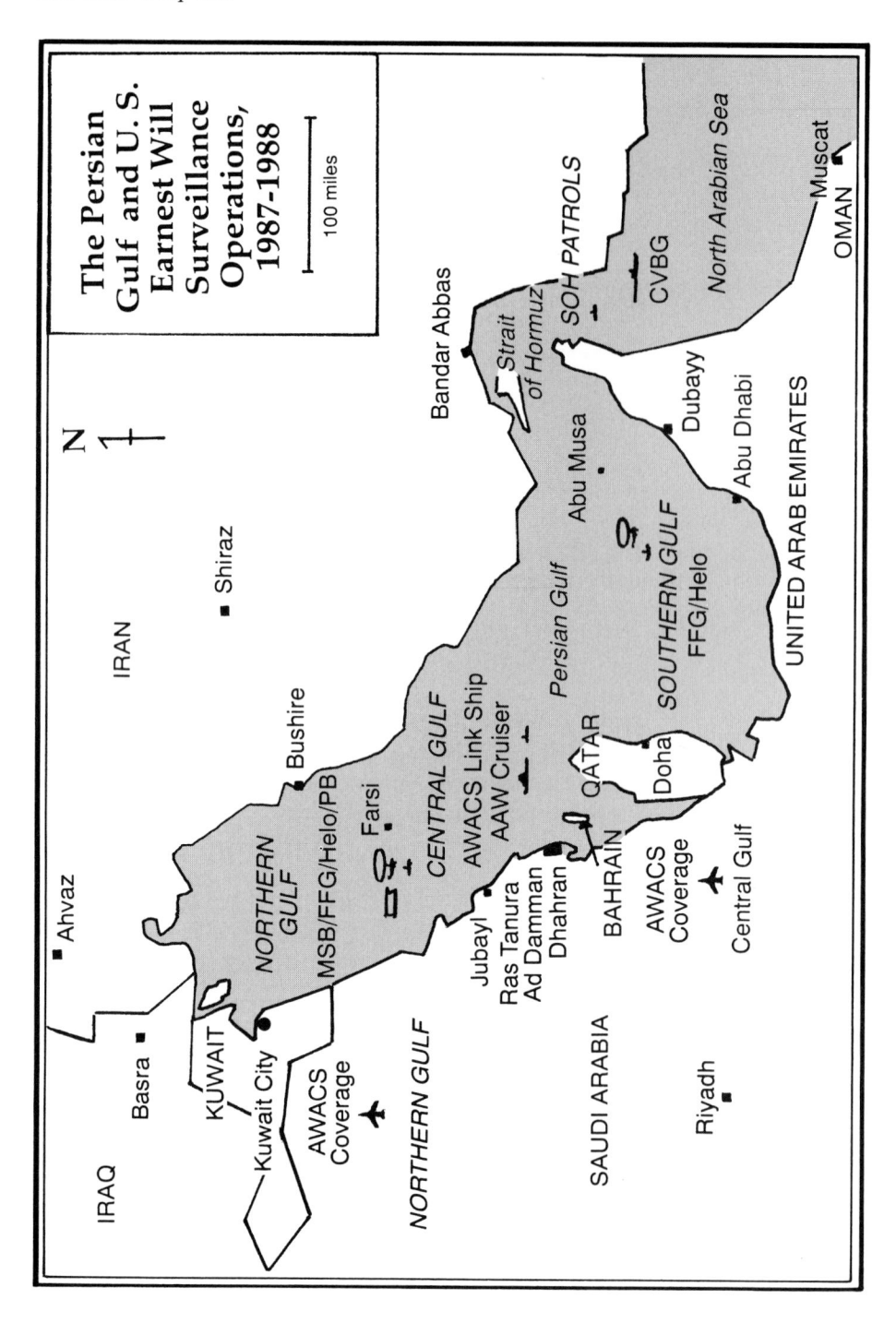

The Persian Gulf and U.S. Earnest Will Surveillance Operations, 1987-1988

12

The United States and the Tanker War

Initially, the Reagan administration's hope that its actions would deter further Iranian escalation appeared well founded. Secretary of Defense Caspar Weinberger and Chairman of the Joint Chiefs of Staff Admiral William J. Crowe, Jr., appearing before a congressional committee on 17 June 1987, noted the drop-off in both Iranian and Iraqi attacks against shipping that followed the *Stark* incident.[1] Public statements emanating from Teheran seemed to reflect a cautious response to the American actions. Michael H. Armacost, Undersecretary of State for Political Affairs, told the Senate Armed Services Committee:

> Iran has not attacked any U.S. naval vessel. It has consistently avoided carrying out attacks on commercial ships when U.S. naval vessels have been in the vicinity. In its recent actions, it has displayed no interest in provoking incidents at sea with the United States. Of course, it would be foolhardy for them to attack an American flag vessel. Those ships would have American masters—that is, the reflagged vessels. They will carry no contraband. They pose no danger to Iran. They will be defended if attacked.[2]

TABLE 9

Attacks by Iran and Iraq on Ships in the Persian Gulf, 1987

	Jan	Feb	Mar	Apr	May	Jun	Jul	Aug	Sep	Oct	Nov	Dec	Total
Iran	6	3	4	4	10	5	4	5	16	7	10	17	91
Iraq	6	8	5	7	5	2	3	4	12	13	8	15	88

SOURCE: Ronald O'Rourke, "The Tanker War," U.S. Naval Institute *Proceedings* 114 (May 1988): 32.

The American military in both Washington and the gulf viewed the Strait of Hormuz as the most likely focus of Iranian attack. Accordingly, U.S. Navy forces in the theater concentrated their efforts on this narrow passage, where ships would have to steam within range of Chinese-manufactured Silkworm antiship missiles. The U.S. Navy traditionally concentrated its attention on maritime choke points, and the Strait of Hormuz was an obvious point of transit for all ships entering or leaving the Persian Gulf.

The Iran-Iraq War

The Strait of Hormuz also seemed to be the most logical place for an Iranian mine campaign.[3] Nevertheless, the Joint Chiefs of Staff and the U.S. Navy did not consider the Iranian threat to be so serious. During congressional hearings Senator Dan Quayle asked about the threat posed by mines. "Do we have any minesweepers that are going to go up in there?" Quayle asked. "No; we do not," Undersecretary Armacost admitted. Armacost then downplayed the danger of Iranian attack.

> I can tell you what the Chairman of the Joint Chiefs [Crowe] told me in answer to that question. He said, it was very small, because we do not feel that they are there yet. If they are there, then obviously we would have to reconsider how we were going to go about transiting the gulf.[4]

Armacost also stated that the Silkworm, a Chinese version of the old Soviet Styx missile, posed few problems for the U.S. Navy: "We can defeat, and have defeated, the STYX missile with the weapons systems that are on board ... [although] the protection of a protected [convoyed] ship is somewhat more difficult."[5]

American disregard of the possibility of Iranian military action and its lack of minesweepers in the Strait of Hormuz is understandable. The strait, although narrow, was also deep and swept by strong currents that would make effective mining difficult.[6] Besides, the Iranian Silkworm sites located near the strait were not yet operational, although those located farther north were.

Unfortunately for the United States, the political geography of the war made the entire gulf a narrow strait. Iran had declared a wartime exclusion zone, within which all non-Iranian ships were subject to attack; it extended south and west into the gulf from the Iranian coast and Iran's many island possessions. Since the bottom of the Persian Gulf is convex and slopes downward towards the Iranian coast, deep-draft vessels such as the large, reflagged Kuwaiti tankers were effectively confined to a relatively narrow corridor of deep water in the central gulf which hugged the boundary of the exclusion zone. There were thus numerous locations where the Iranians could seed minefields that the American-flagged tankers and escorts were likely to pass through on their way to or from gulf positions.

The Iranian threat of mine warfare in the gulf should have been apparent to American military leaders. Following a CENTO exercise in 1973 General George J. Eade, U.S. Army, and the senior American observer at MIDLINK 73, informed JCS Chairman Admiral Thomas Moorer, that the Iranian exercise commander had "expressed some concern to me privately about the vulnerability of the Persian Gulf to Guerilla mine warfare. He remarked that this tactic 'could play havoc with merchant ships and flow of oil'"[7] Obviously, the Shah's naval officers had thought through the possibilities of mine warfare in the gulf, and mining studies and plans remained in the files of the various Iranian naval commands.

The Tanker War

Bridgeton steams under her own power after hitting a mine in the Persian Gulf a month earlier, August 1987.

In late July Iran became more daring and confrontational, adopting an escalatory course that, by the end of the summer, increased the number of Iranian attacks against gulf shipping by a factor of three. On 24 July the reflagged tanker *Bridgeton*, the first Kuwaiti ship to be escorted through the Persian Gulf by the U.S. Navy, struck an Iranian-laid mine about eighteen miles west of Farsi Island. To Admiral Crowe the mining of *Bridgeton* meant that deterrence had failed and that the United States would have to build up its forces in the gulf rapidly. "If there's one profession in which you can't mount an error-free operation, it's the military," Admiral Crowe later admitted.[8]

The new Iranian mood of confrontation quickly became obvious. On 31 July Shia pilgrims making the traditional Haj pilgrimage to Mecca in Saudi Arabia rioted. In the melee that erupted between edgy Saudi security forces and a massive crowd driven by Iranian provocateurs, hundreds were killed. Iranian official statements issued before and after the Mecca riots indicated that Teheran remained a threat to the gulf Arabs.[9] In August Iranian television broadcast the "Martyrdom Maneuvers," a fairly extensive, dramatically staged extravaganza depicting mock attacks by Iranian patrol boats and commandos obviously directed at the United States. In Teheran, according to journalist Robin Wright, a sign reading,

The Iran-Iraq War

"The Persian Gulf will be the graveyard of the United States," adorned the headquarters of the Revolutionary Guards.[10]

Because the United States had failed to deter Iran's escalation of the war in the gulf (although the Iranians had avoided direct attacks on American ships), the Reagan administration decided to accelerate the military buildup in the region. "We had to put some capability there that we had hoped to avoid," Chairman Crowe remarked.[11] Minesweeping helicopters and ships rushed to the gulf. Middle East Force, which began 1987 at a strength of six ships, grew to thirteen by year's end. The warships of the battle group in the Gulf of Oman brought American strength to between twenty-five and thirty vessels, a level at which it would remain until late 1988. Other forces operating in and over the gulf included eighteen Navy patrol boats, several P-3 Orion patrol aircraft, and two Mobile Sea Bases [12] in the northern Persian Gulf, about eight Marine Corps helicopters and a 400-man Marine Air Ground Task Force, several U.S. Army MH-6 "Seabats" and AHIPS helicopters operating from naval platforms at Admiral Crowe's personal direction, and U.S. Air Force ELF One AWACS and aerial tankers operating from Saudi Arabia.[13]

To control this expanding force, the Department of Defense established a new command—Joint Task Force Middle East (JTFME)—on 21 August 1987. Rear Admiral Dennis M. Brooks, flying his flag with the carrier battle group in the Gulf of Oman, became JTFME's first commander. Brooks answered to USCENTCOM, commanded by Marine Corps General George B. Crist (USCINCCENT) in Tampa, Florida.

The Reagan administration also secured substantial international support for its role in the Persian Gulf. Virtually all of the Arab gulf states had granted the United States temporary support or access of some kind. Former Secretary Weinberger noted:

> Kuwait was the primary source of contract fuel for all of our naval aircraft and ships in the region during the actual escort operations. The government of Kuwait also partially absorbed the cost of fuel for our ships and aircraft involved in escorting the American-flagged Kuwaiti oil tankers.[14]

By the end of 1987 west European naval forces in or en route to the gulf included the United Kingdom's ten-ship ARMILLA Patrol and two Dutch, two Belgian, seven Italian, and thirteen French ships;[15] the French ships included a carrier. With the Americans concentrating more and more naval forces in the gulf and Indian Ocean, West Germany sent three warships to the Mediterranean. The Japanese agreed to fund improved navigation capabilities necessary for minehunting. A February 1988 Center for Naval Analyses (CNA) symposium on the gulf war presciently concluded that U.S. ability to mobilize such international support would compel the Iranians to recognize their isolation and could become a critical factor in forcing them to end the war.[16]

The Tanker War

The ocean minesweeper *Illusive* (MSO–448) and the dock landing ship *Mount Vernon* (LSD–39) at anchor off Sitrah, Bahrain.

A self-defense force on board the amphibious assault ship *Okinawa* (LPH–3) stands watch as the ship performs its escort missions in the gulf.

The Iran-Iraq War

As American military strength in the region increased, the United States adopted a less passive concept of operations in the Persian Gulf. To deter further mining and to demonstrate to the international community that, despite denials, Iran was responsible for the threat to shipping in the gulf, the United States planned an operation to catch the Iranians in the act of laying mines. Varied intelligence assets allowed American forces in the gulf to monitor and track an Iranian minelaying effort. On the night of 21 September U.S Army helicopters flying from the U.S. Navy frigate *Jarrett* (FFG–33) caught the small Iranian amphibious ship *Iran Ajr* laying mines in the shipping channel and attacked the vessel with rockets. *Iran Ajr* was boarded by Navy SEALs, and her cargo of mines was photographed and made public.[17] On 8 October Navy-based Army helicopters surprised four Iranian speedboats operating fifteen miles southwest of Farsi Island.[18] The Army helos attacked after the Iranians opened fire, sinking one speedboat and damaging and capturing two others. On 15 and 16 October the Iranians fired Silkworm antiship missiles from launching sites in the Fao Peninsula against tankers at Kuwait's Mina al-Ahmadi terminal. One of the missiles struck the reflagged Kuwaiti Oil Tanker Company (KOTC) tanker *Sea Isle City*. Admiral Crowe proposed a retaliatory attack on an Iranian ship, but the Reagan administration rejected the plan and directed U.S. Navy forces in the gulf to attack and destroy two Iranian oil platforms used as military outposts.[19]

In early 1988, in an effort to command and control an increasingly active and growing multiservice force, the United States improved its somewhat cumbersome command structure in the region. Since September 1987 the overall command of American forces in the North Arabian Sea and the Persian Gulf had been vested in Rear Admiral Brooks, the Commander Joint Task Force Middle East (CJTFME), who rode with the battle group. A second Rear Admiral, Harold J. Bernsen, commanded MEF within the Persian Gulf. In February Rear Admiral Anthony A. Less became CJTFME as well as CMEF and shifted his flag to *Coronado* (AGF–31) in the gulf.[20] Less recalled:

> In order to streamline location, command and control functions, it was decided to consolidate the two geographically separated staffs and install a single commander who would be responsible for the region.... My job was to plan, coordinate and direct joint and combined operations in the Arabian Gulf, the Gulf of Oman, and the Northern Arabian Sea. This included protecting U.S. flagged ships, and others as directed, providing a military presence in the region and coordinating operations and training with allied and friendly forces. We were tasked to operate a regional joint force.[21]

Rear Admiral Less directed operational procedures developed to counter myriad threats, including aerial, missile, small boat, naval, and mine attacks; the procedures were well established by early 1988.

The Tanker War

Four U.S. Navy destroyers shelled this Iranian command and control platform following an Iranian missile attack on a reflagged Kuwaiti super tanker.

The principal air threat came from the Iraqis. Their accidental attack on the frigate *Stark* exemplified the nature of the threat to American forces in the gulf. The continual threat was driven home on 12 February when an Iraqi aircraft mistakenly attacked, fortunately without success, the destroyer *Chandler* (DDG–996).[22] Throughout the gulf war the United States worked with the Iraqis to improve "deconfliction" procedures meant to make such attacks unlikely, although the possibility was never totally eliminated. But because such attacks were accidental in nature, rather than planned, they did not represent an operational challenge to the successful execution of the Navy's mission in the Persian Gulf.

The Iranians posed the greatest threat to the U.S. Navy's operations in the gulf. Weapons in Iran's military arsenal included aircraft, Silkworm missiles, Boghammers and other small fast-attack boats manned by the Pasdaran (Revolutionary Guards), and the remnants of the Shah's Imperial Iranian Navy. Iran's few attempts to use aircraft against American forces failed completely, and the Iranians were unable to execute any successful small boat or naval attacks against the U.S. Navy. After the retalia-

The Iran-Iraq War

Destroyer *Chandler* passes a burning Greek tanker attacked by small Iranian gunboats.

An RA–53D Sea Stallion helicopter and the ocean minesweeper *Inflict* (MSO–456) conduct minesweeping operations in the Persian Gulf. The Sea Stallion in the foreground is parked on board amphibious assault ship *Okinawa*.

tory strike of the United States on 19 October 1987 against the Rostam oil platform following the Silkworm attack on *Sea Isle City*, the Iranians chose not to employ antiship missiles against American or American-escorted ships. Only in the area of mine warfare did the Iranians achieve even marginal successes.

For many critics and analysts the mine problem became, and has remained, central to any discussion of the American naval campaign in the Persian Gulf. Many analysts have portrayed the U.S. Navy as a service unprepared to deal with such a "primitive threat" from "World War I-design" weapons.[23] The United States was in fact caught woefully unprepared in the gulf for the Iranian mining campaign. Naval mine countermeasure (MCM) forces were not on hand to meet the mine threat when escorting began in July 1987. In fact, until late in the year, U.S. strategy relied more on the hope that the Iranians would avoid a confrontation with Americans than on the deterrent effect of its expanding forces within the gulf. It is not inconceivable that the U.S. Navy would have had just as much difficulty protecting escorted tankers from Silkworm attacks in the Strait of Hormuz had the Iranians been prepared to use the antiship missiles. The true significance and most troubling aspect of the mining of *Bridgeton* was not the U.S. Navy's apparent inability to counter the mine threat but the American failure to deter Iran from attacking at all.[24]

A discussion of mine warfare in the Persian Gulf cannot be limited to technical MCM capabilities, but must also address the overall context within which American naval operations were conducted. In 1987 the U.S. Navy's priority focus was on the Soviet Union, and justifiably so. The American fleet was designed primarily to fight within an alliance structure that included a sensible division of labor that assigned most overseas MCM tasks to European and Asian navies. Indeed, several MCM vessels from NATO navies were redeployed to the Persian Gulf in 1987 and 1988. U.S. Navy assets did include MCM forces, but they were deployed in American ports that would have to be swept in the event of a war. These forces were quickly redeployed to the Persian Gulf after the need there became apparent.

Although these ships were old, having been built in the early 1950s, their technological capability was up to date, if not state of the art. Moreover, the MCM job in the gulf did not involve minesweeping in the traditional sense; rather, it called for minehunting, that is, using remote-controlled devices to locate, identify, and record the location of bottom debris and mines. The mines would then be destroyed by Explosive Ordnance Disposal (EOD) divers.

It is also a mistake to assume that mine warfare was a risk-free option for Iran. Iranians talked of the "hand of God," and many Reagan administration critics viewed Teheran's mining effort as "an effective way to confront the U.S. Navy and other navies at low risk of immediate discovery and retaliation."[25] But there was never any actual doubt about who was laying

The Iran-Iraq War

A Mark III patrol boat returns to its mobile sea base after all-night surveillance of Iranian small boat activity in the gulf.

mines in the gulf. And the Iranians had no guarantee that their mines would damage or destroy only reflagged Kuwaiti or American vessels. Blowing up British or Soviet ships would hardly have advanced Iran's war aims.

Iran's mine warfare campaign ultimately proved to be a dismal failure. The Iranians were quickly caught in the act when U.S. Army helicopters observed *Iran Ajr* laying mines in the gulf. Iranian mining of shipping routes prompted the dispatch of an international force of MCM vessels and accompanying warships into the gulf, where they cooperated with the United States. Finally, the retaliatory operation that followed the mining of the frigate *Samuel B. Roberts* (FFG–58) (discussed later) cost Iran half of its operational navy.

The U.S. Navy's operations in the Persian Gulf and the Gulf of Oman recognized that the counter to the Iranian mine campaign was not simply technical MCM. Minehunting is a slow, dangerous, costly process. MCM is a capability that a navy hopes it will not have to use because the last place one wants to deal with a mine is in the water. Thus, to say that the U.S. Navy ignored the mine threat is incorrect; the American concept of naval operations in the gulf was designed to preclude mining as well as other "guerrilla" methods of naval warfare.

The Navy's philosophy of operations involved deterrence, intelligence, surveillance, presence, retaliation, and, lastly, MCM. The Navy hoped to deter attacks

The Tanker War

The crane on board the barge *Hercules* prepares to lift a patrol boat into gulf waters.

by its presence in the gulf and a not-so-veiled threat of retribution. If deterrence failed, intelligence and reconnaissance could reveal Iranian preparations for an attack. To detect Iranian minelaying throughout the gulf, the Navy established a presence from Kuwait to the Gulf of Oman that included aerial reconnaissance from AWACS flying from Saudi Arabia, E–2C Hawkeyes flying from the carrier battle group in the Arabian Sea, and P–3C patrol aircraft. JTFME divided the gulf itself into several sectors, each one usually patroled by a destroyer or frigate. In the northern Persian Gulf two mobile sea bases (MSB), accompanied by minesweepers and a frigate, operated as floating islands from which Mark III patrol boats and helicopters conducted surveillance activities. Cruisers in the gulf coordinated the antiair warfare effort to provide safety from Iraqi or Iranian air attack. Additional frigates performed the actual escort of the reflagged tankers (and occasional tag-alongs) during the 127 Earnest Will missions that ran between the Gulf of Oman and Kuwait between July 1987 and December 1988.[26]

The most significant aspect of the U.S. Navy's operations during 1987 and 1988 was its ability to establish a presence throughout the gulf rather

The Iran-Iraq War

than its actual conduct of individual Earnest Will missions. By the end of 1987 every tanker that passed through the gulf came through areas patroled and secured by American naval forces and thereby benefitted from the protection of the U.S. Navy. The passage along shipping routes that were neither mined nor subject to harassment or attack by Iranian small boats or men-of-war was the principal fruit of the Navy's work in the gulf. By early 1988 the Navy focused less on the physical escort mission itself, which had become more symbolic than real, than on the safety of the corridor through which the tankers steamed. The shift from multiship escorts during the early Earnest Will missions to single frigate escorts later in the war marked this transition in the American naval effort.

The tremendous strain the Iran-Iraq war placed on the U.S. Navy led to expressions of concern about just how long the effort would have to be maintained.[27] The successful but reactive nature of operations in the gulf offered no avenue to force an end to the war. In early 1988 many in the Navy began to ponder: "How do we get out?" The answer was as frank as it was pessimistic. U.N. efforts were critical to the peace process but unlikely to produce a quick resolution of the conflict. Therefore the "outcome/resolution of Iran-Iraq war is the key.... The sheer scale of the land war makes it apparent that the Persian Gulf war is, ultimately, a *sideshow* to the war that counts for the two protagonists."[28]

Unfortunately, in early 1988 the end of the war seemed to be nowhere in sight. The tempo of the tanker war slowed after December 1987, although Iranian attacks rose from seven in February 1988 to thirteen in March. Following their accidental attack on *Chandler* in February, the Iraqis temporarily suspended their shipping strikes. The Iranian effort slowed as well, but Iran nevertheless continued, as it had late in 1987, to be responsible for most of the antishipping attacks in the gulf.

TABLE 10

Attacks by Iran and Iraq on Ships in the Persian Gulf, 1988

	Jan	Feb	Mar	Apr	May	Jun	Jul-Aug	Total
Iran	7	7	13	7	5	3	10	52
Iraq	8	5	6	0	7	1	11	38

SOURCE: Ronald O'Rourke, "Gulf Ops," U.S. Naval Institute *Proceedings* 114 (May 1988): 33.

Despite American concerns about the prospects of a prolonged struggle in the gulf, the war was actually reaching its crisis point as Iran suffered a series of reverses on land and sea. On 27 February the "war of the cities"

The Tanker War

U.S. Navy aircraft attacked the Iranian frigate *Sahand* in retaliation for the mining of the guided missile frigate *Samuel B. Roberts*.

resumed, reaching a new level of destruction. On 29 February seventeen Iraqi Scud-B surface-to-surface missiles (SSM) hit Teheran. By 20 April, when the barrage ended, at least 140 SSMs had hit the Iranian capital.[29] In March the Iraqis began using mustard gas and nerve agents along the front in Kurdistan. On 18 April the Iraqis retook the Fao Peninsula, again using gas. That same day in the gulf, the U.S. Navy fought its largest surface action since the Second World War.

The American action came in retaliation for the near-sinking of the frigate *Samuel B. Roberts*, which hit a mine in the gulf on 14 April (see appendix A). Four days later JTFME executed Operation Praying Mantis, a plan that called for the destruction of two Iranian oil platforms and a frigate. During the course of the operation, the Iranians attempted a counterattack that led to the destruction of about half of their operational ships.[30] Then on 22 April the United States announced the expansion of the rules of engagement of American forces in the gulf.[31] Henceforth U.S. Navy ships would provide "distress assistance" to neutral vessels that were under Iranian attack outside the exclusion zone and that requested help.

In Iran war weariness became apparent, even to the governing regime. Antiwar demonstrations broke out in Isfahan and Tabriz. As foreign arms and supplies and Arab petrodollars flowed into Iraq, Iran rapidly headed towards bankruptcy. The economy had all but collapsed under the pressures of eight years of war. Unemployment rates soared. Inflation was rampant.[32]

The Iran-Iraq War

The Dutch heavy lift ship *Mighty Servant 2* carries its cargo, *Samuel B. Roberts*, to its home port in Newport, Rhode Island.

Iran's efforts to strike at Iraq had failed, had drawn the Americans into the war, and had left Teheran increasingly isolated internationally.

As the Iraqis continued their advance in May and June, the Iranians weakened. A letter critical of both the war and Khomeini's leadership that had been written by former premier Mehdi Bazargan, circulated openly in Teheran.[33] On 2 June Rafsanjani became Commander in Chief of the Iranian armed forces. In a 2 July speech he spoke of the possibility of a "nonmilitary" end to the war.[34] The movement in Iran towards the acceptance of U.N. Resolution 598 was unmistakable. The next day, 3 July, the U.S. Navy cruiser *Vincennes* (CG–49) mistakenly shot down an Iranian civilian airliner, killing 290 people.[35]

According to Robin Wright the Airbus incident provided the war-weary Iranians with the "pretext" they needed to end hostilities.[36] On July 18, with Khomeini's acquiescence, the Iranians accepted the U.N. cease-fire resolution. The Iran-Iraq war and the U.S. gulf war had come an end.

Conclusion

Over the course of two centuries the United States has accumulated interests in the region in a series of layers: commercial since the late 1780s, strategic since the Second World War, and petrostrategic since the late 1940s. The pursuit of each set of interests led the United States more deeply into the affairs of both the gulf and the Middle East.

American commercial interests in the Persian Gulf, although certainly extensive by the 1930s, did not require any significant diplomatic or military involvement by the U.S. Government. Time and again between the 1850s and the 1930s, American policymakers rejected suggestions that the United States play a larger role in the affairs of the region.

Not until the Second World War did the United States undertake political commitments to the two most important Persian Gulf states—Saudi Arabia and Iran. Those commitments quickly led to even more involvement as the Cold War began, and between 1946 and 1989 strategic interests dominated American policy. The Iran crisis of March 1946 demonstrated both the possibility of a Soviet military advance from the Caucasus towards the Persian Gulf as well as the potential for political meddling in the affairs of an unstable region. Containing the Soviet Union politically and militarily became the cornerstone of American policy in the Middle East.

In the late 1940s, the economic recovery of Western Europe, the political containment of the Soviet Union, and the continued prosperity of the United States necessitated an increased reliance by the West on the petroleum of the Persian Gulf as oil itself became a strategic and not solely a commercial commodity. Petrostrategic interests, combined with strategic interests, led to ever-deeper American involvement in the gulf.

The British withdrawal from east of Suez between 1968 and 1971 and the collapse of the Iranian monarchy in 1978 left the United States as the only power capable of defending Western interests in the region. Following the Soviet invasion of Afghanistan in 1979, the Carter administration decided that the United States would have to accept military responsibility for the security of the gulf.

Within a decade, the strategic threat receded as the likelihood of a Soviet advance towards the gulf or the political spread of communism into the Middle East became remote. The late 1980s found the Soviet Union struggling with the political and economic processes of reform. In 1989 the Joint Chiefs of Staff and Central Command began to shift the focus of planning

Conclusion

from the need to stop a Soviet invasion of the Middle East to the possibility of a military challenge to Western interests by one of the gulf states.

Over the course of several decades American policymakers did have a difficult time managing these changes in priorities within the U.S. policies in the gulf and, more broadly, in the Middle East. The historical record demonstrates that events within the gulf took the United States by surprise with fair regularity. Nevertheless, American policymakers did, for the most part, achieve goals they set for themselves in shaping Persian Gulf policy.

That policy included three basic and interrelated objectives: containing the Soviet Union, increasing flow of oil from the gulf to the West, and aiding the economic and political development of the Middle East.

The United States and its allies, both in Europe and in the gulf, successfully contained the political and military spread of Soviet influence in the gulf and throughout the Middle East. Thus over the course of a half-century, the Soviets made but fleeting gains in the region and never were able to halt or even impede the flow of oil to the West through their own efforts. Indeed the Western economic machines that ultimately buried Soviet communism were fueled by the oil of the Persian Gulf.

And as United States policymakers had planned in the 1940s, Western Europe, first, then eventually the capitalist states of East Asia, and ultimately the United States itself became increasingly reliant on the oil of the gulf. Although that dependency is often viewed as a failure of American policy, it was in fact planned. American policymakers recognized as early as 1943 that the United States could no longer supply Europe with oil. The Middle East was the only alternative.

This growing Western dependence on the oil of the gulf became a dilemma because U.S. policy rested on a faulty assumption. American diplomats and economists of the 1940s—products of the New Deal era—honestly believed that the higher oil royalties that would accompany the expansion of the gulf's oil industry would bring not only economic benefits to the region, but also social and political advances that would lead to more progressive, democratic, and stable states in the Persian Gulf.

Nearly a half-century later a new generation of American policymakers vainly search the horizon for a stable, progressive, democratic, Islamic state in the Middle East. Thus as the United States enters the last decade of the twentieth century, it finds itself, along with much of the West, growing increasingly dependent on energy sources located in a volatile region. As Operations Desert Shield and Desert Storm clearly demonstrated, the disappearance of a Soviet threat has not lessened the need for a strong American role in the Persian Gulf. After all, United States policy was never driven solely by perceptions of the Soviet menace. The U.S. Navy's Middle East Force was not sent to the gulf—as was the Sixth Fleet to the Mediterranean—to serve as a deterrent force. MEF ships have cruised the

Conclusion

gulf and the Indian Ocean principally to ensure the continued flow of oil, not to deter or meet a Soviet attack.

The receding of the Soviet threat over the last decade has been offset by the increasing instability of the region. The 1979 Soviet invasion of Afghanistan may have been the catalyst for the Carter Doctrine, but it was the Iran-Iraq war—a regional struggle—that prompted the United States to "pledge" itself to the continued passage of oil through the Strait of Hormuz. In 1987 and 1988 the Central Command structure set up to deter and confront a Soviet attack, oversaw operations directed against Iran. And during Operation Desert Shield, the United States demonstrated its political strength in the Persian Gulf by leading a broad international coalition that confronted Saddam Hussein following his invasion of Kuwait. In Operation Desert Storm, the United States demonstrated its military power in the gulf by driving Saddam's army back into Iraq. That process had begun a decade or more before. Thus the U.S. political-military effort in Operations Desert Shield and Desert Storm was the predictable, if not inevitable result of an extended and complex process of deepening involvement. Nothing on the horizon, not even the decline of the Soviet Union, appears likely to reverse that trend any time soon. Even when most of the American forces deployed to the gulf return to their bases in Europe or the United States, the ships of the U.S. Navy's Middle East Force will remain on station, patroling the waters they have patroled for the last forty-plus years, ensuring that the oil of the gulf continues to flow to the West.

Appendixes

A. Operation Praying Mantis
by Hans S. Pawlisch

Upholding the U.S. commitment to maintain freedom of navigation in the troubled waters of the Persian Gulf in 1987 and 1988, elements of the U.S. Central Command, directed by the Commander Joint Task Force, Middle East, actively patroled the gulf to prevent belligerent mining of international shipping lanes.

While executing this mission on 14 April 1988, the crew of the guided missile frigate *Samuel B. Roberts* detected three Iranian mines floating near the water's surface approximately fifty-five miles northeast of the Qatar Peninsula. As the vessel reversed engines to back away from the danger, it struck a fourth submerged mine. The 253 pounds of explosive packed into the device tore a massive 21-foot hole below the engine room along the port side of the ship's keel, causing extensive fires and flooding. Only heroic damage-control efforts by the ship's crew kept the vessel afloat. Ten American sailors were injured by the explosion.

Iranian Mines in the Gulf

In early 1987 evidence emerged to suggest that the Iranians were laying mines in Persian Gulf shipping lanes outside Iran's declared war-exclusion zones. At the beginning the Iranian government may have favored this policy for its nonattributable character, the so-called "invisible hand." But on 21 September 1987 U.S. forces caught an Iranian naval vessel, *Iran Ajr*, laying mines off the Bahrain coast. Despite the humiliating capture of *Iran Ajr* by American forces and the international condemnation that followed, the *Samuel B. Roberts* incident demonstrated that the Iranian government had no intention of abandoning its practice of mining international waterways. It is also possible that the Iranians may have deliberately laid the minefield to target U.S. forces in the gulf. Within ten days of the incident, American and allied naval forces discovered another eight mines of Iranian manufacture.

Dr. Pawlisch is Command Historian for the U.S. Central Command at MacDill Air Force Base in Tampa, Florida. He received his B.A. and M.A. in history from the University of Wisconsin-Milwaukee and his Ph.D. from the University of London. He is the author of Sir John Davis and the Conquest of Ireland: A Study in Legal Imperialism *(Cambridge University Press, 1985), which won the John Ben Snow award given by the North American Conference in British Studies for the best book in British history and social sciences.*

Appendixes

In response to the mining of *Samuel B. Roberts*, the National Command Authority directed General George B. Crist (USCINCCENT) and Rear Admiral Anthony B. Less (CJTFME) to plan and execute a measured retaliatory blow. Codenamed Praying Mantis, the purpose of U.S. retaliation, as explained by Pentagon spokesman Daniel Howard on 21 April, was to neutralize Sassan and Sirri gas-oil separation platforms (GOSP) and to target an Iranian naval vessel in recompense for damage inflicted on *Samuel B. Roberts*.

The Plan

Staff officers from the Tampa-based U.S. Central Command carefully assessed the decision to target the Sassan and Sirri GOSPs in the central and southern portions of the Persian Gulf. Like the Rashadat platform, destroyed in response to the Iranian Silkworm attack on the Kuwaiti reflagged tanker *Sea Isle City* in October 1987, both Sirri and Sassan were manned by Iranian forces and were used as platforms to coordinate attacks on merchant shipping. The two targets were armed with ZU–23mm automatic guns, rocket-propelled grenades, and assorted small arms. Sirri was also known to produce 180,000 barrels of oil per day. In selecting an Iranian naval target, attention focused on the British-built 1,540-ton Vosper Mark V-class frigate *Sabalan*. During the previous two years *Sabalan* had committed numerous attacks on merchant shipping, featuring concentrated fire on the crew quarters of tankers and other vessels. In view of this propensity Pentagon spokesman Daniel Howard readily conceded that *Sabalan* "was a target of opportunity."

Following U.S. Central Command Directives, JTFME tasked three Surface Action Groups (SAG) with assigned air support to accomplish the mission. SAGs Bravo, Charlie, and Delta; a pair of A–6E Intruders; two EA–6B Prowlers; and four F–14 Tomcats flying Surface Combat Air Patrol (SUCAP) from the carrier *Enterprise* (CVA–65) in the North Arabian Sea made up the American force. U.S. Air Force KC–10 tankers furnished continuous air refueling to fleet aircraft. Air Force E–3A Sentry Airborne Warning and Control System (AWACS) and carrier-based E–2C Hawkeye aircraft provided radar surveillance of hostile air space.

Praying Mantis

The retaliatory strikes began about 0800 local time (0100 EDT) on 18 April 1988. Directed by the commander of Destroyer Squadron 9, SAG Bravo—the destroyers *Merrill* (DD–976) and *Lynde McCormick* (DDG–8) and the amphibious ship *Trenton* (LPD–14)—attacked the Sassan platform. Five minutes before the assault, the American commander issued a warning, in Farsi and in English, for Iranians aboard the platform to abandon the facility. Twenty-nine Iranians disembarked in two tugboats. When the destroyer *Merrill* opened fire with its 5-inch gun, other Iranians still on Sassan replied with their

Appendix A

ZU–23mm. *Merrill* and *Lynde McCormick* quickly silenced the Iranian fire and continued the bombardment until an Iranian tugboat radioed for permission to retrieve the other twenty-eight to thirty crewmen still aboard the platform. Following evacuation a Marine assault element of MAGTF 2–88 and a Navy Explosive Ordnance Disposal (EOD) detachment fast-roped from UH–1 and CH–46 helicopters to Sassan. After securing the platform, the Americans found antiaircraft guns, rocket-propelled grenades, ammunition, and communication gear. The boarding party then destroyed the Sassan with explosives.

SAG Charlie—the guided missile cruiser *Wainwright* (CG–28), the guided missile frigate *Simpson* (FFG–56), and the frigate *Bagley* (FF–1069)—attacked the Sirri platform about 0815. Led by the commanding officer of *Wainwright*, SAG Charlie also warned platform occupants to abandon their posts before opening fire. During the ensuing barrage, American forces held their fire and allowed Iranian forces to pick up personnel who had initially refused to abandon the platform. At one point an American helicopter even dropped a raft to six surviving Iranians. Extensive fires and secondary explosions prevented a landing party from boarding Sirri.

While SAGs Bravo and Charlie attacked the GOSPs, SAG Delta—the *Spruance*-class destroyer *O'Brien* (DD–975), the guided missile frigate *Jack Williams* (FFG–24), and the guided missile destroyer *Joseph Strauss* (DDG–16)—cruised toward the Strait of Hormuz in search of *Sabalan*. But SAG Delta, led by the commander of Destroyer Squadron 22, was unable to engage the Iranian warship, which had abandoned the Strait of Hormuz once the platform strikes began; the ship had retired to the port of Bandar Abbas, where it positioned itself between two tankers. According to Pentagon spokesman Daniel Howard, the anchorage proved especially convenient because it provided protection against Harpoon antiship missile attacks. Because the Harpoon's guidance system homes on the largest target, *Sabalan's* commanding officer apparently reasoned that a U.S.-launched missile would strike one of the tankers.

Other Iranian warships were more aggressive. Within several hours of the American strikes against the platforms, Iranian gunboats rampaged through the southern gulf, attacking oil facilities and commercial vessels. At 1146 hours, Iranian Boghammar speedboats attacked the American-flagged supply ship *Willie Tide* with rocket-propelled grenades. Iranian speedboats also shot up *Scan Bay*, a Panamanian-flagged ship with fifteen Americans on board, near the Mubarak oil field. The British-flagged tanker *York Marine* was also attacked. In response *Jack Williams* vectored American SUCAP Intruders into an attack position. The A–6Es dropped Rockeye MK 20 cluster bombs, sinking one speedboat and damaging the four others.

This initial sparring quickly escalated into a major engagement when the Iranian Combattante II fast-attack craft *Joshan*, armed with a 76mm gun and an American-made Harpoon, closed to within thirteen nautical miles of

Appendixes

SAG Charlie. Ignoring four separate warnings to turn away, *Joshan* continued to approach *Wainwright* and launched a Harpoon antiship missile at the American cruiser. *Wainwright* and *Simpson* responded promptly, firing five SM–1 missiles in surface-to-surface mode at *Joshan*. *Bagley* then launched a Harpoon. All five SM–1 missiles fired by U.S. combatants found their mark, leaving *Joshan* a burning, sinking hulk over which *Bagley*'s Harpoon passed. *Wainwright* successfully evaded *Joshan*'s Harpoon.

In the midst of this short engagement an Iranian F–4 sortied from Bandar Abbas to menace SAG Charlie. As the aircraft maneuvered to attack *Wainwright*, the cruiser launched a pair of SM–2 surface-to-air missiles (SAM), damaging the Phantom. The aircraft limped back to its base at Bandar Abbas.

The destruction of the 147-foot *Joshan* once again raised the tempo of fighting. At 1459 hours *Sahand*, sister ship to *Sabalan*, steamed out of Bandar Abbas to confront elements of SAG Delta. The action began when *Sahand* fired SAMs at two A–6E aircraft flying cover for *Joseph Strauss*. In response the Intruders launched two Harpoons and four laser-guided Skipper bombs while *Joseph Strauss*, in a coordinated attack, fired another Harpoon. All the weapons found the target, leaving *Sahand* dead in the water with decks afire and a large hole in the starboard side. Witnesses on *Joseph Strauss* felt the shock waves as *Sahand*'s magazines caught fire and blew up. By early evening *Sahand* disappeared beneath the waters of the Persian Gulf.

As SAG Delta and its supporting aircraft dispatched the *Sahand*, *Sabalan* ventured into the gulf. Cruising just south of Larak Island in the Strait of Hormuz, *Sabalan* engaged American forces, firing antiaircraft artillery at one of *Enterprise*'s Intruders. A laser-guided bomb, dropped from one of the orbiting A–6Es, hit *Sabalan* amidships, exploding inside the vessel. U.S. naval forces did not interfere as Iranian tugs took *Sabalan*, dead in the water with stern down, in tow to Bandar Abbas.

Final Assessment

Monday, 18 April 1988, proved a milestone in the history of American naval combat. For the first time since the Battle of Leyte Gulf on 23–26 October 1944, U.S. naval forces and supporting aircraft fought a major surface action against a determined and fanatical enemy. Losses inflicted on the Iranians were impressive. During the day SAGs Bravo, Charlie, and Delta destroyed both the Sirri and Sassan GOSPs. The Iranian frigates *Sabalan* and *Sahand* and missile patrol boat *Joshan* were sunk or put out of action. In further combat A–6E aircraft from *Enterprise* sank one Boghammar and neutralized four more of the Swedish-made speedboats in the Mubarak oil field.

Against this toll the Iranians made questionable claim to one American helicopter. During the evening of 18 April an AH–1T Sea Cobra from Marine Light Attack Helicopter Squadron 167 failed to return from a recon-

Appendix A

naissance mission. An Iranian television broadcast monitored in Cyprus on 27 April said that Iranian forces had destroyed the helicopter during fighting on the afternoon of 18 April. But examination of the recovered wreckage on 15 May evidenced no battle damage to the downed helicopter. When queried by the media on 2 June as to whether the aircraft may have hit the water while evading hostile fire, General George Crist replied that "we don't know and probably never will."

The success of Praying Mantis owed much to the quality of American weapons systems and to the skill of American aviators and seamen. Particularly effective were the Harpoon and Standard missiles—the backbone of the U.S. Navy's antiship and antiaircraft defense systems.

The Navy bore the brunt of fighting on 18 April, but other services operating jointly under the direction of CJTFME were also involved. Marines from Contingency Marine Air Ground Task Force 2–88 from *Trenton* boarded the Sassan GOSP alongside Navy demolition experts. While Air Force KC–10 tankers refueled fleet aircraft from *Enterprise*, Navy E–2C Hawkeye surveillance aircraft controlled F–14s flying combat air patrol over the gulf, linking their radar picture with ship-based radar systems to coordinate operations. Throughout this complex operation, communications between the Commander Joint Task Force Middle East, the U.S. Central Command, and the Joint Chiefs of Staff never failed. The communications relay is best illustrated by the attack on *Sabalan*. As A–6E aircraft circled over the stricken Iranian vessel, the aircraft commander asked permission from Rear Admiral Less, CJTFME, to deliver a final blow. Admiral Less communicated the request to General Crist, who relayed it to Admiral William J. Crowe, Jr., Chairman of the Joint Chiefs of Staff. Admiral Crowe then discussed the issue with Secretary of Defense Frank C. Carlucci, who decided to spare *Sabalan* any further harm.

Expanded U.S. Coverage

The week of 18 April 1988 brought other disasters for Iran. In a lightning offensive launched on 17 April, the first day of the Moslem holy month of Ramadan, units of the Iraqi VIIth Corps recovered the Fao peninsula, ending a two-year Iranian occupation. The swift victory led Speaker of the Iranian parliament, Ali Akbar Hashemi Rafsanjani, to comment that time was no longer on Iran's side in the lengthy war with Iraq. The American victory in the gulf further underscored the declining Iranian position. On 29 April Secretary Carlucci announced that American forces would extend distress assistance to friendly and neutral nonbelligerent shipping operating outside recognized war exclusion zones. Because the bulk of Iranian attacks on merchant shipping occurred outside their declared war zones, the implications of this policy could not have been lost on Iran's Supreme Defense

Appendixes

Council. In the past Iranian patrol boats had attacked foreign commercial vessels, even those adjacent to U.S. Navy warships, with the knowledge that U.S. protection extended only to American-flagged vessels.

In combination with the U.S. government's decision to extend distress assistance to neutral shipping, Operation Praying Mantis reassured not only the states of the Persian Gulf, but also the world, of American resolve. U.S. forces refused to accept mining of international waterways and would no longer tolerate hostile attacks on innocent commercial shipping transiting the international waters of the Persian Gulf.

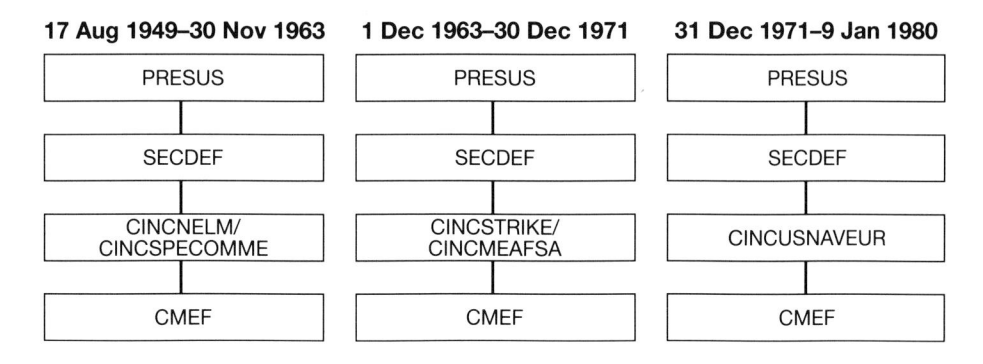

B. Middle East Force Chain of Command, 1949–1988

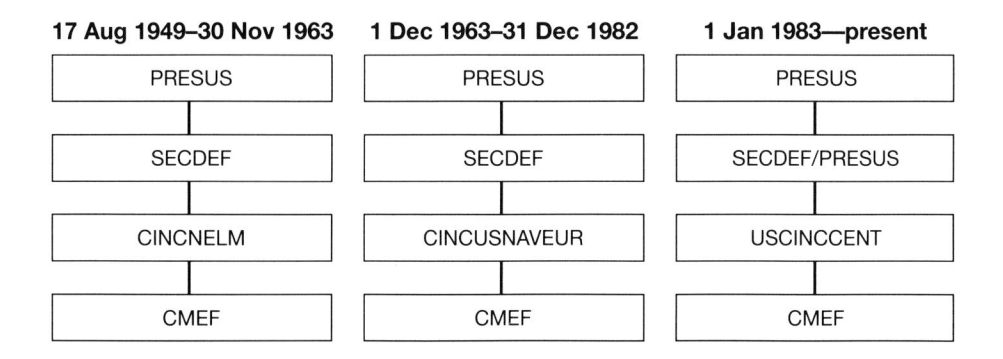

17 Aug 1949–30 Nov 1963

```
PRESUS
  |
SECDEF
  |
CINCNELM
  |
CMEF
```

1 Dec 1963–31 Dec 1982

```
PRESUS
  |
SECDEF
  |
CINCUSNAVEUR
  |
CMEF
```

1 Jan 1983—present

```
PRESUS
  |
SECDEF/PRESUS
  |
USCINCCENT
  |
CMEF
```

Contingency Chain of Command

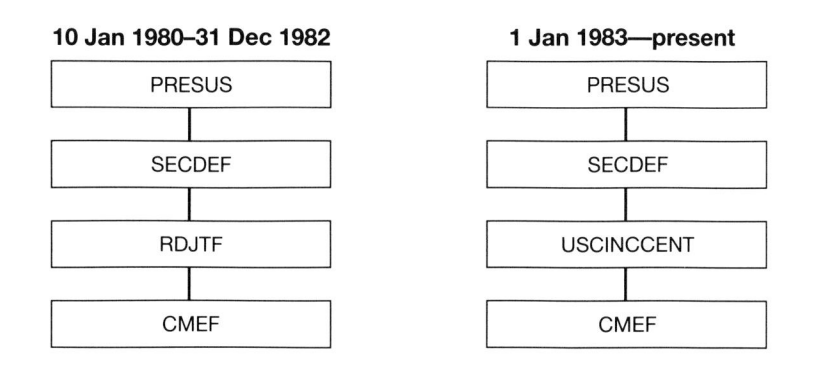

17 Aug 1949–30 Nov 1963

```
PRESUS
  |
SECDEF
  |
CINCNELM/
CINCSPECOMME
  |
CMEF
```

1 Dec 1963–30 Dec 1971

```
PRESUS
  |
SECDEF
  |
CINCSTRIKE/
CINCMEAFSA
  |
CMEF
```

31 Dec 1971–9 Jan 1980

```
PRESUS
  |
SECDEF
  |
CINCUSNAVEUR
  |
CMEF
```

10 Jan 1980–31 Dec 1982

```
PRESUS
  |
SECDEF
  |
RDJTF
  |
CMEF
```

1 Jan 1983—present

```
PRESUS
  |
SECDEF
  |
USCINCCENT
  |
CMEF
```

C. Commanders, Middle East Force, 1949–1988

CAPT William V. O'Regan*	1 January 1949–12 August 1949
CAPT Karl G. Hensel	17 August 1949– 6 March 1950
CAPT William T. Rassieur	8 March 1950–18 August 1950
CAPT Ernest M. Eller	18 August 1950–21 April 1951
RADM Harry D. Felt	21 April 1951–2 October 1951
RADM Rufus E. Rose	2 October 1951–18 April 1952
RADM Francis M. Hughes	18 April 1952–3 November 1952
RADM George C. Towner	3 November 1952–29 June 1953
RADM Wallace M. Beakley	29 June 1953–4 January 1954
RADM William G. Beecher	4 January 1954–14 June 1954
RADM Harry H. Henderson	14 June 1954–15 December 1954
RADM Allen Smith, Jr.	15 December 1954–1 January 1955
CAPT Robert J. C. Maulsby (acting)	1 January 1955–22 July 1955
RADM Paul L. Dudley	22 July 1955–22 January 1956
RADM John Quinn	22 January 1956–3 August 1956
RADM Jack P. Monroe	3 August 1956–4 September 1957
RADM Harold M. Briggs	4 September 1957–2 September 1958
RADM Michael F. D. Flaherty	2 September 1958–22 July 1959
RADM James R. Lee	22 July 1959–9 September 1960
RADM Andrew McB. Jackson, Jr.	9 September 1960–9 August 1961

*O'Regan commanded Task Force 126, U.S. Naval Force, Persian Gulf, established 20 January 1948, and Persian Gulf Forces, established 26 June 1949. The U.S. Navy established Middle East Force on 16 August 1949.

Appendix C

RADM Elonzo G. Grantham, Jr.	9 August 1961–30 May 1962
RADM Benedict J. Semmes, Jr.	30 May 1962–9 July 1963
RADM Arnold F. Schade	9 July 1963–17 July 1964
RADM John H. Maurer	17 July 1964–26 April 1966
RADM Earl R. Eastwold	26 April 1966–1 May 1967
RADM Walter L. Small, Jr.	1 May 1967–11 June 1968
RADM Ed R. King	11 June 1968–21 April 1970
RADM Marmaduke G. Bayne	21 April 1970–9 December 1972
RADM Robert J. Hanks	9 December 1972–20 February 1975
RADM Thomas J. Bigley	20 February 1975–30 June 1976
RADM William J. Crowe, Jr.	30 June 1976–4 July 1977
RADM Samuel H. Packer II	4 July 1977–25 June 1979
RADM Robert W. Chewning	25 June 1979–11 June 1981
RADM Charles E. Gurney	11 June 1981–6 July 1983
RADM John F. Addams	6 July 1983–5 July 1986
RADM Harold J. Bernsen	5 July 1986–27 February 1988
RADM Anthony A. Less	27 February 1988–16 March 1989

Abbreviations

AAW	Antiair Warfare
AHIPS	Army Helicopter Improvement Program
AIOC	Anglo-Iranian Oil Company
ALINDIEN	French military command in the Indian Ocean
APOC	Anglo-Persian Oil Company
Aramco	Arab-American Oil Company
AWACS	Airborne Warning and Control Systems
Bapco	Bahrain Petroleum Company
CENTCOM	Central Command
CENTO	Central Treaty Organization
CINC	Commander in Chief
CINCLANT	Commander in Chief, Atlantic
CINCLANTFLT	Commander in Chief, Atlantic Fleet
CINCME	Commander in Chief, Middle East
CINCNELM	Commander in Chief, Northeastern Atlantic and Mediterranean
CINCPAC	Commander in Chief, Pacific
CINCSPECOMME	Commander in Chief, Specified Command, Middle East
CINCUSNAVEUR	Commander in Chief, U.S. Naval Forces, Europe
CJTFME	Commander Joint Task Force, Middle East
CMEF	Commander Middle East Force
CNA	Center for Naval Analyses

Abbreviations

CNO	Chief of Naval Operations
COMIDEASTFOR	Commander Middle East Force
COMNAVEU	Commander Naval Forces, Europe
COMNAVMED	Commander Naval Forces, Mediterranean
COMSEVENTHFLT	Commander Seventh Fleet
CVBG	Carrier Battle Group
EOD	Explosive Ordnance Disposal
ERP	European Recovery Program
EUCOM	European Command
FFG	Guided Missile Frigate
GCC	Gulf Cooperation Council
GOSP	Gas-Oil Separation Platform
INSMAT	Inspector of Naval Material
IPC	Iraqi Petroleum Company
JCS	Joint Chiefs of Staff
JSSC	Joint Strategic Survey Committee
JTFME	Joint Task Force, Middle East
JWPC	Joint War Plans Committee
KOTC	Kuwaiti Oil Tanker Company
LSM	Landing Ship, Medium
MAGTF	Marine Air-Ground Task Force
MCM	Mine Countermeasures
MEB	Marine Expeditionary Brigade
MEDO	Middle East Defense Organization
MEF	Middle East Force
MIDEASTFOR	Middle East Force

Abbreviations

MPS	Maritime Prepositioning Ship
MSB	Mobile Sea Base
NATO	North Atlantic Treaty Organization
NEA	Near Eastern and African Affairs Office, U.S. State Department
NSC	National Security Council
ONI	Office of Naval Intelligence
OPNAV	Office of the Chief of Naval Operations
PACOM	Pacific Command
PB	Patrol Boat
POL	Petroleum Oil Lubricants
RDF	Rapid Deployment Force
RDJTF	Rapid Deployment Joint Task Force
ROE	Rules of Engagement
SACEUR	Strategic Air Command, Europe
SAG	Surface Action Group
SAM	Surface-to-Air Missile
SECDEF	Secretary of Defense
SECSTATE	Secretary of State
SLOC	Sea Line of Communication
Socal	Standard Oil of California
SOPA	Senior Officer Present Afloat
SSM	Surface-to-Surface Missile
STRAC	Strategic Army Corps
STRIKCOM	Strike Command
SUCAP	Surface Combat Air Patrol

Abbreviations

SWNCC	State-War-Navy Coordinating Committee
TPC	Turkish Petroleum Company
UAE	United Arab Emirates
UAR	United Arab Republic
USCENTCOM	U.S. Central Command
USCINCENT	U.S. Commander in Chief, Central Command
VTOL	Vertical Take-Off and Landing

Notes

Chapter 1

1. Captain Charles Derby brought the brig *Cadet* from Salem to Muscat, Oman, in 1795. Captain Joseph Beadle, returning to Salem in the barque *Eliza* in May 1805, reported on piracy in the gulf. See James Duncan Phillips, *Salem and the East Indies: The Story of the Great Commercial Era of the City* (Boston, 1947), pp. 186, 238.

2. Master Commandant David Geisinger to Secretary of the Navy Levi Woodbury, 17 Jan 1834, #108, Masters Commandants Letters to the Secretary of the Navy, Jan–Jun 1834, Record Group 45, National Archives; Edmund Roberts, *Embassy to the Eastern Courts of Cochin-China, Siam, and Muscat; in the U.S. Sloop-of-War Peacock, David Geisinger, Commander, during the Years 1832–3–4* (New York, 1938), pp. 351–63; J. B. Kelly, *Britain and the Persian Gulf, 1795–1880* (Oxford, 1968), p. 236; Charles I. Bevans, ed., *Treaties and Other International Agreements of the United States of America, 1776–1949*, 13 vols. (Washington, 1968–1976), 9:1291–93; David F. Long, *Gold Braid and Foreign Relations: Diplomatic Activities of U.S. Naval Officers, 1798–1883* (Annapolis, 1988), pp. 261–62.

3. For background on the history of the Persian Gulf, see Roger M. Savory's "The Ancient Period," "A.D. 600–1800," and Malcolm Yapp's "The Nineteenth and Twentieth Centuries," in Alvin J. Cottrell, ed., *The Persian Gulf States: A General Survey* (Baltimore and London, 1980), pp. 3–13, 14–40, 41–69.

4. Kelly, *Britain and the Gulf*, p. 2. See also Charles Rathbone Low, *History of the Indian Navy, 1613–1863*, 2 vols. (London, 1977) for the view from the perspective of the East India Company and the Indian navy.

5. Kelly, *Britain and the Gulf*, p. 66. Until the Indian Mutiny of 1857–1858 the East India Company, not the British government, bore responsibility for the region.

6. Ibid., pp. 236–38.

7. An American consular report of December 1851 noted that ten to twelve American ships were trading in the gulf proper, using Zanzibar as their depot. See John F. Webb, William H. Jelly, and Samuel R. Masury to John Aulick, 5 Dec 1851, in Norman R. Bennett and George E. Brooks, Jr., eds., *New England Merchants in Africa: A History Through Documents, 1802 to 1865* (Boston, 1965), pp. 488–90.

8. See David Gillard, *The Struggle for Asia, 1828–1914: A Study in British and Russian Imperialism* (London, 1977).

9. James A. Field, Jr., *America and the Mediterranean World, 1776–1882* (Princeton, 1969), pp. 256–61; Kelly, *Britain and the Gulf*, p. 458.

10. Field, *America and the Mediterranean*, p. 261.

11. Frederick C. Drake, *The Empire of the Seas: A Biography of Rear Admiral Robert Wilson Shufeldt, USN* (Honolulu, 1984).

12. Ibid., p. 220; and Kelly, *Britain and the Gulf*, pp. 775–76.

13. Drake, *Shufeldt*, pp. 220, 224.

14. Quoted in ibid., p. 220.

15. Ibid., pp. 221, 222–23.

Notes to Pages 6–9

16. Quoted in ibid., p. 227.

17. Ibid., p. 223.

18. See Alfred Thayer Mahan, *The Problem of Asia and Its Effect upon International Policies* (Boston, 1900), p. 77; and "The Persian Gulf and International Relations," in *Retrospect & Prospect: Studies in International Relations, Naval and Political* (Boston, 1902), pp. 209–51. Mahan's personal knowledge of the gulf was limited. He had visited Muscat as a young officer in the *Iroquois* in 1867, but had not actually entered the gulf proper. Alfred Thayer Mahan, *From Sail to Steam: Recollections of Naval Life* (New York, 1907), pp. 223–25.

19. Petroleum Industry Research Foundation, Inc., *World Oil, Fact and Policy: The Case for a Sound American Petroleum Policy* (New York, 1944), pp. 10–11, estimated the world's oil reserves in 1944: United States, 39 percent; Middle East, 32 percent; and the Soviet Union, 11 percent. Fifteen years later, Middle East reserves were estimated at 26,000 million tons of oil, or over 62 percent of the world's total. See Stephen Hemsley Longrigg, *Oil in the Middle East: Its Discovery and Development*, 2d ed. (London, New York, and Toronto, 1961), p. 350.

20. Leonard M. Fanning, *American Oil Operations Abroad* (New York and London, 1947), pp. 256–59. American companies alone produced between 60 and 70 percent of the world's crude between 1890 and 1918. Only briefly, between 1898 and 1901, did Russia outproduce the United States; in that period, the latter's proportion of world production fell to about 40 percent.

21. Longrigg, *Oil in the Middle East*, pp. 17–21.

22. Arthur J. Marder, *From Dreadnought to Scapa Flow: The Royal Navy in the Fisher Era, 1904–1919*, 5 vols. (London, 1961–70), 1:45.

23. See Sir John Fisher, *Memoirs and Records of Admiral of the Fleet Lord Fisher*, 2 vols. (London, New York, and Toronto, 1919), 2:189–203; Sir John Fisher, *The Papers of Admiral Sir John Fisher*, P. K. Kemp, ed., 2 vols. (Navy Records Society, 1960–1964), 1:80–81; and Jon Tetsuro Sumida, *In Defence of Naval Supremacy: Finance, Technology and British Naval Policy, 1889–1914* (Boston, London, Sydney, Wellington, 1989), pp. 259–61.

24. Marder, *Dreadnought to Scapa Flow*, p. 269.

25. Ibid., 1:270; Ruddock F. Mackay, *Fisher of Kilverstone* (Oxford, 1973), p. 438; and Richard Hough, *Admiral of the Fleet: The Life of John Fisher* (New York, 1969), pp. 318–19.

26. Longrigg, *Oil in the Middle East*, pp. 25–32.

27. Benjamin Shwadran, *The Middle East, Oil and the Great Powers* (New York, Toronto, and Jerusalem, 1973), pp. 197–98.

28. Longrigg, *Oil in the Middle East*, p. 25.

29. Ibid., pp. 33–35. Historian Malcolm Yapp writes that Britain's "supremacy in the Gulf in 1919 was a flash in the pan; not the inevitable result of a steady program of historic advance, but an accident of war." Malcolm Yapp, "The Nineteenth and Twentieth Centuries," in Cottrell, ed., *The Persian Gulf*, pp. 58–59. British hegemony, obviously, also came at the expense of the Arabs whose "revolt" during the First World War had assisted Britain's drive on Damascus and left the Arabs bitterly disappointed after the war.

30. E. H. Davenport and Sidney Russell Cooke, *The Oil Trusts and Anglo-American Relations* (New York, 1924), pp. 40–41; Shwadran, *Middle East, Oil, and the Great Powers*, pp. 28–29.

31. Longrigg, *Oil in the Middle East*, pp. 36–37.

32. Gerald D. Nash, *United States Oil Policy, 1890–1964: Business and Government in Twentieth Century America* (Pittsburgh, PA, 1968), p. 52; Herbert Feis, *Petroleum and American Foreign Policy* (Stanford, CA, 1944), pp. 8–9; Aaron David Miller, *Search for Security: Saudi Arabian Oil and American Foreign Policy, 1939–1949* (Chapel Hill, 1980), p. 10; Longrigg, *Oil in the Middle East*, p. 44; Shwadran, *Middle East, Oil, and the Great Powers*, p. 201.

33. The Americans ran afoul of both British and Russian interests in north Persia. But the main problem was geographical—moving oil from the north necessitated overland transportation either through southern Iran, where the British had an exclusive concession that included oil transport, or through the Soviet Union, which claimed the rights to the concession in the northern provinces of the Persian empire itself. Shwadran, *Middle East, Oil, and the Great Powers*, pp. 71–83.

34. Nash, *United States Oil Policy*, pp. 24–32.

35. Ibid., pp. 42, 43, 50, 53–55.

36. Ibid., p. 56.

37. Shwadran, *Middle East, Oil, and the Great Powers*, p. 219.

38. Longrigg, *Oil in the Middle East*, pp. 46, 66–70; Miller, *Search for Security*, pp. 11–12; Shwadran, *Middle East, Oil, and the Great Powers*, p. 238.

39. Ibid., pp. 390–91; Longrigg, *Oil in the Middle East*, pp. 98–105; and Miller, *Search for Security*, pp. 14–15.

40. Abbas Faroughy, *The Bahrein Islands, 750–1951: A Contribution to the Study of Power Politics in the Persian Gulf* (New York, 1951), pp. 103–7.

41. Miller, *Search for Security*, pp. 15–16; Longrigg, *Oil in the Middle East*, pp. 110–13; Shwadran, *Middle East, Oil, and the Great Powers*, pp. 407–9.

42. Ibid., p. 301, 302; Miller, *Search for Security*, p. 18.

43. Shwadran, *Middle East, Oil, and the Great Powers*, pp. 18–21, Longrigg, *Oil in the Middle East*, pp. 106–113. Longrigg represented the IPC during the negotiations.

44. The United States remained the source of about 60 percent of the world's petroleum in 1939. The percentage of total world production for the gulf region increased from 0.017 percent to 0.055 percent. Fanning, *American Oil Operations*, pp. 256–69.

Chapter 2

1. A 1940 long-range air attack against oil installations on Bahrain, launched from an Italian base in the Dodecanese Islands in the Aegean, caused little damage but brought the war to the gulf. Faroughy, *Bahrein*, p. 111.

2. Iraq, a victim of external pressures as well as its own internal difficulties, saw annual oil production fall from 32,643,000 barrels in 1938 to 12,650,000 in 1941 before recovering to a level of 32,112,000 by 1945. Shwadran, *Middle East, Oil, and the Great Powers*, p. 241. Iranian oil production declined from 213,737 barrels per day in 1938 to 138,704 in 1941 before rising to 280,000 in 1944. Fanning, *American Oil Operations Abroad*, p. 257.

3. Longrigg, *Oil in the Middle East*, pp. 117–29; 136–38.

4. In Bahrain, with well-developed facilities and an in-place refinery, production declined (though not as markedly as it did elsewhere) from 8,298,000 barrels per year in 1938 to 6,241,000 in 1942 before recovering by war's end. Shwadran, *Middle East, Oil, and the Great Powers*, p. 392.

Production in Saudi Arabia continued to increase into 1940, when annual production reached 5,075,000 barrels, up from 580,000 in 1938. Production then fell to 4,310,000 in 1941, but rose to 21,311,000 by 1945. Ibid., p. 349.

5. Longrigg, *Oil in the Middle East*, p. 137.

6. Nash, *United States Oil Policy*, pp. 129–57.

Notes to Pages 12–17

7. Ibid., p. 265. See also "Foreign Petroleum Policy of the United States," 11 Apr 1944, U.S. Department of State, *Foreign Relations of the United States* (hereafter *FRUS*), *1944,* 5:27–33.

8. Nash, *United States Oil Policy,* pp. 170–72. See also the Petroleum Industry Research Foundation, *World Oil, Fact and Policy: The Case for a Sound American Petroleum Policy*; and Feis, *Petroleum and American Foreign Policy.* Both short studies supported a more detailed government-industry relationship in the pursuit of a coherent postwar U.S. oil policy. However, on the issue of direct U.S. government participation in the construction and operation of a transarabian pipeline to carry oil from the Persian Gulf region to the eastern Mediterranean, a pet project of Secretary Ickes, Feis argued in support of the proposal, while PIRINC argued against such involvement.

9. John W. Frey and H. Chandler Ide, eds., *A History of the Petroleum Administration for War, 1941–1945* (Washington, 1946), p. 1.

10. Ibid., pp. 277–78.

11. Ibid., pp. 265–68.

12. Nash, *United States Oil Policy,* pp. 175–79; Frey and Ide, *Petroleum Administration for War,* pp. 279–87.

13. T. H. Vail Motter, *The Persian Corridor and Aid to Russia*, United States Army in World War II (Washington, 1952), pp. 15–18, 27.

14. James A. Bill, *The Eagle and the Lion: The Tragedy of American-Iranian Relations* (New York and London, 1988), pp. 29–30.

15. Ibid., pp. 162–63. The American in charge of building up the Iranian gendarmerie was H. Norman Schwarzkopf, father of General H. Norman Schwarzkopf, Jr., commander of US-CENTCOM during Operations Desert Shield and Desert Storm in 1990–91.

16. The Persian Gulf Service Command was established in August 1942. Ibid., pp. 227, 437.

17. Motter, *The Persian Corridor,* p. 444.

18. Miller, *Search for Security,* pp. 34–36.

19. Ibid., p. 130.

20. Ibid., pp. 37–44.

21. Ibid., p. 50.

22. Ibid., pp. 70–108.

23. Ibid., p. 129–31; Robert E. Sherwood, *Roosevelt and Hopkins: An Intimate History* (New York, 1948), pp. 871–72.

24. Memo, Thomas T. Handy to Assistant Secretary of War, 5 Feb 1945, Annex B to Appendix A, SWNCC 19, Operational Archives, Naval Historical Center, Washington, DC (hereafter OA).

25. Memo, State Department to SWNCC, 14 Jun 1945, SWNCC 19/13, OA.

26. SWNCC 19/18D, 23 Aug 1945, OA.

27. Report, SWNCC Subcommittee for the Near and Middle East, 20 Sep 1945, SWNCC 19/20, OA. SWNCC was an attempt to coordinate the efforts of the State, War, and Navy Departments and a precursor of the National Security Council.

28. Grew to Truman, 26 Jun 1945, *FRUS, 1945,* 8: 915–17.

29. Memo, Truman to Dean Acheson, 28 Sep 1945, SWNCC 19, OA.

Chapter 3

1. Knox's speech is quoted in Vincent Davis, *Postwar Defense Policy and the U.S. Navy, 1943-1946* (Chapel Hill, 1962), p. 27. American planners had no intention of maintaining postwar bases in the Mediterranean or the Middle East. See JCS 570/2, 10 Jan 1944, OA. Palmer, *Origins of the Maritime Strategy*, pp. 3–8, 17–18; and Elliott Vanvelt Converse, "United States Plans for a Postwar Overseas Military Base System, 1942-1948" (Ph.D. dissertation, Princeton University, 1984), p. 214.

2. Bernhard H. Bieri, interview by John T. Mason, Jr., 1970, pp. 211–17, U.S. Naval Institute Oral History (hereafter Bieri Oral History). Bieri, who would later command American naval forces in the Mediterranean, was attached to the SHAEF staff in Europe in 1944. See also Bruce Robellet Kuniholm, *The Origins of the Cold War in the Near East: Great Power Conflict and Diplomacy in Iran, Turkey, and Greece* (Princeton, 1980), pp. 96–98.

3. JCS 1518, 19 Sep 1945, OA.

4. JIC 341, 31 Jan 1946, *Records of the Joint Chiefs of Staff*, Part II: *1946-1953, The Soviet Union* (Washington, 1979), reel 1.

5. Kuniholm, *Origins of the Cold War in the Near East*, p. 336.

6. Language of the article could easily be taken to imply that the Allies were to withdraw from Iran within six months of the surrender of Germany, not Japan. It reads: "The forces of the Allied Powers shall be withdrawn from Iranian territory not later than six months after all hostilities between the Allied Powers and Germany and her associates have been suspended by the conclusion of an armistice or armistices, or on the conclusion of peace between them, whichever date is the earlier." In January 1942 the Soviet Union was not at war with Japan. When Germany surrendered in May 1945, the Iranians demanded Allied withdrawal. Loy Henderson was sympathetic to the Iranian interpretation, and the Americans and the British ultimately agreed to speed their withdrawal if the Soviets would likewise comply. See Henderson memo, 1 Jun 1945, *FRUS, 1945*, 8:374–75; and Murray to Secretary of State, 14 Sep 1945, ibid., pp. 408–9.

7. Murray to Brynes, 20 Nov 1945, ibid., pp. 437–38.

8. Kuniholm, *The Origins of the Cold War in the Near East*, pp. 274–75.

9. See McFarland, "A Peripheral View of the Origins of the Cold War," pp. 333–51. McFarland focuses on the substantial Iranian role in the crisis, writing that they "laid the foundation for the confrontation and worked to enlarge it for Iran's advantage." Ibid., p. 351.

10. Kennan to Byrnes, 1 Oct 1945, *FRUS, 1945*, 8:424.

11. Wilson to Brynes, 18 Mar 1946, Ibid., 7:818–9.

12. Harry S. Truman, *Memoirs*, vol. 2, *Years of Trial and Hope* (Garden City, NY, 1955), p. 94.

13. According to Rossow, General Bagramian had replaced Lieutenant General Glinsky, the former garrison commander in Iran, in command. Rossow to Byrnes, 6 Mar 1946, *FRUS, 1946*, 7:342–43. Bagramian, a Red Army commander of Armenian descent, had commanded a front against the Germans during the latter stages of the 1941-1945 war.

14. Robert Rossow, Jr., "The Battle of Azerbaijan, 1946," *The Middle East Journal* 10 (Winter 1956): 17–32. Quote on p. 17.

15. The text of Churchill's speech appeared in the *New York Times*, 6 March 1946, p. 4. It is excerpted in Barton J. Bernstein and Allen J. Matusow, ed., *The Truman Administration: A Documentary History* (New York and London, 1966), pp. 215–19.

16. Byrnes to Kennan, 5 Mar 1946, *FRUS, 1946*, 7:340–42.

Notes to Pages 23–27

17. Press Release, 6 Mar 1946, U.S. Department of State, *The Department of State Bulletin* 14 (17 Mar 1946): 447. For the Navy's initial plans for a show of force, see Palmer, *Origins of the Maritime Strategy*, pp. 21–22; and Hansen W. Baldwin's "U.S. Fleet Parade in Europe Dropped," *New York Times*, 17 Mar 1946, pp. 1, 3.

18. Rossow to Byrnes, 5 Mar 1946, *FRUS 1946*, 7:340; Rossow to Byrnes, 6 Mar 1946, ibid., pp. 342–43; Rossow to Byrnes, 7 Mar 1946, ibid., pp. 344–45.

19. See editorial note, ibid., pp. 346–48.

20. Byrnes to Kennan, 8 Mar 1946, ibid., p. 348.

21. Kennan to Byrnes, 17 Mar 1946, ibid., pp. 362–64.

22. Kennan to Brynes, 22 Feb 1946, ibid., vol. 4, *Eastern Europe: The Soviet Union* (Washington, 1969), pp. 696–709, Quote from p. 707.

23. The Soviets informed the Iranians of their intention to withdraw on the evening of 24 March. Murray to Byrnes, 25 Mar 1946, ibid., 7:379–80. Andrei Gromyko made the official announcement before the United Nations on the 26th, ibid., pp. 381–82. See also Truman, *Memoirs*, 2:95–96; and Robert James Maddox, *From War to Cold War: The Education of Harry S. Truman* (Boulder, CO, & London, 1988), p. 176.

24. CNO to CINCPAC, CINCLANT, COM7THFLT, COM12THFLT, COMNAVMED, 23 Sep 1946, box 12, Series II, Dispatch Files, Operations Division—COMINCH, OA.

25. Truman, *Memoirs*, vol. 1, *Year of Decisions*, p. 552. A solid, balanced article on the Iran crisis is Gary R. Hess, "The Iranian Crisis of 1945–46 and the Cold War," *Political Science Quarterly* 89 (Mar 1974): 117–46. Hess concludes:

> While the importance of commercial and economic objectives cannot be discounted, the dominant factor shaping American policy was that Soviet actions were seen against the background of a vivid memory of Munich. Americans thus regarded their position in Iran as a test of Western firmness and especially as a means of demonstrating the workability of the international peace-keeping system centered in the United Nations. Obviously coincidence was an important element in the shaping of American policy: the Iranian situation intensified just at the moment that disenchantment with the Soviet Union became part of the American consensus and when the convening of the United Nations presented an opportunity to prove the effectiveness of collective action to prevent war (Ibid., p. 146).

26. Truman listed Rumania, Bulgaria, Iran, the Kiel Canal, the Rhine-Danube Waterway, the Black Sea Straits, Japan, China, Korea, and the Lend-Lease debt of the Soviet Union as areas where the United States should take a harder line.

27. Byrnes to JCS, 6 Mar 1946, JCS 1641, OA. The letter was approved and signed by Truman.

28. JCS 1641/3 13 Mar 1946, OA.

29. Memo, JCS to Truman, 12 Mar 1946, JCS 1643, OA.

30. JCS 1641/5, 11 Apr 1946, OA.

31. JCS 1641/6, 18 May 1946, OA.

32. JCS 1714/1, 4 Oct 1946, OA. Great Britain drew 40 percent of its oil from the Abadan fields in Iran.

33. JCS 1714/3, 14 Oct 1946, OA.

34. The department had prepared a policy statement in July 1946. See Policy and Information Statement on Iran, 15 Jul 1946, *FRUS, 1946*, 7:507–9.

35. Clayton to Byrnes, 27 Sep 1946, *FRUS, 1946*, 7:516–17; Allen to Brynes, 28 Sep 1946, ibid., pp. 517–18; Allen to Byrnes, 30 Sep 1946, ibid., pp. 518–20; Acheson to Byrnes, 1 Oct 1946, ibid., p. 520; Henderson to Acheson, 18 Oct 1946, enclosing memo of the same date, ibid., pp. 533–36.

36. Memo, Loy Henderson, 21 Oct 1946, enclosing Memorandum on Turkey, ibid., pp. 893–97.

37. McFarland, "A Peripheral View of the Origins of the Cold War," p. 334.

Chapter 4

1. Henderson Memo, undated, *FRUS, 1946*, 7:1–6.

2. Joyce and Gabriel Kolko, *The Limits of Power: The World and United States Foreign Policy, 1945–1954* (New York, Evanston, San Francisco, and London, 1972), p. 236; Yergin, *Shattered Peace*, pp. 179–80. Yergin quotes Henderson on the importance of the region "especially in view of the oil reserves," but Henderson's concerns were much broader. For example, his 19 November 1945 memorandum on the Iranian situation for Assistant Secretary of State Dunn, which runs for nearly two complete pages in the *Foreign Relations* series, mentions oil once, and then in a short concluding paragraph that reads, "Apart from our interest in the international security aspect [which is the subject of extensive discussion in the memo], this country has a direct interest in this problem because of our oil, economic, and strategic interest in this area." Henderson to Dunn, 19 Nov 1945, *FRUS, 1945*, 8:430–31.

3. Henderson to Acheson, 18 Oct 1946, enclosing memorandum of the same date, ibid., *1946*, 7:533–36.

4. The Joint War Plans Committee's "Strategic Study of the Area between the Alps and the Himalayas," conducted as a study in the Pincher series, concluded in Nov 1946 that "the greatest strategic objectives in the Alps to Himalayas area, for both the Soviets and the Allies, are the control of the eastern Mediterranean area and the Middle East oil resources." See JWPC 475/1, 2 Nov 1946, p. 3, *Records of the Joint Chiefs of Staff*, Part II: *1946–1953, The Soviet Union*.

5. "Foreign Petroleum Policy of the United States," 11 Apr 1944, *FRUS, 1944*, 5:27–33.

6. Some historians portray the oil problem as critical immediately after the war. See Yergin, *Shattered Peace*, pp. 179–80.

7. Walter Millis, ed., *The Forrestal Diaries* (New York, 1951), p. 272.

8. Forrestal to Secretary of State, 11 Dec 1944, Middle East, box 13, Political-Military Policy Division, OA.

9. Memos, Notes on Middle East Oil, 16 Apr 1946 and 17 Oct 1946, Middle East, box 13, Political-Military Policy Division, OA. The April memorandum concluded that Soviet interests in Iran were rooted more in "political reasons than for oil and that she will use her oil rights to seek an outlet on the Persian Gulf." Also note that while it has been U.S. policy since the oil embargo of 1973 to decrease American "reliance" on foreign oil supplies, American policy in the late 1940s was quite the opposite.

10. *New York Times*, 18 Jan 1948, pp. 1, 51.

11. "Forrestal Diaries," 9:2026–27, Privileged Manuscript Collection, OA. Princeton University Library holds the original copy of the Forrestal diaries.

12. *New York Times*, 20 Jan 1948, pp. 1, 14.

13. Millis, *Forrestal Diaries*, p. 323.

14. Navy press release, 2 Jul 1948, Press Release Files, OA.

15. The Navy began to buy Persian Gulf oil in late 1945, purchasing Navy Special Fuel Oil from Aramco refineries in Saudi Arabia for $1.05 per barrel, when the corresponding Western

Hemisphere price was about $1.48. Again, the Persian Gulf rates were significantly lower than the price for Western Hemisphere oil products.

Price per Barrel

	Persian Gulf	United States
Navy Special Fuel	$1.48	$2.63
Navy Diesel	2.11	3.51
Motor Gasoline	3.39	3.57

See statement by Secretary of the Navy John L. Sullivan, 28 Apr 1948, Press Release Files, OA; Navy press release, 24 Jun 1948, ibid.

16. Millis, *Forrestal Diaries*, p. 551.

17. Address to the Nation, 18 Apr 1977, Jimmy Carter, *Public Papers of the Presidents of the United States: Jimmy Carter, 1977*, vol. 1, *January 20 to June 24, 1977* (Washington, 1977), p. 656; Jimmy Carter, *Keeping Faith: Memoirs of a President* (Toronto, New York, London, Sydney, 1982), p. 91.

Chapter 5

1. During the last half of 1946, 35 percent of the petroleum products moved by the U.S. Navy came from the Persian Gulf; during 1947, 41.5 percent; during 1948, 30 percent; during 1949, 38 percent; and during 1950, 32 percent. U.S. Navy, *Logistics Summary Reports*, Logistics Reports, Command File, OA.

2. DCNO (Logistics) Narrative Report, 1 Jul 1946–30 Jun 1947, p. 13, Logistics Division Reports, Command File, OA.

3. Between 1 July and 1 November 1950, "64 government owned and/or operated tankers called at Bahrein or Ras Tanura," an average of sixteen per month.

4. CNO to COMNAVEU, 17 Oct 1946, Chronological, CNO, Command File, OA. Conolly's headquarters, originally established early in World War II, first bore the title U.S. Naval Forces, Europe. On 1 November 1947, the command, answerable to the JCS under the Unified Command Plan, was redesignated U.S. Naval Forces, Eastern Atlantic and Mediterranean. Conolly's cumbersome title, CINCNAVEASTLANTMED, was mercifully shortened in May 1948 to CINCNELM.

5. Richard L. Conolly, interview by Donald F. Shaughnessy, 1960, p. 294, Columbia University Oral History Project, New York, NY.

6. CINCNELM Command History, Oct 1947–Mar 1948, Middle East Force, Command File, OA.

7. CINCNELM Command History, Oct 1948–Mar 1949, ibid.

8. CINCNELM to CNO, Annual Report of Operations, 1 Jul 1948–30 Jul 1949 [sic], 30 Nov 1949, ibid.

9. CMEF to CNO (OP–09B9), 29 Jul 1960, enclosing Command History, from commissioning through 31 December 1958, ibid.

10. Memo, E. T. Woolridge to Radford, 2 Apr 1948, A4/QG1–2 (Near East), box 2, Operations Division—CNO, OA. Woolridge discussed the development of the American naval force in the gulf with the State Department's Loy Henderson who agreed.

11. Memo, OP–03 regarding NELM Conference, 5 Jun 1948, 4/FF7 (NELM), box 1, ibid.

12. DCNO (Logistics), Historical Narrative, 1 Jul 1947–30 Sep 1947, p. 11, Logistics Reports, Command File, OA.

13. Chief of Naval Communications, Earl E. Stone to CNO, 28 Apr 1948, folder 1, 1948, Chronological, CNO, ibid; I. N. Kiland to DCNO (Operations), 1 Oct 1948, A4 (General), box 1,

Operations Division-CNO, ibid.; CINCNELM Command History, Apr–Sep 1948), 14 Oct 1948, Middle East Force, Command File, OA.

14. CINCLANTFLT to CNO, 24 Oct 1947, A4/QG1–2 (Near East), box 2, Operations Division-CNO, ibid; CNO to CINCPAC, CINCNELM, CINCLANT, 16 Jan 1948, ibid; memo, OP–33 to OP–03, 24 May 1948, A4 (General), box 1, ibid.

15. Memo, OP–03 to CNO, 15 Feb 1948, ibid.; memo, B. H. Rodgers to OP–03, 11 Feb 1948, ibid.; memo, OP–33 to OP–09, 17 May 1948, A4 (General), box 1, ibid.

16. Commander *Pawcatuck* (AO–108) to Commander Service Force, U.S. Atlantic Fleet, 2 Sep 1948, Report File, OA.

17. Report, *Greenwich Bay* (AVP–41), 12 Aug 1948, ibid.

18. Commander *Pawcatuck* (AO–108) to Commander Service Force, U.S. Atlantic Fleet, 2 Sep 1948, ibid.

19. Commander Carrier Division Five to CINCNELM, 3 May 1948, ibid.

20. Command History of Middle East Force through 31 Dec 1958, 29 Jul 1960, Middle East Force, Command File, OA.

21. E. M. Eller to Sherman, folder 2, box 1, Sherman Papers, 1950, Records of the Immediate Office of the Chief of Naval Operations (hereafter 00 File), OA.

Chapter 6

1. For the relevant correspondence see *FRUS, 1945*, 8:1034–1218.

2. Dean Acheson, *Present at the Creation: My Years in the State Department* (New York, 1969), p. 169.

3. Compare Acheson, *Present at the Creation*, p. 169, and Millis, *Forrestal Diaries*, p. 347.

4. Ibid., p. 169. See also Robert J. Donovan, *Conflict and Crisis: The Presidency of Harry S Truman, 1945–1948* (New York, 1977), pp. 312–31.

5. See, for example, Steven L. Rearden, *History of the Office of the Secretary of Defense*, vol. 1, *The Formative Years, 1947–1950* (Washington, 1984), pp. 545–46.

6. SWNCC memo of 21 Jun 1946 in JCS 1684/1, 18 Jun 1946, OA.

7. JCS 1684/3, 10 Oct 1947, OA.

8. See memo, Nimitz to JCS, 10 Oct 1947, JCS 1684/6, later added to 1684/3, OA.

9. Memo, CNO to JCS, 7 Feb 1948, in JCS 1684/8, 9 Feb 1948, OA.

10. JCS 1684/11, 31 Mar 1948; JCS 1684/14, 13 May 1948, OA.

11. JCS 1684/27, 7 Mar 1949, OA.

12. JCS 1684/28, 6 May 1949, report of JSSC of 1 Apr 1949 accepted, ibid. For an Israeli view of American efforts in the region and the potential contribution of Israel, see Dore Gold, *America, The Gulf and Israel: CENTCOM (Central Command) and Emerging US Regional Security Policies in the Mideast* (Jerusalem and Boulder, CO, 1988).

13. The United States also believed that Israel could pay reparations for any territory held beyond that assigned in the original United Nations partition. See Kenneth W. Condit, *The History of the Joint Chiefs of Staff*, vol. 2, *The Joint Chiefs of Staff and National Policy, 1947–1949* (Washington, 1978), pp. 103–4.

14. See pp. 38–39.

15. Commander *Rendova* to CINCNELM, 16 Jul 1948, Report File, OA.

16. See Louis, *The British Empire in the Middle East*, pp. 25, 26, 583.

Notes to Pages 47–54

17. Report of the Near East Regional Conference in Cairo, 16 Mar 1950, *FRUS, 1950*, 5:2–8.

18. Re-evaluation of US Plans for the Middle East, *FRUS, 1951*, 5:6–11. For a good review of McGhee's role in the development of thinking about British capability, see Peter H. Hahn, "Containment and Egyptian Nationalism: The Unsuccessful Effort to Establish the Middle East Command, 1950–1953," *Diplomatic History* 11 (Winter 1987): 23–40.

19. As late as October, the State Department noted that "we understand that the JCS are opposed to any measures which would commit or tend to commit U.S. forces to the Middle East in the event of global war." McGhee to Jessup, 19 Oct 1950, *FRUS, 1950*, 5:217–21 (218). For evidence of the apparent lack of enthusiasm among the JCS and American military planners for Middle East defense and anything that might lead to increased American involvement, see Jernegan to Henderson, 9 Nov 1953, *FRUS, 1952–1954*, 9, Part 1:424–28.

Chapter 7

1. Shwadran, *Middle East, Oil, and the Great Powers*, p. 341. For an excellent discussion of Anglo-American perceptions regarding oil concessions in the Middle East and the Aramco agreement of December 1950, see Louis, *The British Empire in the Middle East*, pp. 596–603.

2. Acheson to Embassy Iran, 17 Mar 1951, *FRUS, 1951*, 10:25–26.

3. Memo, JCS to SECDEF, 10 Oct 1951, ibid., pp. 220–22.

4. Draft policy statement, NSC 107, 14 Mar 1951, *FRUS, 1952–1954*, 10:21–23. Nearly a year later as the situation in Iran continued to deteriorate, the Turkish Prime Minister informed George McGhee, U.S. Ambassador to Turkey: "We must not remain a spectator but must do something about the situation." McGhee had responded that "the situation was too dangerous to allow to drift, and that we must attempt to determine, rather than merely to react to the course of events." See McGhee's memo of conversation, 10 Feb 1952, *FRUS, 1952–1954*, 8:873–80.

5. NSC 107/2, 27 Jun 1951, ibid., pp. 71–76.

6. For example, see Allen to Jernegan, 26 Dec 1947, *FRUS, 1947*, 5:996–98.

7. JCS 1887/20, 27 Apr 1951, OA.

8. Eller to Sherman, 5 Feb 1951, folder #2, box 1, 1950, 00 File.

9. For example, see telegrams from Ambassador Allen to Marshall, 27 Mar and 9 Sep 1947, *FRUS, 1947*, 5:901–2, 948–50.

10. Allen to Marshall, 9 Sep 1948, *FRUS, 1948*, 5:948–50.

11. Allen to Marshall, 14 Jun 1947, *FRUS, 1947*, 5:913–14.

12. Allen to Marshall, 10 Nov 1947, ibid., pp. 977–79.

13. JCS 1887/6, 25 Oct 1950, OA.

14. JCS 1887/29, 5 Dec 1951, OA.

15. NSC 136/1, 20 Nov 1952, *FRUS, 1952–1954*, 10:529–34.

16. Robert J. Watson, *History of the Joint Chiefs of Staff*, vol. 5, *The Joint Chiefs of Staff and National Policy, 1953–1954* (Washington, 1986), p. 333.

17. JCS 1714/45, 18 Nov 1952, OA.

18. Watson, *The JCS and National Policy, 1953–1954*, p. 333; JCS 1714/46, 26 Jan 1953, OA.

19. JCS 1714/48, 16 Apr 1953, ibid. Medium landing ships (LSM) and seaplane tenders (AVP) were often used as command ships by the early 1950s.

20. JCS 1714/49, 13 May 1953, OA.

21. Paul H. Nitze, *From Hiroshima to Glasnost: At the Center of Decision* (New York, 1989), p. 135.

22. See Gifford to SECSTATE, 9 Jan 1953, *FRUS 1952–1954*, 10:596–97 for positive movement in Britain. The review of the published documents in the State Department's new Iran volume make clear that an agreement seemed near in January and early February.

23. Acting SECSTATE to Embassy UK, 3 Feb 1953, ibid, pp. 659–62.

24. J. F. Dulles to Embassy Iran, 10 Feb 1953, ibid, 662–64.

25. The American ambassador in Teheran noted that Mossadegh also contemplated breaking off negotiations. Henderson to State, 14 Feb 1953, ibid., pp. 665–67.

26. See Henderson to State, two messages of 28 Feb 1953, ibid, pp. 685–88, and 688–89.

27. Nitze suggests that Mossadegh thought he could get a better deal from Eisenhower. See p. 54; and Nitze, *From Hiroshima to Glasnost*, p. 135. More likely, Mossadegh had simply lost control of the nationalist movement and realized that any agreement acceptable to the British would be unacceptable to many of his supporters. Even the Shah was loathe to replace Mossadegh before he finalized an agreement with the British, fearing that the onus for the settlement would fall on the monarchy instead of on the prime minister who had engineered the crisis.

28. Henderson to State, 28 Feb 1953, *FRUS, 1952–1954*, 10:688–89.

29. CIA memo, 1 Mar 1953, ibid., pp. 689–91.

30. Memo of Discussion, 135th Meeting of NSC, 4 Mar 1953, ibid., pp. 692–701. See also CIA Special Estimate, 12 Mar 1953, *FRUS, 1952–1954*, 8:1125–29, which concluded: "The new Soviet regime probably fears that, while it is in the process of consolidating its power, the West may make aggressive moves against the Bloc. It would probably view with extreme suspicion any new moves made by the West, particularly involving long-range air forces or military forces close to Bloc frontiers."

31. Draft policy statement, NSC 107, 14 Mar 1951, *FRUS, 1952–1954*, 10:21–23.

32. C. M. Woodhouse, *Something Ventured* (London, 1982), pp. 111, 117. The idea for a coup in Britain originated in the Foreign Office of Herbert Morrison of a Labor government, not with the Tory government of Winston Churchill, which subsequently executed the plan.

33. Ibid., p. 122.

34. Ibid., p. 124.

35. Henderson to State, 10 Mar 1953, *FRUS, 1952–1954*, 10:706–8. Kenneth Love, a *New York Times* reporter in Iran sympathetic to the Iranian prime minister, nevertheless wrote that Mossadegh "had eliminated all means of an orderly change of government and achieved dictatorial powers before his overthrow." See *New York Times*, 21 Aug 1953, p. 1.

36. Henderson to State, 6 Mar 1953, *FRUS, 1952–1954*, 10:701–2.

37. The decision to go ahead with the coup was taken in early March 1953. See Woodhouse, *Something Ventured*, p. 124.

38. Henderson to State, 20 May 1953, *FRUS, 1952–1954*, 10:727–28.

39. Woodhouse later drew a comparison between what the British and Americans feared in 1953 for Iran and what happened a quarter of a century later in Afghanistan: "The overthrow of a weak monarchy by nationalist forces, which would then be overtaken by indigenous Communists, who would then be overwhelmed by the Red Army." Woodhouse, *Something Ventured*, p. 131.

40. A 21 August 1953 *New York Times* editorial (p. 16) commented:

> There lies Iran today: weak, soft, torn by internal strife, but enormously valuable in material and strategic terms.... Neither democratic West nor Communist East dare intervene *overtly* [italics added] in a situation where such vital interests are involved. If the Russians, for instance, were to enter Iran "to restore order" they would be courting World War III and they know it.

41. A record of a phone conversation between the Dulles brothers on 24 July makes clear that the Eisenhower administration still had doubts about the Shah:

> The Secy called and said in your talk about Iran yesterday at the meeting you did not mention the other matter, is it off? AWD said he doesn't talk about it, it was cleared directly with the President, and is still active.
>
> ... AWD said it is moving along reasonably well but the young many [man?] may pull out at the last minute, he is an unaccountable character but the sister has agreed to go.

See memorandum of telephone conversation by the Secretary of State, 24 Jul 1953, *FRUS, 1952–1954*, 10:737–38.

42. Kermit Roosevelt, *Countercoup: The Struggle for the Control of Iran* (New York, 1979), p. 210. Roosevelt believed that the coup succeeded because, he said, "we believed—and we were proven right—that if the people and the armed forces were shown that they must choose, that Mossadegh was forcing them to choose, between their monarch and a revolutionary figure backed by the Soviet Union, they could, and would, make only one choice." Kenneth Love, a *New York Times* reporter in Iran, made the same point, writing, "Mossadegh's big mistake was to push the nation and the army closer and closer to a choice between him and the Shah." *New York Times*, 23 Aug 1953, p. 5E.

43. The British codename for the operation was "Boot." See Woodhouse, *Something Ventured*, p. 117.

44. For an excellent contemporary British account of the coup, see memo on "Persia: Political Review of the Recent Crisis," 2 Sep 1953, *FRUS, 1952–1954*, 10:780–88.

45. Ibid., pp. 128–29; Roosevelt, *Countercoup*, pp. 190–93; Helen Chapin Metz, ed., *Iran: A Country Study* (Washington, 1989), p. 31. Woodhouse wrote: "In fact, probably for the first time, the Communists' technique of spontaneous demonstration was successfully turned against them." Woodhouse, *Something Ventured*, p. 129.

46. British memo on "Persia: Political Review of the Recent Crisis," 2 Sep 1953, *FRUS, 1952–1954*, 10:780–88.

47. As early as 17 August Iranians were already blaming the United States for what was at that point an attempted, failed coup. See *New York Times*, 18 Aug 1953, p. 1. On the 20th, *Pravda* reported that the "American agents who operated within Iran hatched new diversionary plans directed towards the overthrow of the Government." See *New York Times*, 20 Aug 1953, p. 3.

48. Bill, *The Eagle and the Lion*, p. 97.

49. Dulles to Wilson, 8 Nov 1954, *FRUS, 1952–1954*, 10:1063–66.

50. Because of the ongoing crisis, MEF ships were often directed to remain in the gulf and to forego routine visits to Indian Ocean and Red Sea ports in order to maintain a presence in the Persian Gulf in the event of an emergency.

51. Watson, *The JCS and National Policy*, pp. 334–35; JCS 1714/51, 26 Aug 1953, OA.

52. Watson, *The JCS and National Policy*, p. 335.

Chapter 8

1. Report on the Near East by Secretary of State John Foster Dulles, *Department of State Bulletin* 28 (15 Jun 1953), pp. 831–35.

2. Dulles saw MEDO as a Middle East parallel to the European Pact, which eventually matured into a broader association—NATO—and gained American adherence. See memorandum of conversation by the Counselor in Pakistan, 24 May 1953, *FRUS, 1952–1954*, 9, Part 1:134–36. For Dulles's views on the futility of relying on the Arab states and his conviction that Turkey would have to be the "backbone" of any pact, see memorandum of conversation by

the Counselor of Embassy in Turkey, 26 May 1953, ibid., pp. 137–47; memorandum of discussion, NSC 1 Jun 1953, ibid., pp. 379–86.

3. A reappraisal of American policy in the Near East concluded that "the US must in its own interest take more initiative than it has to date in the determination of policies relative to the area." See Hoskins to Byroade, reappraisal of US policies in the NEA area, 7 Apr 1952, ibid., pp. 204–13.

4. The American focus on the Northern Tier represents a progression of thought that dates back to McGhee's memo of late 1950 on the need to push the West's defensive ring outward, and to earlier concepts that originated immediately after the end of the Second World War. For example, the U.S. Navy's Sixth Task Fleet's Operation Plan 1–48 of late 1948-early 1949 stated: "Italy, Greece, Turkey and Iran form a strategic barrier against expansion by a hostile power into the Mediterranean and the Middle East." See OPLAN 1–48 (rev), Annex Dog (Intelligence), Sixth Fleet, Plans File, OA. Commander Sixth Task Fleet at the time was Vice Admiral Forrest P. Sherman who, as Deputy Chief of Naval Operations (Operations), had been the Navy's chief strategist during 1946 and 1947 and would become CNO (1949–1951). See Michael A. Palmer, *Origins of the Maritime Strategy*, (Washington, 1989), pp. 21–32.

5. See memorandum of conversation, 1 Oct 1952, *FRUS 52–54*, 9, Part 1, pp. 279–81 for Bradley's discussion of the inner and outer ring and his preference for the latter. JCS historian Robert J. Watson writes: "The futile effort to build a defense around Egypt had been abandoned. A strategy tied to the northern tier would take advantage of the excellent defensive terrain along the southwestern boundary of the Soviet Union and of the willingness of the countries of that region to cooperate with a minimum of prodding from the West." Watson, *The JCS and National Policy*, p. 347.

6. Statement of policy by the National Security Council, 23 Jul 1954, NSC 5428, *FRUS, 1952–1954*, 9, part 1:525–36.

7. Memorandum by the Deputy Director of the Office of British Commonwealth and Northern European Affairs, 16 Apr 1952, ibid., pp. 213–18. For Bradley's assessment that MEDO would be "largely political," see minutes of State-JCS meeting, 28 Nov 1952, ibid., pp. 319–26. See also National Intelligence Estimate, Conditions and Trends in the Middle East Affecting US Security, 15 Jan 1953, ibid., pp. 334–43, which concluded that "Middle East armed forces are incapable, individually or collectively, of effectively resisting attack by a major power."

8. Memorandum of conversation by the Politico-Military Adviser, Bureau of Near Eastern, South Asian, and African Affairs, 24 Apr 1952, ibid., pp. 218–21.

9. National Intelligence Estimate, Prospects for the creation of a Middle East defense grouping and probable consequences of such a development, 22 Jun 1954, ibid., pp. 516–20. The NIE also concluded:

> Such a loose grouping would not result in any significant reduction of the area's military vulnerability. However, together with US military aid programs, it would create greater opportunities than in the past for reducing existing Middle East defense deficiencies. The requirements for outside ground forces might eventually be reduced. However, achievement of even this limited goal would be a long and costly operation, involving considerable training and equipment over a period of years, and effective Middle East defense will continue to depend for the foreseeable future on substantial Western force contributions.

10. Transcript of 29 Jan 1972 press conference held by the Shah of Iran, in Rouhollah K. Ramazani, *The Persian Gulf: Iran's Role* (Charlottesville, VA, 1972), p. 146.

11. Memorandum to the Assistant Secretary of State for European Affairs, 12 Jan 1954, *FRUS, 1952–1954*, 9:450–52.

Notes to Pages 63–68

12. See 25 Mar 1965 memorandum from Captain Murray B. Frazee, Jr., USN, to Colonel Hidalgo of the Joint Staff discussing the problems of naval command in CENTO, CENTO file, box 259, Political-Military Affairs Division Records, OA.

13. MEF Command History, from Commissioning to 31 Dec 1958, 29 Jul 1960, MEF, Command File, OA.

14. MEF, Report of Operations and Conditions of Command, 1 Jul 1959 to 18 Feb 1960, 14 Jan 1960, ibid.

15. See memorandum of conversation in the White House, 30 Jan 1956, *FRUS, 1955–1957*, 15:101–7; and Anderson to State, 19 Jan 1956, ibid., 28–36.

16. Gamal Abdel Nasser's Nationalization Speech of 26 Jul 1956, in Carol A. Fisher and Fred Krinsky, eds., *Middle East in Crisis: A Historical and Documentary Review* (Syracuse, NY, 1959), p. 139.

17. See Anthony Adamthwaite, "Suez Revisited," *International Affairs* 64 (Summer 1988): 449–64.

18. Memorandum of Discussion, National Security Council, 30 Aug 1956, *FRUS, 1955–1957*, 16:324–32.

19. Memorandum of Discussion, Department of State-Joint Chiefs meeting, 31 Aug 1956, ibid., pp. 342–44.

20. For an assessment of the situation and its impact on U.S. policy see Special National Intelligence Estimate 30–4–56, "Probable Repercussions of British-French Military Action in the Suez Crisis," 5 Sep 1956, ibid., pp. 382–91.

21. *Oglethorpe* cruised the eastern Mediterranean in the late summer of 1956 loaded with arms for Egypt that were to be delivered in the event of an Israeli attack. See Radford to Secretary of Defense Charles E. Wilson, 19 Sep 1956, ibid., pp. 523–24; and Dulles to Reuben B. Robertson, Jr., 28 Sep 1958, ibid., pp. 610–11.

22. David Lee, *Wings in the Sun: A History of the Royal Air Force in the Mediterranean, 1945–1986* (London, 1989), p. 106.

23. Extracts from David Ben-Gurion's diary, in Selwyn Ilan Troen and Moshe Shemesh, eds., *The Suez-Sinai Crisis, 1956: Retrospective and Reappraisal* (New York, 1990), p. 322.

24. Memorandum of conversation between the President and the Secretary of State, 12 Nov 1956, *FRUS, 1955–1957*, 16:1112–14.

25. Dwight D. Eisenhower's broadcast on the Middle East crisis, 31 Oct 1956, in Fisher and Krinsky, *Middle East in Crisis*, p. 169.

26. Kennett Love, *Suez: The Twice Fought War* (New York and Toronto, 1969), p. 568.

27. George Lenczowski, *Oil and State in the Middle East* (Ithaca, NY, 1960), pp. 334–38.

28. Shwadran, *The Middle East, Oil and the Great Powers*, pp. 268–71; Longrigg, *Oil in the Middle East*, pp. 262–64, 302–3, 313.

29. Resolution on the Middle East, 5 Mar 1957, in Fisher and Krinsky, *Middle East in Crisis*, pp. 175–76.

30. JCS 2268, Joint Middle East Emergency Defense Plan 1–57, 8 May 1957, OA.

31. Memorandum of discussion at Department of State—Joint Chiefs of Staff meeting, 31 August 1956, *FRUS, 1955–1957*, 16:342–44.

32. On the 18th and 19th, the United States became aware of Soviet and Warsaw Pact troops movements along the Turkish border, apparently ordered by Khrushchev. See ibid., p. 252.

Notes to Pages 68–77

33. For an excellent account of the Marines' participation in the Lebanon operation see Jack Shulimson, *Marines in Lebanon* (Washington, 1966).

34. See Lee, *Wings in the Sun*, p. 143; and George S. Dragnich, *The Lebanon Operation of 1958: A Study of the Crisis Role of the Sixth Fleet* (Center for Naval Analyses Research Contribution 153, 1970), p. A–3.

35. Dwight D. Eisenhower, *The White House Years* (Garden City, New York, 1963–1965), vol. 2, *Waging Peace, 1956–1961*, p. 278.

36. CMEF, Report of Operations and Conditions of Command, 1 Jul 1959 to 18 Feb 1960, 14 Jan 1960, MEF, Command File, OA.

37. Eisenhower, *Waging Peace*, p. 290.

38. Quandt, "Lebanon, 1958, Jordan, 1970," pp. 251–52.

39. MEF Command History, 1 Jan 1963–31 Dec 1963, 9 Feb 1964, Command File, OA.

40. During this period MEF generally consisted of the flagship and two to four destroyers. Ships rotated into and out of the command throughout the year. In all eighteen ships served under Middle East Force command during the year.

41. MEF Command History, 1966, 18 Feb 1967, ibid.

42. MEF Command History 1967, 25 Feb 1968, ibid; and William B. Quandt, *Decade of Decisions: American Policy toward the Arab-Israeli Conflict, 1967–1976* (Berkeley, Los Angeles, and London, 1977), pp. 39–59.

43. MEF Command History 1967, 25 Feb 1968, MEF Command File, OA; and Command History, Arab-Israeli Crisis, 1967, 26 Aug 1967, MEF, Report File, OA.

44. MEF Command History, 1968, 21 Nov 1969, MEF, Command File, OA.

45. MEF Command History, 1973, 30 Apr 1974, ibid.

Chapter 9

1. C. J. Bartlett, *The Long Retreat: A Short History of British Defense Policy, 1945–1970* (London and Basingstoke, 1972). See also Kelly, *Arabia, the Gulf and the West*, pp. 48–51, who views lack of will as the principal cause of the withdrawal; and Phillip Darby, *British Defense Policy East of Suez, 1947–1968* (London, 1973), pp. 307–326, 334, who focuses on lack of resources.

2. R. M. Burrell and Alvin J. Cottrell, *Iran, the Arabian Peninsula, and the Indian Ocean* (New York, 1972).

3. Darby, *British Defense Policy East of Suez*, pp. 219–21; and Charles W. Koburger, Jr., "The Kuwait Confrontation of 1961," U.S. Naval Institute *Proceedings* 100 (Jan 1974): 42–49.

4. Kelly, *Arabia, the Gulf and the West*, p. 49–50.

5. Soviet concerns about a possible American naval buildup in the Indian Ocean, including the establishment of a U.S. Navy "Fifth Fleet," date back to the late 1950s. See Office of Naval Intelligence, "Soviet Interest in the Nonexistent Indian Ocean Fleet," *ONI Review* 14 (Aug 1959): 357–59.

6. *Public Papers of the Presidents of the United States: Richard M. Nixon, 1969* (Washington, 1971), p. 549. See also Richard Nixon, *RN: The Memoirs of Richard Nixon* (New York, 1978), pp. 394–95.

7. *Nixon Papers, 1970*, p. 9.

8. Henry Kissinger, *White House Years* (Boston and Toronto, 1979), p. 1264.

9. In testimony before the Subcommittee on the Near East, House Foreign Affairs Committee, on 8 August, Assistant Secretary of State for Near Eastern and South Asian Affairs Joseph

Notes to Pages 77–80

Sisco testified: "In addition to the tradition of Anglo-American cooperation throughout the world and the parallel nature of American and British interests in the Persian Gulf, the United States has had a long and fruitful tradition of cooperation with the two major regional powers, Iran and Saudi Arabia." See *State Department Bulletin* 57 (4 Sep 1972), pp. 241–45. See also Anthony H. Cordesman, *The Gulf and the Search for Strategic Stability: Saudi Arabia, the Military Balance in the Gulf, and Trends in the Arab-Israeli Military Balance* (Boulder, CO, and London, 1984), pp. 158–62. Following the expulsion of the Soviets from Egypt in 1972, and the 1973 Arab-Israeli October War when President Anwar Sadat brought his country into the Western camp, Egypt became the third pillar of the American position in the Middle East.

10. See Bill, *The Eagle and the Lion*, pp. 197–200.

11. William D. Brewer, "Yesterday and Tomorrow in the Persian Gulf," *The Middle East Journal* 23 (Spring 1969): 149–58.

12. Ibid.

13. Edward M. Kennedy, "The Persian Gulf: Arms Race or Arms Control?" *Foreign Affairs* 54 (Oct 1975): 14–35. Kennedy believed that a relatively advanced Iran might be able to survive the race, but that the less advanced, smaller Arab countries, forced to try to keep up, would strain both their budgets and their social fabric, perhaps to the breaking point.

14. Professor James A. Bill was an outspoken academic critic of the Shah. See, for example, Bill, *The Eagle and the Lion*, pp. 245–46.

15. CNO Mideast Tripbook, 1974, memo of 31 Oct 1974 on US/UK talks of 29–30 Oct 1974, box 263, Political-Military Affairs Division, OA. John Thomson, Britain's Assistant Secretary at the Foreign Office, stated that he expected that the Shah would be secure for the "short term," which he defined as from three to five years.

16. Department of State Research Study, Bureau of Intelligence and Research, 12 Apr 1973, "Iran and Saudi Arabia—The Odd Couple," box 286, ibid.

17. Ibid., p. ii.

18. "Saudi Arabia-Iran: Problems of Regional Cooperation," 3 Aug 1973, Department of State, Bureau of Intelligence and Research Intelligence Note, Iran 1973, box 286, ibid.

19. Defense Intelligence Agency, Defense Intelligence Estimate, 12 Apr 1973, "Iran's Military Buildup: Response to Apprehensions and Aspirations," p. 33, ibid.

20. Transcript of 29 Jan 1972 press conference held by the Shah of Iran, in Ramazani, *The Persian Gulf*, pp. 143–48.

21. DIA Defense Intelligence Estimate, 12 Apr 1973, "Iran's Military Buildup: Response to Apprehensions and Aspirations," pp. 31–34, Iran 1973, box 286, Political-Military Affairs Division, OA.

22. Ibid., p. 27.

23. Intelligence note, Department of State Bureau of Intelligence and Research, 31 Jan 1974, Iran 1974, ibid.

24. Quoted in Monoronjan Bezboruah, *U.S. Strategy in the Indian Ocean: The International Response* (New York and London, 1977), p. 1920.

25. Kennedy, "The Persian Gulf," p. 24.

26. Iran point paper of 23 Oct 1974, CNO Mideast Trip Book, box 263, Political-Military Affairs Division, OA.

27. "The Imperial Iranian Armed Forces: An Assessment," 19 September 1973, draft, Office of the Director of Defense Program Analysis and Evaluation, Special Regional Studies Division, Iran 1973, box 286, ibid.

28. Cordesman, *The Gulf and the Search for Strategic Stability*, p. 160.

29. Ibid., p. 156. Saudi military manpower increased from 62,000 in 1969 to 94,000 in 1978. The corresponding figures for Iraq are 78,000 and 272,000; and for Iran, 221,000 and 413,000.

30. Ibid., p. 160.

31. Ibid., pp. 174–75.

32. Ibid., pp. 173–75, 220–23.

33. Bezboruah, *U.S. Strategy in the Indian Ocean*, pp. 50–56.

34. *New York Times*, 25 Mar 1969; CNO to CINCLANTFLT, draft, c. 11 May 1968, Bahrain, box 272, Political-Military Affairs Division, OA; VCNO memo, F. J. Blouin, 30 Aug 1968, ibid.; CNO to CINCLANTFLT, late 1968 draft paper, CMEF, box 261, ibid.

35. CNO to CINCLANTFLT, nd [Sep 1968], Bahrain, box 272, ibid. Moorer would later serve as chairman of the Joint Chiefs of Staff.

36. G. Warren Nutter to Joseph J. Sisco, 18 Jun 1968, ibid.

37. CNO Point Papers, 1970, CMEF, box 259, ibid.

38. Secretary of the Navy memorandum for the Assistant Secretary of Defense for International Security Affairs, 15 Oct 1971, Bahrain 1970, box 272, ibid.

39. CMEF Command History, 1971, 29 Aug 1972, MEF, Command File, OA.

40. Point paper on MEF and Bahrain, 27 May 1972, Bahrain, box 273, Political-Military Affairs Division, OA.

41. Memo for the Director, Command Support Programs, on Political Factors Affecting Fleet Communications, enclosure 4, Bahrain, Mar 1972, ibid.

42. For a study of Navy long-range planning and the Long Range Objectives Group (OP–93) formed under Burke, see David A. Rosenberg, "Historical Perspectives in Long Range Planning in the Navy: Part I: The Planning Process Overview, 1900–1978," Draft, CNO, Command File, OA.

43. MEF Command History, 1968, 21 Nov 1969, MEF, Command File, OA.

44. MEF Command History, 1971, 29 Aug 1972, ibid.

45. MEF Command History, 1972, 1 May 1973, ibid.

46. MEF Command History, 1973, 30 Apr 1974; CMEF Command History 1974, 15 Apr 1975, ibid.

47. MEF Command History, 1975, 16 Mar 1976, ibid.

48. Quandt, "Lebanon, 1958, and Jordan, 1970," p. 285.

49. MEF Command History, 1973, 30 Apr 1974, MEF, Command File, OA.

50. Comment on memo on MEF "Where do we go from here?" session, 30 Oct 1973, Bahrain 1973, box 273, Political-Military Affairs Division, OA.

51. Draft memo for Chairman, JCS, from VCNO, 7 Nov 1973, ibid.

52. MEF Command History, 1975, 16 Mar 1976, MEF, Command File, OA.

53. Memo, VCNO for CNO, 30 Dec 1974, Bahrain 1974, box 273, Political-Military Affairs Division, OA.

54. Draft memo for the Secretary of Defense on U.S. Self-Imposed Indian Ocean Restrictions, file 3120, box 58, 1974, 00 File, OA.

55. MEF Command History, 1974, 15 Apr 1975, MEF, Command File, OA.

56. House, "Naval Petroleum Reserves," 93/1, HASC, 17, 18 Oct 1973.

57. Memo, E. R. Zumwalt, Jr., to ASD ISA, 10–20 Nov 1973; memo, CNO to W. D. Gaddis, DCNO (Log), 15 Nov 1973, uncataloged files, Middle East, box 130, 00 File, OA.

Chapter 10

1. *Business Week*, 13 Jan 1975, pp. 66–76.

2. Memo, DCNO Plans and Policy to CNO, enclosing "a survey of military options in response to an Arab oil embargo, 24 Aug 1974, Middle East, box 155, 1974, 00 File, OA; "An Examination of Direct Economic/Military Actions in Response to Arab Oil Leverage," 12 Sep 1974, uncataloged Middle East, box 156, ibid.

3. Zbigniew Brzezinski, *Power and Principle: Memoirs of the National Security Adviser, 1977–1981* (New York, 1983), p. 177.

4. Ibid.

5. David A. Quinlan, *The Role of the Marine Corps in Rapid Deployment Forces* (Washington, 1983), pp. 1–2.

6. See p. 67.

7. OP–61 Point Paper on MEAFSA Command Evolution, 25 Nov 1970, MEAFSA Command Evolution File, 1960–1970, box 254, Political-Military Affairs Division, OA.

8. James A. Bowden, "The RDJTF and Doctrine," *Military Review* 62 (Nov 1982): 51–64.

9. Memo, Gen. David C. Jones, USAF, Chairman, JCS, to SECDEF Brown, 28 Feb 1979, with attached appendix, increased presence in the Red Sea and Indian Ocean, Increased Indian Ocean Presence file, Indian Ocean, Area File, OA.

10. Peter M. Swartz, interview with the author, 24 Aug 1990, Washington, DC. Brown was a proponent of small carriers operating vertical take-off and landing (VTOL) aircraft such as the Harrier.

11. Memo, OP–60 to OP–06, Briefing on Increased Indian Ocean Presence, 18 Apr 1979, Indian Ocean, Area File, OA.

12. Swartz interview, 24 Aug 1990.

13. According to Zbigniew Brzezinski, *The Grand Failure: The Birth and Death of Communism in the Twentieth Century* (New York, 1990), p. 92, the Soviet leadership made the decision to invade Afghanistan while in a state of intoxication.

14. Bill, *The Eagle and the Lion*, pp. 245–46.

15. The Iranian navy purchased oil from the Iranian National Oil Company and then sold it to the U.S. Navy, some 1.5 million barrels that the U.S. Navy sources considered "critical" to its operations. See Kissinger, *White House Years*, p. 1262; and 23 Oct 1974 memo on Iran, CNO Mideast Tripbook, 1974, box 263, Political-Military Affairs Division, OA; 16 Oct 1974 memo on POL supplies from Iran, Iran 1974, box 286, ibid.

16. Kissinger, *White House Years*, p. 1260.

17. Theodore H. Moran, "Iranian Defense Expenditure and the Social Crisis." *International Security* 3 (Winter 1978/1979): 181.

18. Amitav Acharya, *U.S. Military Strategy on the Gulf* (London and New York, 1989), p. 32. The United States was well aware of many of these problems including the growing problem in agriculture and accelerating and "worrisome" inflation, which as early as 1973 had topped 10 percent. See Economic Trends Report from the American Embassy in Teheran, 1 Dec 1973, Iran 1973, box 286, Political-Military Affairs Division, OA.

19. Bill, *The Eagle and the Lion*, pp. 158–61.

20. Kennedy, "The Persian Gulf," p. 19.

21. Toast by President Carter to the Shah at the state dinner, Teheran, 31 Dec 1977, U.S. Department of State, *American Foreign Policy: Basic Documents, 1977–1980* (Washington, 1983), #328.

It was during this toast that Carter issued his oft-quoted statement: "Iran, because of the great leadership of the Shah, is an island of stability in one of the more troubled areas of the world."

22. The Shah himself later wrote: "At the time [1977] foreign policy issues occupied most of my attention." See Mohammad Reza Pahlavi, *Answer to History* (New York, 1980), p. 150.

23. See R. K. Ramazani, "Who Lost America? The Case of Iran," *The Middle East Journal* 36 (Winter 1982): 5–21.

24. Khosrow Fatemi, "Leadership by Distrust: The Shah's *Modus Operandi*," *The Middle East Journal* 36 (Winter 1982): 49–61. Gary Sick, *All Fall Down: America's Tragic Encounter with Iran* (New York, 1986), pp. 191–2, adds that the Shah may have realized that his own schemes had failed to achieve what he had expected.

25. James A. Bill, "Power and Religion in Revolutionary Iran," *The Middle East Journal* 36 (Winter 1982): 22–47 (28).

26. Kissinger, *White House Years*, p. 1260.

27. Cordesman, *The Gulf and the Search for Strategic Stability*, p. 213.

28. *New York Times*, 14 Nov 1979, p. 17; *Washington Star*, 21 Nov 1979, p. 1.

29. Carter State of the Union Address, 23 Jan 1980, State Department, *Basic Documents, 1977–1980*, #15.

30. The third carrier, *Nimitz*, was relieving *Kitty Hawk* which shortly thereafter steamed for home. *Washington Star*, 18 Jan 1980, p. 4.

31. Address of Secretary of Defense Brown, 6 Mar 1980, State Department, *Basic Documents 1977–1980*, #253.

32. Memo, Jones to Brown, 6 May 1980, JCS, Command File, OA; and Paul B. Ryan, *The Iranian Rescue Mission: Why It Failed* (Annapolis, 1985).

33. *Washington Star*, 24 Sep 1980, p. 11; *Washington Post*, 30 Sep 1980, p. 14; *New York Times*, 15 Oct 1980, p. 14.

34. The flagship *LaSalle* and six combatants.

35. *Washington Post*, 16 Oct 1980, p. 1.36. Remarks of President Carter to reporters at the White House, 24 Sep 1980, State Department, *Basic Documents, 1977–1980*, #256.

37. Address by Secretary of State Edmund Muskie, 14 Oct 1980, Muskie, ibid., #258.

Chapter 11

1. For example, while giving testimony before the House Foreign Affairs committee on 12 November 1981, Representative Paul Findley (R-Illinois) asked Secretary of State Alexander Haig: "President Carter made a statement that seemed to imply that the United States alone would meet any Soviet advance to the Persian Gulf. Was that a commitment?" Haig responded: "That is not our policy." But Haig remarked:

> [Y]ou have got to create an atmosphere of confidence in American reliability, and our willingness to share our leadership responsibility in the Middle East and everywhere, and we have been in the process of doing that. We are not seeking in the Middle East to structure archaic historic alliances, Baghdad Pacts or reestablishment of CENTO (Testimony of Haig before the House Foreign Affairs Committee, 12 Nov 1981, State Department, *Current Documents, 1981*, #292).

2. Statement of Secretary of Defense Weinberger before the Senate Armed Services Committee, 28 Jan 1981, ibid., #23.

Notes to Pages 103–106

3. Defense Guidance for fiscal years 1983–1987, 18 May 1981, 3060/1, 1981, 00 File, OA. The report also called for improved capabilities of indigenous forces to respond to Soviet attack, greater access of American forces to local facilities, and out-of-area cooperation from America's European allies.

4. Transcript of interview with Secretary of State Haig, 5 Mar 1981, State Department, *Current Documents, 1981*, #280.

5. Statement by Deputy Secretary of Defense Carlucci before the Senate Armed Services Committee, 9 Mar 1981, ibid., #281. For examples of studies in the early 1980s of American interests in the Persian Gulf and the Rapid Deployment Force see Robert J. Hanks, *The U.S. Military Presence in the Middle East: Problems and Prospects* (Cambridge, MA, and Washington, 1982); Lewis C. Sowell, Jr., *Base Development and the Rapid Deployment Force: A Window to the Future* (Washington, 1982); Maxwell Orme Johnson, *The Military as an Instrument of U.S. Policy in Southwest Asia: The Rapid Deployment Joint Task Force, 1979–1982* (Boulder, CO, 1983); U.S. Congress, Congressional Budget Office, *Rapid Deployment Forces: Policy and Budgetary Implications* (Washington, 1983); and Alvin J. Cottrell and Michael L. Moodie, *The United States and the Persian Gulf: Past Mistakes and Present Needs* (New York, 1984).

6. In a 2 February 1981 interview with the *New York Times*, Reagan acknowledged that he himself had attacked the Carter Doctrine as a commitment not backed by credible force. See transcript of interview with President Reagan, 2 Feb 1981, State Department, *Current Documents, 1981*, #279.

7. Jeffrey Record, *The Rapid Deployment Force and U.S. Military Intervention in the Persian Gulf* (Cambridge, MA, and Washington, 1981), pp. 1–2. Record remained consistent in his opposition to the RDF concept. In testimony before the Senate Armed Services Committee in 1987, he remarked: "The most recent example of what I would term strategic irresponsibility was the Carter administration's extension of containment to the vast and logistically remote region of Southwest Asia, a commitment that has yet to be accompanied by appropriate increases in our military power." See Senate, Committee on Armed Services, *National Security Strategy*, S. Hrg. 100–257, 100th Cong., 1st sess., 1987, p. 707.

8. In a 2 February 1981 interview with the *New York Times*, Reagan implied that the administration sought deterrence through threats of vertical, that is, nuclear, escalation. Horizontal escalation involves military retaliation in another theater. See transcript of an interview with President Reagan, 2 Feb 1981, State Department, *Current Documents, 1981*, #279.

9. Joshua M. Epstein, *Strategy and Force Planning: The Case of the Persian Gulf* (Washington, 1987).

10. Brzezinski, *Power and Principle*, p. 445.

11. Address of Secretary of Defense Brown, 6 Mar 1980, State Department, *Basic Documents, 1977–1980*, #253.

12. Ibid.

13. Strategic Mobility Requirements and Programs in a Persian Gulf Contingency (SMRP–84), Joint Chiefs of Staff, p. IX–95, JCS, Command File, OA.

14. Record, *The Rapid Deployment Force*, pp. 73–74.

15. OP–60 Point Paper, Unified Command Plan and RDJTF Command Arrangements, 22 Jan 1981, 3060/1, 1981, 00 File, OA. The Navy did not favor the establishment of a unified command in Southwest Asia at the time but preferred the establishment of a sub-unified commander under EUCOM or the reassignment of the Persian Gulf, but not the Red Sea, to PACOM.

16. Robert C. Kingston, "From RDF to CENTCOM: New Challenges?" *RUSI Journal* 129 (Mar 1984): 14–17 (16). Kingston was writing about NATO CENTCOM.

Notes to Pages 106–111

17. Kingston was the commander of RDJTF until the establishment of USCENTCOM.

18. On paper, CENTCOM controlled substantial forces although, in the event of a wider war with the Soviet Union, not all would be available for deployment in Southwest Asia.

19. Kingston, "From RDF to CENTCOM," p. 16.

20. For an overview of the war and its impact on American interests, see Edgar O'Ballance, *The Gulf War* (London, 1988; Anthony H. Cordesman, *The Iran-Iraq War and Western Security, 1984–1987: Strategic Implications and Policy Options* (London and New York, 1987); Thomas Naff, ed., *Gulf Security and the Iran-Iraq War* (Washington, 1985); Ronald E. Bergquist, *The Role of Airpower in the Iran-Iraq War* (Maxwell Air Force Base, AL, 1988); and William J. Olson, ed., *US Strategic Interests in the Gulf Region* (Boulder, CO, and London, 1987).

21. *Wall Street Journal*, 2 Oct 1981, p. 3. The attack on 30 September followed previous attacks on 12 and 16 November 1980 and 13 June 1981, and ended an oil truce between the belligerents that had been unofficially recognized after similar attacks by both sides against petroleum facilities early in the war.

22. Presidential press conference, 1 Oct 1981, *Current Documents, 1981*, #405.

23. *New York Times*, 2 Oct 1981, p. 1.

24. Statement by Deputy Assistant Secretary of State for Near Eastern and South Asian Affairs before the House Foreign Affairs Subcommittee, 26 Sep 1983, State Department, *Current Documents, 1983*, #278.

25. Official State Department statement, 5 Mar 1984, ibid, #222.

26. Iraq's only outlet to the gulf—the Shatt al-Arab—was closed to all shipping as a result of the war.

27. Statement by the Deputy Representative of the United States to the U.S. Security Council, 30 May 1984, State Department, *Current Documents, 1984*, #223; United Nations Resolution 552, 1 Jun 1984, ibid., #224.

28. Statement by the Assistant Secretary of State for Near Eastern and South Asian Affairs, 11 Jun 1984, ibid., #225.

29. Statement by the Assistant Secretary of State for Near Eastern and South Asian Affairs, 25 Jul 1984, ibid., #197.

30. Statement by the Assistant Secretary of State for Near Eastern and South Asian Affairs, 18 Sep 1985, ibid, #256.

31. Ibid.

32. Response by President Reagan to a question asked during an 11 Jun 1985 interview, ibid., #245.

33. Statement by Secretary of State George Shultz, 1 Oct 1985, ibid., #247.

34. Shireen T. Hunter, "The Gulf Economic Crisis and Its Social and Political Consequences," *The Middle East Journal* 40 (Autumn 1986): 593.

35. Ronald O'Rourke, "The Tanker War," U.S. Naval Institute *Proceedings* 114 (May 1988): 31.

36. The Shah recognized the Iranian vulnerability and accordingly built up the Iranian navy. See Pahlavi, *Answer to History*, p. 142.

37. David Segal, "The Iran-Iraq War: A Military Analysis," *Foreign Affairs* 66 (Summer 1988): 960.

38. O'Rourke, "The Tanker War," p. 34. During 1987, and before reflagging, twenty-four such ships were attacked; after reflagging, the number fell to sixteen. The Iranians and Iraqis together sank only a handful of ships, reaching a high of six in 1987, but damaged more than 30 million tons of shipping.

Notes to Pages 111–116

39. Prepared statement by the Secretary of State, 19 Feb 1986, State Department, *Current Documents, 1986*, #172; statement by the Assistant Secretary of State for Near Eastern and South Asian Affairs, 16 Apr 1986, ibid., #203.

40. Statement by President Reagan's press secretary, 7 May 1986, ibid., #204.

41. Caspar Weinberger, *Fighting for Peace: Seven Critical Years in the Pentagon* (New York, 1990), p. 363.

42. Caspar W. Weinberger, interview with author, 24 Jul 1990, Washington, DC.

43. Statement by Secretary of State Shultz, 27 Jan 1987, State Department, *Current Documents, 1987*, #253.

44. Statement by President Reagan, 25 Feb 1987, ibid., #254.

45. Weinberger, *Fighting for Peace*, p. 387.

46. Ships fly the flag of the country of registration, not the nationality of the owner. During wartime ships frequently seek reflagging as a means of escape. During the American Civil War, for example, owners of many American ships registered their vessels overseas to escape the predations of Confederate commerce raiders. Today, many American-owned ships fly Panamanian and Liberian flags because the regulations imposed on ship owners by those countries are far less stringent than those demanded by the U.S. government. These regulations govern inspections, safety, crew size, wages, etc. The regulations relative to ships registered in the United States are, like everything else in the country, rather extensive and costly to comply with.

As neutrals, the Kuwaitis had the legal right under American and international law to register their ships as long as they were willing to meet the regulations established by the U.S. government. The Reagan administration became involved in the reflagging because the Kuwaitis would not, and could not in a timely fashion, meet all the restrictions imposed by American law. To reflag their ships, the Kuwaitis had to meet U.S. Coast Guard inspection standards and hire American masters and radiomen. The crews of the reflagged ships remained foreign. Thus the issue was not really reflagging per se, but the administration's decision to relax existing regulatory standards to allow the reflagging.

47. Weinberger, *Fighting for Peace*, pp. 396–397; and Weinberger interview, 24 Jul 1990.

48. Ibid., p. 397. To Weinberger, the Kuwaiti request for Soviet assistance "lent a little more urgency" to the American debate, but was not the major factor in the administration's decision. Weinberger interview, 24 Jul 1990.

49. Statement by the Assistant Secretary of State for Near Eastern and South Asian Affairs, 21 Apr 1987, State Department, *Current Documents, 1987*, #255.

50. Statements by the Assistant Secretary of State for Near Eastern and South Asian Affairs, 19 May 1987, ibid., #259; and 29 May 1987, ibid., #263.

51. Murphy commented: "I think those who argue that others, not the United States, have the oil problem or should be concerned about the Gulf situation miss the point. Our economic well-being is involved, particularly since our economy is the most oil intensive of the major industrialized nations. That others may suffer more is not a persuasive argument for us to do less than our interests require."

52. Statement by President Reagan, 29 May 1987, State Department, *Current Documents, 1987*, #262.

53. See Weinberger's "The Military Underpinnings of Diplomacy: The Case of the Persian Gulf," delivered to the Portland World Affairs Council, 21 Sep 1987, Persian Gulf 1987, box 10 (of 19) 1988, 00 File (unprocessed), OA.

54. Statement read by President Reagan's Assistant for Press Relations, 30 Jun 1987, State Department, *Current Documents, 1987*, #266.

55. U.N. Security Council Resolution 598, 20 Jul 1987, ibid., #268; and statement by President Reagan, 20 Jul 1987, ibid., #269.

56. Joint statement issued by the Venice Summit participants, 9 Jun 1987, ibid., #74.

57. For examples of the Soviet reaction, see V. Markov, "The War in the Persian Gulf, Freedom of Navigation, and International Law," *Morskoi Sbornik* (Feb 1988): 83–87; M. Abramov, "U.S. Navy Aggravates Persian Gulf Situation," ibid. (Mar 1988): 78–81; Sergei Turchenko, "Sinister Armada," *Soviet Military Review* (Jul 1988): 52–54; and Norman Cigar, "The Soviet Navy in the Persian Gulf: Naval Diplomacy in a Combat Zone," *Naval War College Review* 42 (Spring 1989): 56–88.

58. Quoted in Shahram Chubin and Charles Tripp, *Iran and Iraq at War* (Boulder, CO, 1988), p. 217.

59. Senate, Committee on Foreign Relations, "War in the Persian Gulf: The U.S. Takes Sides," Oct 1987, pp. 5–8.

60. Weinberger, *Fighting for Peace*, pp. 391, 397.

61. Ibid., p. 402.

62. Statement by the Assistant Secretary of State for Near Eastern and South Asian Affairs, 29 May 1987, State Department, *Current Documents, 1987*, #263.

63. Statement by the Undersecretary of State for Political Affairs, 16 Jun 1987, ibid., #265.

64. Caspar W. Weinberger, "A Report to the Congress on Security Arrangements in the Persian Gulf," unclassified version, 15 Jun 1987, p. iv.

65. To Secretary Weinberger, the reflagging of the Kuwaiti tankers itself was just a detail. "I don't think it made any difference which flag they carried. If they wanted to put them under the American flag, I was perfectly agreeable to that. If they didn't, I also thought we should protect them. It was the idea of shipping—neutral, innocent, non-belligerent shipping—in an international body of water of immense importance, [so] it didn't make the slightest difference to me which flag they flew. I thought they should be protected. And if they felt better about putting them under our flag, fair enough." Weinberger interview, 24 Jul 1990.

Chapter 12

1. *New York Times*, 10 Jun 1987, p. 3.

2. Senate, Committee on Armed Services, *U.S. Military Forces to Protect "Re-flagged" Kuwaiti Oil Tankers*, S. Hrg. 100–269, 100th Cong., 1st sess., 5, 11, 16 Jun 1987, p. 29.

3. Cordesman, *The Iran-Iraq War*, p. 558.

4. Senate, *U.S. Military Forces to Protect "Re-flagged" Kuwaiti Oil Tankers*, S. Hrg. 100–269, 100/1, Committee on Armed Services, 5, 11, and 16 Jun 1987, p. 60.

5. Ibid., p. 61.

6. Cordesman, *The Iran-Iraq War*, p. 558.

7. CMEF Command History, 1973, 30 Apr 1974, enclosing letter of Gen. G. J. Eade, USA, to Chairman JCS, 10 Dec 1973, MEF, Command File, OA.

8. *Wall Street Journal*, 8 Feb 1988, p. 1.

9. Robin Wright, *In the Name of God: The Khomeini Decade* (New York, London, Toronto, Sydney, Tokyo, 1989), pp. 165–66.

10. Ibid., p. 167.

11. *Wall Street Journal*, 8 Feb 1988, p. 1.

Notes to Pages 124–134

12. Sea bases are barges outfitted as forward bases from which SEALs, patrol boats, and helicopters conducted surveillance operations.

13. "The Persian Gulf: Commitment and Objectives in Troubled Waters," OP–60 unclassified brief, Mar 1988, Iran-Iraq, vol. 2 1988, USNATO Persian Gulf files (unprocessed), OA.

14. Weinberger, *Fighting for Peace*, p. 390.

15. *The Independent*, 11 Sep 1987.

16. CNA working paper, 12 Feb 1988, USNATO Persian Gulf files (unprocessed), OA.

17. Cordesman, *The Iran-Iraq War*, p. 318, states that Rear Admiral Harold Bernsen, Commander Middle East Force, and Admiral Crowe, Chairman of the Joint Chiefs of Staff, planned the operation in early September during the latter's tour of the gulf. According to Robin Wright, *In the Name of God*, p. 168, the *Iran Ajr* "had been tracked for several days after intelligence indicated that it had loaded 'suspect devices' at an Iranian port." Weinberger, *Fighting for Peace*, pp. 414, noted: "That we caught the ship was no accident."

18. O'Rourke, "The Tanker War," p. 33.

19. *Wall Street Journal*, 8 Feb 1988, p. 1; Wright, *In the Name of God*, p. 170.

20. *Washington Times* 16 Dec 1987, p. 4; *Washington Post*, 18 Dec 1987, p. 18; *New York Times*, 18 Dec 1987, p. 1.

21. Interview with Anthony A. Less, "Mideast Perspective," *Wings of Gold* 15 (Spring 1990): 50–52.

22. Ronald O'Rourke, "Gulf Ops," U.S. Naval Institute *Proceedings* 115 (May 1989): 44.

23. Senate, Committee on Foreign Relations, Staff Report, "War in the Persian Gulf: The U.S. Takes Sides," Oct 1987, p. 50.

24. For the failure of the American deployment to deter the Iranians, see Janice Gross Stein, "The Wrong Strategy in the Right Place: The United States in the Gulf," *International Security* 13 (Winter 1988/89): 155, 155n.

25. Senate Committee on Foreign Relations, Staff Report, "War in the Persian Gulf: The U.S. Takes Sides," Oct 1987, p. 51.

26. O'Rourke, "Gulf Ops," p. 49.

27. In early 1988 U.S. Navy officials reportedly pressed for a reduction of American forces in the gulf, but the administration decided not to reduce the size of the force. See *Washington Post*, 7 Jan 1988, p. 12.

28. "The Persian Gulf: Commitment and Objectives in Troubled Waters," OP–60 unclassified brief, Mar 1988, Iran-Iraq, vol. 2 1988, USNATO Persian Gulf files (unprocessed), OA.

29. Wright, *In the Name of God*, pp. 173–75.

30. Ibid., p. 176; O'Rourke, "Gulf Ops," pp. 44–47; Bud Langston and Don Bringle, "Operation Praying Mantis: The Air View," U.S. Naval Institute *Proceedings* 115 (May 1989): 54–65; J. B. Perkins III, "Operation Praying Mantis: The Surface View," ibid., pp. 66–70; John H. Admire, "A Report on the Gulf," *Marine Corps Gazette* 72 (Dec 1988): 56–61; and William M. Rakow, "Marines in the Gulf—1988," ibid., pp. 62–68.

31. Statement by Secretary of Defense Carlucci, 29 Apr 1988, State Department, *Basic Documents, 1988*, #245. Carlucci also announced continued and deeper cooperation in the gulf between the United States and its European allies.

32. Wright, *In the Name of God*, pp. 180–85.

33. Ibid., p. 176.

34. Ibid., pp. 185–86.

35. For the Airbus incident see Norman Friedman, "The *Vincennes* Incident," U.S. Naval Institute *Proceedings* 115 (May 1989): 72–79; and William M. Fogarty, *Investigation Report: Formal Investigation into the Circumstances Surrounding the Downing of Iran Air Flight 655 on 3 July 1988* (Washington, 1988).

36. Wright, *In the Name of God*, p. 186.

Bibliography

Primary Sources

Manuscript (Only unclassified and declassified records were used for this study.)

Naval Historical Center, Operational Archives Branch. Washington, DC.

> Records of the Immediate Office of the Chief of Naval Operations, the 00 (Double Zero) File.
>
> Political-Military Affairs Division Records.
>
> Files of the CNO Secretariat, Joint Staff (JCS files).
>
> Dispatch Files, Operations Division, COMINCH.
>
> World War II, Post–1 Jan 1946, and Post–1 Jan 1974, Command Files.
>
> World War II, Post–1 Jan 1946, and Post–1 Jan 1974, Plans Files.
>
> World War II, Post–1 Jan 1946, and Post–1 Jan 1974, Report Files.
>
> Privileged Manuscript Collection.
>
> Press Release Files.

National Archives and Records Administration. Washington, DC.

> Record Group 45. Masters Commandants Letters to the Secretary of the Navy, January–June 1834.

Published

Bennett, Norman R., and George E. Brooks, Jr., eds. *New England Merchants in Africa: A History Through Documents, 1802 to 1865*. Boston: Boston University Press, 1965.

Bernstein, Barton J., and Allen J. Matusow, eds. *The Truman Administration: A Documentary History*. New York and London: Harper & Row Publishers, 1966.

Bevans, Charles I., ed. *Treaties and Other International Agreements of the United States of America, 1776–1949*. 13 vols. Washington: Department of State, 1968–1976.

Carter, Jimmy. *Public Papers of the Presidents of the United States: Jimmy Carter*. 12 vols. Washington: GPO, 1977–1982.

Fisher, Sir John. *The Papers of Admiral Sir John Fisher*. P. K. Kemp, ed. 2 vols. Navy Records Society, 1960–1964.

Joint Chiefs of Staff. *Records of the Joint Chiefs of Staff, 1946–1953*. Washington: University Publications of America, 1979.

Bibliography

Nixon, Richard M. *Public Papers of the Presidents of the United States: Richard M. Nixon*. 6 vols. Washington: GPO, 1971–1975.

U.S. Congress. Senate. Committee on Armed Services. *National Security Strategy*. 100th Cong., 1st sess., 1987.

U.S. Department of State. *American Foreign Policy: Basic Documents, 1977– 1980*. Washington: Department of State, 1983.

———. *American Foreign Policy: Current Documents*. Washington: Department of State, 1982–.

———. *Foreign Relations of the United States*. Washington: GPO, 1861–.

———. *U.S. Department of State Bulletin*.

Wattenberg, Ben J., ed. *The Statistical History of the United States: From Colonial Times to the Present*. New York: Basic Books, 1976.

Interviews and Oral Histories

Interviews with author, Naval Historical Center, Washington, DC.

Swartz, Peter M. 24 August 1990.

Weinberger, Caspar W. 24 July 1990.

United States Naval Institute Oral History Collection. Annapolis, MD.

Bieri, Bernhard H. Interview by John T. Mason, Jr. 1970.

Columbia University Oral History Project. New York, NY.

Conolly, Richard L. Interview by Donald F. Shaughnessy. 1960.

Secondary Sources

Books

Abrahamsson, Bernhard J., and Joseph L. Steckler. *Strategic Aspects of Seaborne Oil*. Beverly Hills and London: Sage Publications, 1973.

Acharya, Amitav. *U.S. Military Strategy on the Gulf*. London and New York: Routledge, 1989.

Acheson, Dean. *Present at the Creation: My Years in the State Department*. New York: W. W. Norton & Co., 1969.

Bartlett, C. J. *The Long Retreat: A Short History of British Defense Policy, 1945–1970*. London and Basingstoke: The Macmillan Press, 1972.

Baylis, John. *Anglo-American Defense Relations, 1939–1984: The Special Relationship*. Second Edition. New York: St. Martin's Press, 1984.

Bergquist, Ronald E. *The Role of Airpower in the Iran-Iraq War*. Maxwell Air Force Base, AL: Air University Press, 1988.

Best, Richard A., Jr. *"Cooperation with Like-Minded Peoples": British Influences on American Security Policy, 1945–1949*. New York, Westport, CT, and London: Greenwood Press, 1986.

Bezboruah, Monoranjan. *U.S. Strategy in the Indian Ocean: The International Response*. New York and London: Praeger Publishers, 1977.

Bill, James A. *The Eagle and the Lion: The Tragedy of American-Iranian Relations*. New Haven and London: Yale University Press, 1988.

Blechman, Barry M., and Stephen S. Kaplan. *Force without War: U.S. Armed Forces as a Political Instrument*. Washington: The Brookings Institution, 1978.

Brown, Harold. *Thinking about National Security; Defense and Foreign Policy in a Dangerous World*. Boulder, CO: Westview Press, 1983.

Brzezinski, Zbigniew. *Power and Principle: Memoirs of the National Security Adviser, 1977–1981*. New York: Farrar, Straus, Giroux, 1983.

———. *The Grand Failure: The Birth and Death of Communism in the Twentieth Century*. New York: Collier Books, 1990.

Burrell, R. M., and Alvin J. Cottrell. *Iran, the Arabian Peninsula, and the Indian Ocean*. New York: National Strategy Information Center, 1972.

Campbell, John C. *Defense of the Middle East: Problems of American Policy*. Revised Edition. New York: Frederick A. Praeger, Publisher, 1960.

Carter, Jimmy. *Keeping Faith: Memoirs of a President*. Toronto, New York, London, Sydney: Bantam Books, 1982.

Chubin, Shahram, and Charles Tripp. *Iran and Iraq at War*. Boulder, CO: Westview Press, 1988.

Condit, Kenneth W. *The History of the Joint Chiefs of Staff*. Vol. 2., *The Joint Chiefs of Staff and National Policy, 1947–1949*. Washington: Joint Chiefs of Staff, 1978.

Cordesman, Anthony H. *The Gulf and the Search for Strategic Stability: Saudi Arabia, the Military Balance in the Gulf, and Trends in the Arab-Israeli Military Balance*. Boulder, CO, and London: Westview Press/Mansell Publishing, 1984.

———. *The Iran-Iraq War and Western Security, 1984–1987: Strategic Implications and Policy Options*. London and New York: Jane's, 1987.

Cottrell, Alvin J., ed. *The Persian Gulf States: A General Survey*. Baltimore and London: The Johns Hopkins University Press, 1980.

Cottrell, Alvin J., and Michael L. Moodie. *The United States and the Persian Gulf: Past Mistakes and Present Needs*. New York: National Strategy Information Center, 1984.

Bibliography

Darby, Phillip. *British Defense Policy East of Suez, 1947–1968*. London: Oxford University Press, 1973.

Davenport, E. H., and Sidney Russell Cooke. *The Oil Trusts and Anglo-American Relations*. New York: The Macmillan Company, 1924.

Davis, Vincent. *Postwar Defense Policy and the U.S. Navy, 1943–1946*. Chapel Hill: University of North Carolina Press, 1962.

Donovan, Robert J. *Conflict and Crisis: The Presidency of Harry S. Truman, 1945–1948*. New York: W. W. Norton & Co., 1977.

Dragnich, George S. *The Lebanon Operation of 1958: A Study of the Crisis Role of the Sixth Fleet*. Alexandria, VA: Center for Naval Analyses, 1970.

Drake, Frederick C. *The Empire of the Seas: A Biography of Rear Admiral Robert Wilson Shufeldt, USN*. Honolulu: University of Hawaii Press, 1984.

Epstein, Joshua M. *Strategy and Force Planning: The Case of the Persian Gulf*. Washington: The Brookings Institution, 1987.

Fanning, Leonard M. *American Oil Operations Abroad*. New York and London: McGraw-Hill Book Co., 1947.

Faroughy, Abbas. *The Bahrein Islands, 750–1951: A Contribution to the Study of Power Politics in the Persian Gulf*. New York: Verry, Fisher & Co., 1951.

Feis, Herbert. *Petroleum and American Foreign Policy*. Stanford, CA: Food Research Institute, Stanford University, 1944.

Field, James A., Jr. *America and the Mediterranean World, 1776–1882*. Princeton: Princeton University Press, 1969.

Fisher, Carol A., and Fred Krinsky, eds. *Middle East in Crisis: A Historical and Documentary Review*. Syracuse, NY: Syracuse University Press, 1959.

Fisher, Sir John. *Memoirs and Records of Admiral of the Fleet Lord Fisher*. 2 vols. London, New York, and Toronto: Hodder and Stoughton, 1919.

Fogarty, William M. *Investigation Report: Formal Investigation into the Circumstances Surrounding the Downing of Iran Air Flight 655 on 3 July 1988*. Washington: Department of Defense, 1988.

Frey, John W., and H. Chandler Ide, eds. *A History of the Petroleum Administration for War, 1941–1945*. Washington: GPO, 1946.

Gaddis, John Lewis. *The United States and the Origins of the Cold War*. New York: Columbia University Press, 1972.

Gillard, David. *The Struggle for Asia, 1828–1914: A Study in British and Russian Imperialism*. London: Methuen & Co., 1977.

Gold, Dore. *America, The Gulf and Israel: CENTCOM (Central Command) and Emerging US Regional Security Policies in the Mideast*. Jerusalem and Boulder, CO: The Jerusalem Post and Westview Press, 1988.

Bibliography

Hanks, Robert J. *The U.S. Military Presence in the Middle East: Problems and Prospects*. Cambridge, MA, and Washington: Institute for Foreign Policy Analysis, 1982.

Hay, Rupert. *The Persian Gulf States*. Washington: The Middle East Institute, 1959.

Hough, Richard. *Admiral of the Fleet: The Life of John Fisher*. New York: Macmillan, 1969.

Johnson, Maxwell Orme. *The Military as an Instrument of U.S. Policy in Southwest Asia: The Rapid Deployment Joint Task Force, 1979–1982*. Boulder, CO: Westview Press, 1983.

Kelly, J. B. *Arabia, the Gulf and the West*. New York: Basic Books, 1980.

———. *Britain and the Persian Gulf, 1795–1880*. Oxford: Clarendon Press, 1968.

Khadduri, Majid. *The Gulf War: The Origins and Implications of the Iraq-Iran Conflict*. New York and Oxford: Oxford University Press, 1988.

Kissinger, Henry. *For the Record: Selected Statements, 1977–1980*. Boston and Toronto: Little, Brown & Co., 1977–1981.

———. *White House Years*. Boston and Toronto: Little, Brown & Co., 1979.

Kolko, Joyce and Gabriel. *The Limits of Power: The World and United States Foreign Policy, 1945–1954*. New York, Evanston, San Francisco, and London: Harper & Row, 1972.

Kuniholm, Bruce Robellet. *The Origins of the Cold War in the Near East: Great Power Conflict and Diplomacy in Iran, Turkey, and Greece*. Princeton: Princeton University Press, 1980.

Ledeen, Michael, and William Lewis. *Debacle: The American Failure in Iran*. New York: Alfred A. Knopf, 1981.

Lee, David. *Flight from the Middle East: A History of the Royal Air Force in the Arabian Peninsula and Adjacent Territories, 1945–1972*. London: Her Majesty's Stationery Office, 1980.

———. *Wings in the Sun: A History of the Royal Air Force in the Mediterranean, 1945–1986*. London: Her Majesty's Stationery Office, 1989.

LeFeber, Walter. *America, Russia, and the Cold War, 1945–1984*. 5th ed. New York: Alfred A. Knopf, 1985.

Lenczowski, George. *Oil and State in the Middle East*. Ithaca, NY: Cornell University Press, 1960.

———. *Russia and the West in Iran, 1918–1948: A Study in Big-Power Rivalry*. Ithaca, NY: Cornell University Press, 1949.

Long, David F. *Gold Braid and Foreign Relations: Diplomatic Activities of U.S. Naval Officers, 1798–1883*. Annapolis: Naval Institute Press, 1988.

Bibliography

Longrigg, Stephen Hemsley. *Oil in the Middle East: Its Discovery and Development*. 2d ed. London, New York, Toronto: Oxford University Press, 1961.

Louis, William Roger. *The British Empire in the Middle East, 1945–1951: Arab Nationalism, the United States, and Postwar Imperialism*. Oxford: Clarendon Press, 1984.

Love, Kennett. *Suez: The Twice Fought War*. New York and Toronto: McGraw-Hill Book Co., 1969.

Low, Charles Rathbone. *History of the Indian Navy, 1613–1863*. 2 vols. London: Richard Bentley and Son, 1877.

Mackay, Ruddock F. *Fisher of Kilverstone*. Oxford: Clarendon Press, 1973.

Maddox, Robert James. *From War to Cold War: The Education of Harry S. Truman*. Boulder, CO, and London: Westview Press, 1988.

Mahan, Alfred Thayer. *The Problem of Asia and Its Effect upon International Policies*. Boston: Little, Brown, & Co., 1900.

———. *Retrospect & Prospect: Studies in International Relations, Naval and Political*. Boston: Little, Brown & Co., 1902.

———. *From Sail to Steam: Recollections of Naval Life*. New York: Harper & Row, 1907.

Marder, Arthur J. *From Dreadnought to Scapa Flow: The Royal Navy in the Fisher Era, 1904–1991*. 5 vols. London: Oxford University Press, 1961–70.

Meeser, Robert L. *The End of an Alliance: James F. Byrnes, Roosevelt, Truman, and the Origins of the Cold War*. Chapel Hill: University of North Carolina Press, 1982.

Metz, Helen Chapin, ed. *Iran: A Country Study*. Washington: Library of Congress Federal Research Division, 1989.

Miller, Aaron David. *Search for Security: Saudi Arabian Oil and American Foreign Policy, 1939–1949*. Chapel Hill: University of North Carolina Press, 1980.

Millis, Walter, ed., with the collaboration of E. F. Duffield. *The Forrestal Diaries*. New York: Viking Press, 1951.

Motter, T. H. Vail. *United States Army in World War II, The Persian Corridor and Aid to Russia*. Washington: GPO, 1952.

Naff, Thomas, ed. *Gulf Security and the Iran-Iraq War*. Washington: National Defense University Press, 1985.

Nash, Gerald D. *United States Oil Policy, 1890–1964: Business and Government in Twentieth Century America*. Pittsburgh, PA: University of Pittsburgh Press, 1968.

Nitze, Paul H. *From Hiroshima to Glasnost: At the Center of Decision*. New York: Grove Weidenfeld, 1989.

Nixon, Richard. *RN: The Memoirs of Richard Nixon*. New York: Grosset & Dunlap, 1978.

O'Ballance, Edgar. *The Gulf War*. London: Brassey's Defense Publishers, 1988.

Bibliography

Olson, William J., ed. *US Strategic Interests in the Gulf Region*. Boulder, CO, and London: Westview Press, 1987.

Pahlavi, Mohammad Reza. *Answer to History*. New York: Stein and Day, 1980.

Palmer, Michael A. *Origins of the Maritime Strategy: American Naval Strategy in the First Postwar Decade*. Washington: Naval Historical Center, 1988.

Petroleum Industry Research Foundation, Inc. *World Oil, Fact and Policy: The Case for a Sound American Petroleum Policy*. New York: Petroleum Industry Research Foundation, 1944.

Phillips, James Duncan. *Salem and the East Indies: The Story of the Great Commercial Era of the City*. Boston: Houghton Mifflin Co., 1947.

Quandt, William B. *Decade of Decisions: American Policy Toward the Arab-Israeli Conflict, 1967–1976*. Berkeley, Los Angeles, and London: University of California Press, 1977.

Quinlan, David A. *The Role of the Marine Corps in Rapid Deployment Forces*. Washington: National Defense University Press, 1983.

Ramazani, Rouhollah K. *The Northern Tier: Afghanistan, Iran, and Turkey*. New York, London, Toronto, and Princeton, NJ: D. Van Nostrand Co., 1966.

———. *The Persian Gulf: Iran's Role*. Charlottesville: University Press of Virginia, 1972.

Rearden, Steven L. *History of the Office of the Secretary of Defense*. Vol. 1, *The Formative Years, 1947–1950*. Washington: Historical Office of the Secretary of Defense, 1984.

Record, Jeffrey. *The Rapid Deployment Force and U.S. Military Intervention in the Persian Gulf*. Cambridge, MA, and Washington: Institute for Foreign Policy Analysis, 1981.

———. *Revising U.S. Military Strategy: Tailoring Means to Ends*. Washington: Pergamon-Brassey's, 1984.

Roberts, Edmund. *Embassy to the Eastern Courts of Cochin-China, Siam, and Muscat; in the U.S. Sloop-of-War Peacock, David Geisinger, Commander, during the Years 1832–3–4*. New York: Harper & Brothers, 1837.

Roosevelt, Archie. *For Lust of Knowing: Memoirs of an Intelligence Officer*. Boston and Toronto: Little, Brown & Co., 1988.

Roosevelt, Kermit. *Countercoup: The Struggle for the Control of Iran*. New York: McGraw-Hill Book Co. 1979.

Rosenberg, David A. *Historical Perspectives in Long Range Planning in the Navy: Part I: The Planning Process Overview, 1900–1978*. Washington: Office of the Assistant Secretary of the Navy, 1980.

Ryan, Paul B. *The Iranian Rescue Mission: Why It Failed*. Annapolis: Naval Institute Press, 1985.

Bibliography

Saivetz, Carol R. *The Soviet Union and the Gulf in the 1980s.* Boulder, CO, San Francisco, and London: Westview Press, 1989.

Seager, Robert II. *Alfred Thayer Mahan: The Man and His Letters.* Annapolis: Naval Institute Press, 1977.

Sherwood, Robert E. *Roosevelt and Hopkins: An Intimate History.* New York: Harper & Row, 1948.

Shulimson, Jack. *Marines in Lebanon.* Washington: Headquarters, U.S. Marine Corps, 1966.

Shwadran, Benjamin. *The Middle East, Oil and the Great Powers.* New York and Toronto: John Wiley & Sons; Jerusalem: Israel Universities Press, 1973.

Sick, Gary. *All Fall Down: America's Tragic Encounter with Iran.* New York: Penguin Books, 1986.

Siegel, Adam B. *U.S. Navy Crisis Response Activity, 1946–1989: Preliminary Report.* Alexandria, VA: Center for Naval Analyses, 1989.

Siegel, Adam B., Karen Domabyl, and Barbara Lingberg. *Deployment of U.S. Navy Aircraft Carriers and Other Surface Ships, 1976–1988.* Alexandria, VA: Center for Naval Analyses, 1989.

Skrine, Clarmont. *World War in Iran.* London: Constable & Company, 1962.

Sowell, Lewis C., Jr. *Base Development and the Rapid Deployment Force: A Window to the Future.* Washington: National Defense University Press, 1982.

Stoff, Michael B. *Oil, War, and American Security: The Search for a National Oil Policy, 1941–1947.* New Haven, CT, and London: Yale University Press, 1980.

Sumida, Jon Tetsuro. *In Defence of Naval Supremacy: Finance, Technology and British Naval Policy, 1889–1914.* Boston, London, Sydney, Wellington: Unwin Hyman, 1989.

Szaz, Z. Michael, ed. *The Impact of the Iranian Events Upon Persian Gulf & United States Security.* Washington: American Foreign Policy Institute, 1979.

Thomas, Hugh. *Suez.* New York and Evanston, IL: Harper & Row, 1967.

Troen, Selwyn Ilan, and Moshe Shemesh, eds. *The Suez-Sinai Crisis, 1956: Retrospective and Reappraisal.* New York: Columbia University Press, 1990.

Truman, Harry S. *Memoirs.* 2 vols. Garden City, New York: Doubleday & Co., 1955.

United Nations. *Statistical Yearbook, 1949–1950.* New York: United Nations, 1950.

U.S. Congress. Congressional Budget Office. *Rapid Deployment Forces: Policy and Budgetary Implications.* Washington: Congressional Budget Office, 1983.

U.S. Congress. Library of Congress. *Means of Measuring Naval Power with Special Reference to U.S. and Soviet Activities in the Indian Ocean.* Washington: Congressional Research Service, 1974.

U.S. Congress. Senate. Committee on Foreign Relations. *War in the Persian Gulf: The U.S. Takes Sides.* Washington: Senate Foreign Relations Committee, October 1987.

United States. President's Special Review Board [Tower Commission]. *Report of the President's Special Review Board.* Washington: GPO, 1987.

Vance, Cyrus. *Hard Choices: Critical Years in America's Foreign Policy.* New York: Simon and Schuster, 1983.

Watson, Robert J. *History of the Joint Chiefs of Staff.* Vol. 5, *The Joint Chiefs of Staff and National Policy, 1953–1954.* Washington: Joint Chiefs of Staff, 1986.

Weinberger, Caspar. *Fighting for Peace: Seven Critical Years in the Pentagon.* New York: Warner Books, 1990.

―――. *A Report to the Congress on Security Arrangements in the Persian Gulf.* Unclassified version. 15 June 1987.

Woodhouse, C. M. *Something Ventured.* London: Granada, 1982.

Wright, Robin. *In the Name of God: The Khomeini Decade.* New York, London, Toronto, Sydney, Tokyo: Simon and Schuster, 1989.

Yergin, Daniel. *Shattered Peace: The Origins of the Cold War and the National Security State.* Boston: Houghton Mifflin Co., 1977.

Articles

Abramov, M. "U.S. Navy Aggravates Persian Gulf Situation." *Morskoi Sbornik* (March 1988): 78–81.

Adamthwaite, Anthony. "Suez Revisited." *International Affairs* (Summer 1988): 449–64.

Admire, John H. "A Report on the Gulf." *Marine Corps Gazette* 72 (December 1988): 56–61.

Aldrich, Richard, and Michael Coleman. "Britain and the Strategic Air Offensive Against the Soviet Union: The Question of South Asian Bases, 1945–9." *The Journal of the Historical Association* 74 (October 1989): 400–26.

Atherton, Alfred L. "The Soviet Role in the Midddle East: An American View." *The Middle East Journal* 39 (Autumn 1985): 688–715.

Bill, James A. "Power and Religion in Revolutionary Iran." *The Middle East Journal* 36 (Winter 1982): 22–47.

Bowden, James A. "The RDJTF and Doctrine." *Military Review* 62 (November 1982): 51–64.

Brewer, William D. "Yesterday and Tomorrow in the Persian Gulf." *The Middle East Journal* 23 (Spring 1969): 149–58.

Bibliography

Cigar, Norman. "The Soviet Navy in the Persian Gulf: Naval Diplomacy in a Combat Zone." *Naval War College Review* 42 (Spring 1989): 56–88.

DeForth, Peter W. "U.S. Naval Presence in the Persian Gulf: The Mideast Force since World War II." *Naval War College Review* 28 (Summer 1975): 28–38.

Dekmejian, R. Hrair. "The Anatomy of Islamic Revival: Legitimacy Crisis, Ethnic Conflict and the Search for Islamic Alternatives." *The Middle East Journal* 34 (Winter 1980): 1–12.

Fatemi, Khosrow. "Leadership by Distrust: The Shah's *Modus Operandi*." *The Middle East Journal* 36 (Winter 1982): 49–61.

Fish, M. Steven. "After Stalin's Death: The Anglo-American Debate over a New Cold War." *Diplomatic History* 10 (Fall 1986): 333–55.

Friedman, Norman. "The *Vincennes* Incident." U.S. Naval Institute *Proceedings* 115 (May 1989): 72–79.

Hahn, Peter H. "Containment and Egyptian Nationalism: The Unsuccessful Effort to Establish the Middle East Command, 1950–1953." *Diplomatic History* 11 (Winter 1987): 23–40.

Hess, Gary R. "The Iranian Crisis of 1945–46 and the Cold War." *Political Science Quarterly* 89 (March 1974): 117–46.

Hunter, Shireen T. "The Gulf Economic Crisis and Its Social and Political Consequences." *The Middle East Journal* 40 (Autumn 1986): 593–613.

Kennedy, Edward M. "The Persian Gulf: Arms Race or Arms Control?" *Foreign Affairs* 54 (October 1975): 14–35.

Khadduri, Jamid. "The Problem of Regional Security in the Middle East: An Appraisal." *The Middle East Journal* 11 (Winter 1957): 12–22.

Khalidi, Rshid. "Arab Views of the Soviet Role in the Middle East." *The Middle East Journal* 39 (Autumn 1985): 716–32.

Kingston, Robert C. "From RDF to CENTCOM: New Challenges? *RUSI Journal* 129 (March 1984): 14–17.

Koburger, Charles W. Jr., "The Kuwait Confrontation of 1961," U.S. Naval Institute *Proceedings* 100 (January 1974): 42–49.

Langston, Bud, and Don Bringle. "Operation Praying Mantis: The Air View." U.S. Naval Institute *Proceedings* 115 (May 1989): 54–65.

Leffler, Melvyn P. "Adherence to Agreements: Yalta and the Experiences of the Early Cold War." *International Security* 11 (Summer 1986): 88–123.

Less, Anthony A. "Mideast Perspective." *Wings of Gold* 15 (Spring 1990): 50–52.

McFarland, Stephen L. "A Peripheral View of the Origins of the Cold War: The Crises in Iran, 1941–1947." *Diplomatic History* 4 (Fall 1980): 333–51.

Markov, V. "The War in the Persian Gulf, Freedom of Navigation, and International Law." *Morskoi Sbornik* (February 1988): 83–87.

Moran, Theodore H. "Iranian Defense Expenditure and the Social Crisis." *International Security* 3 (Winter 1978/1979): 178–98.

Mosely, Philip E. "The Kremlin's Foreign Policy since Stalin." *Foreign Affairs* 32 (October 1953): 20–33.

O'Rourke, Ronald. "Gulf Ops." U.S. Naval Institute *Proceedings* 115 (May 1989): 42–50.

———. "The Tanker War." U.S. Naval Institute *Proceedings* 114 (May 1988): 30–34.

Perkins, J. B. III. "Operation Praying Mantis: The Surface View." U.S. Naval Institute *Proceedings* 115 (May 1989): 66–70.

Rakow, William M. "Marines in the Gulf—1988." *Marine Corps Gazette* 72 (December 1988): 62–68.

Ramazani, R. K. "Who Lost America? The Case of Iran." *The Middle East Journal* 36 (Winter 1982): 5–21.

Rosenberg, David Alan. "The U.S. Navy and the Problem of Oil in a Future War: The Outline of a Strategic Dilemma, 1945–1950." *Naval War College Review* 29 (Summer 1976): 53–64.

Rossow, Robert Jr. "The Battle of Azerbaijan, 1946." *The Middle East Journal* 10 (Winter 1956): 17–32.

Ryan, Paul B. "Diego Garcia." U.S. Naval Institute *Proceedings* 110 (September 1984): 132–36.

Sapozhnikov, B. "The 'Rapid Deployment Force' as a Weapon of U.S. Neocolonialism." *Morskoi Sbornik* (December 1983): 70–75.

Scharfen, John C. "Interview with Gen George B. Crist, Commander in Chief, U.S. Central Command." *Marine Corps Gazette* 70 (December 1986): 30–37.

Segal, David. "The Iran-Iraq War: A Military Analysis." *Foreign Affairs* 66 (Summer 1988): 946–63.

Stein, Janice Gross. "The Wrong Strategy in the Right Place: The United States in the Gulf," *International Security* 13 (Winter 1988/89): 142–67.

Tibi, Bassam. "The Renewed Role of Islam in the Political and Social Development of the Middle East." *The Middle East Journal* 37 (Winter 1983): 3–13:

Turchenko, Sergei. "Sinister Armada." *Soviet Military Review* (July 1988): 52–54.

Dissertation

Converse, Elliott Vanvelt. "United States Plans for a Postwar Overseas Military Base System, 1942–1948." Ph.D. diss., Princeton University, 1984.

Index

Abadan refinery, 7, 13
Acheson, Dean, 23, 43–44
Aden, 36, 57, 71, 75
Afghanistan, 94, 96–97, 107, 135, 137, 165*n*.39
Al-Hasa, 10
Ali, Ala Hussein, xvii
Allen, George V., 63–64
Amman, 68
Anatolia, 8, 22, 25
Anglo-Persian (Iranian) Oil Company, 7, 8, 9, 49
Anglo-Russian-Persian (Iranian) Treaty of January 1942, 11, 14, 19, 56
Arab-American Oil Company, 49, 50
Arab-Israeli conflicts, 41: and anti-Americanism, 72, 86, 89; Israeli bombing of Iraqi nuclear reactor, xv; Six Day War, 71–72; Yom Kippur War, 86–87, 170*n*.9; U.S. response to, 72, 74, 86–87; 1948 war, 44–45, 46
Arab League, 48, 61
Ardahan, 22, 25
Armacost, Michael H., 121, 122
Armenia, 21
Asmara, 36
Azerbaijan: Soviet presence in, 21–22, 23, 24, 25
Aziz, Abdul. *See* Ibn-Saud

Baghdad Pact, 61–63, 64, 70
Bagley (FF–1069), 143, 144
Bahrain, 5, 10: anti-Americanism in, 72, 89; anti-British sentiments in, 66; Arab hospitality in, 38–39; Iranian claim to, 82; lease-basing agreement with U.S., 83, 87–88, 89; Navy operations from, 38, 45, 46, 70, 79, 82, 83, 87–88; oil development and production, 10, 12, 157*n*.4; special fuels production, 13, 35, 161–62*n*.15; strategic importance, 10, 157*n*.1
Bahrain Petroleum Company, 66
Bandar Abbas, 88, 143, 144
Bandar-e Shahpur, 88
Bartlett, C. J., 75
Basra, 5
Bazargan, Mehdi, 134
Beirut, 43, 107
Ben-Gurion, David, 65
Bernsen, Harold J., 126, 178*n*.17
Bessarabia, 22
Bieri, Bernhard H., 159*n*.2
Bill, James, 59, 94, 96
Bonaparte, Napoleon, 3
Boxer, 3
Brewster, Owen, 30
Brezhnev Doctrine, 94
Bridgeton, 123, 129
British Indian Ocean Territory, 83–84, 99
Brooks, Dennis M., 124, 126
Brown, Harold, 91, 93, 98, 105
Brzezinski, Zbigniew, 105
Bulgaria, 22, 160
Burke, Arleigh, 68, 69, 83
Bushire, 4, 5
Byrnes, James, 22, 23, 24, 25, 26

Cairo conference, 47
California (CGN–36), 104
California-Arabian Standard Oil Company, 10, 15
Caltex, 34
Carlucci, Frank C., 103, 113, 145, 178*n*.30
Carney, Robert B., 51
Carter, Jimmy, administration of: arms sales to Middle East, 108; Carter Doctrine, 98, 99, 100, 101, 103, 105, 108, 135, 137, 174*nn*. 6, 7;

193

Index

grain embargoes against Soviet Union, 96; interests in Middle East, 92, 98; Iran-Iraq war, 99–100; Olympics boycott, 98; Persian Gulf buildup, 91–92, 96, 98, 135
Caucasus, 4, 135
Central Treaty Organization (CENTO), 63, 70, 77, 106, 122
Ceylon, 36
Chagos Archipelago, 83
Chamoun, Camille, 68, 69
Chandler (DDG–996), 127, 128, 132
Cheney, Dick, xvii, xviii
Chester, Colby, 8
Churchill, Winston, 14, 22, 165*n*.32
Cold War: significance of Persian Gulf to, 22, 135
Colombo, 88
Colonialism: British, 8, 10, 48; opposition of Arabs to, 43, 48; U.S. as a counterforce to, 8, 28, 43
Communism: containment policy, 35; Middle East perceptions of threat, 61; threat to Europe, 19; threat to Iran, 50
Congo crisis, 91
Conolly, Richard L., 35–36
Constantinople, 8
Coronado (AGF–31), 126
Crist, George B., 124, 142, 145
Crowe, William J., Jr., 121, 122, 124, 126, 145, 178*n*.17

Damascus, 43
D'Arcy, William Knox, 6
Declaration of the Three Powers Regarding Iran, 14
Denfeld, Louis E., 44
Dhahran, 16–17, 36, 47, 68, 72
Diego Garcia, 83–84, 87, 91, 92, 103
Djibouti, 92
Drew, Joseph C. 17
Dulles, John Foster, 6, 54, 55, 56, 59, 61, 65, 166*n*.2
Duxbury Bay (AVP–38), 110
Dwight D. Eisenhower (CVN–69), xviii, 104
Dyess (DD–880), 72

Eade, George J., 122
East India Company, 3–4, 155*n*.5
Egypt: Anglo-French-Israeli intervention in, 64–65; disputes with British, 48, 61; French military operations, 3–4; Israeli conflicts with, 71–72, 86–87; nationalism in, 61, 63–64, 87; Sadat assassination, 107; Soviet expulsion from, 170*n*.9; strategic value of, 48, 167*n*.5; U.S. military deployments to, 98; World War II operations, 11. *See also* United Arab Republic
Eisenhower, Dwight D., administration of: intervention in Middle East, 67–68, 69; Iranian policy, 54, 56–59, 166*n*.41; "Massive Retaliation" doctrine, 70, 91; Middle East diplomacy, 61; response to Anglo-French-Israeli intervention in Egypt, 64–65; strategic defense policy, 67
Eliza, 155
Eller, Ernest M., 38, 39, 51
Enterprise (CVA–65), 142, 144, 145
Epstein, Joshua, 104
Ertegun, Mehmet Munir, 23
Essex (frigate), 3
Essex (CV–9), 70
Ethiopia, 11, 36

Fahd, King of Saudi Arabia, xvii
Farouk, King, 48
Feisal, King of Iraq, 66, 67
Felt, Harry D., 38, 39
Fisher, John, 7
Fitzwater, Marlin, xvii
Ford, Gerald E., administration of, 90
Forrestal, James, 30–31, 32, 33–34, 44
France, 3–4, 8–9, 43, 86, 124

Gandhi, Indira, 79
Gas King, 125
Geisinger, David, 3
Glaspie, April, xvi
Great Bitter Lake, 16
Great Britain: commercial interests, 3, 6; East India Company, 3–4; intelli-

194

Index

gence contribution of, 85–86; military role in Middle East, 3, 11, 28, 48, 52, 75, 106, 124, 156*n*.29; national oil policy, 8–9; oil interests, 7–8, 10, 11–12; Persian Gulf Squadron, 37; protectorates, 4, 66; Royal Commission on Fuel Oil, 7–8; security agreement, 61; Soviet confrontations with, 21, 29, 34; strategic position in Middle East, 12, 26, 41; U.S. relationship with, 6, 9, 10; withdrawal from east of Suez, 75, 77, 82, 85, 90, 135

Greenwich Bay (AVP–41), 68
Gromyko, Andrei, 160*n*.23
Gulf Cooperation Council, 110
Gulf of Aden, 3, 11
Gulf of Aqaba, 68–69, 72
Gulf of Oman, 111, 130
Gulf Oil Corporation, 10
Ghvam, Premier, 25

Haig, Alexander, 103, 173*n*.1
Hanks, Robert J. 87
Hayward, Thomas B., 93
Henderson, Loy, 23, 29, 56–57, 159*n*.6, 161*n*.2, 162*n*.10
Hiss, Alger, 23–24
HMS *Wild Goose*, 37
HMS *Wren*, 37
Holder (DD–819), 68
Holloway, James L. III, 89
Hormuz island, 3
Hormuz Strait, 100, 110–13, 121–22, 137
Howard, Daniel, 142, 143
Humphrey, George M., 56
Hussein, King of Jordan, 68, 69
Hussein, Saddam, xv-xix, 109, 111

Ibn-Saud, Abdul Aziz, xviii, 10, 15–16
Ickes, Harold, 12–14, 158*n*.8
Independence (CVA–62), xviii
Indian Mutiny of 1857–1858, 155*n*.5
Indian Ocean: French deployments, 92; recommended presence of Western allies, 92; Soviet military presence in, 75–77, 84–85, 90, 94; strength of U.S. Navy in, 97, 98, 103; U.S. basing infrastructure, 83–84, 87, 89, 91, 92, 103
Indochina, 41, 71, 74, 87
Industrial revolution, 6
Inflict (MSO–456), 128
Intelligence: British contribution to, 85–86; and capture of *Iran Ajr*, 126, 178*n*.17; Iranian assessments, 21, 25, 79; Middle East Force activities, 39; on Soviet presence in Indian Ocean, 85–86
Iran: abdication of Shah, 94, 96, 135; Allied withdrawal after World War II, 159*n*.6; American population in, 95; anti-Shah campaign, 54; arms sales to, 77, 80, 111–12; arsenal, 127; Bahrain territory claim, 82; British role in, 9–10; coup (U.S.-backed), 56–59, 165; crisis of 1946, 21–28, 31, 135, 160*n*.25; government, 50–51; hostage crisis, 93–94, 96, 98; internal discord, 41, 53–55, 93–95; Lend-Lease programs, 14, 160*n*.26; Majlis, 50–51, 56; military aids to, 53, 63; military buildup, 77, 79–80, 94–95, 170*n*.19; modernization crisis, 94, 172*n*.17; *movazaneh* strategy, 28; National Front, 53; nationalism in, 22, 48, 49, 56, 62; navy, 80, 127; oil price increases, 79, 94; oil production and resources, 8, 49–50, 157*n*.2; oil sales to U.S. Navy, 172*n*.15; oil shipments, 111; Pasdaran (Revolutionary Guards), 127; ports open to U.S. ships, 88; replacement of British presence with, 76; resistance to communist threat, 51; revolution of 1979, 93–94, 96; Saudi partnership with, 77–79; security agreements, 61, 63; Shah leadership, 50, 52, 55, 63, 70, 77, 79–80, 95–96, 165*n*.27, 166*n*.41, 170*n*.15, 173*nn*. 21, 22, 24; Soviet intervention in, 19, 22, 23–24, 50, 53, 55, 56, 57–58, 135, 161*n*.9; Status of Forces Agreement, 95; strategic importance, 11, 13, 27, 49–50, 61,

195

Index

165*n*.40; Tudeh party, 53, 56, 58; U.S. relationship with, 14–15, 25, 27–28, 29, 49–59, 62–63, 94, 101, 106, 158*n*.15, 170*n*.13 *See also* Persia
Iran Ajr, 126, 130, 141, 178*n*.17
Iran-Iraq war: antiwar demonstrations, 133–34; attacks on ships in Persian Gulf, 121, 127, 132; chemical warfare, xv, xvii, 133; "cities war," 132–33; civilian airliner incident, 134; escalation, 109, 122; Fao Peninsula campaigns, 110, 133, 145; international support of U.S. position, 116–17, 124; Kuwait involvement, 107–8, 112–17, 122, 126; "Martyrdom Maneuvers," 123–24; mine campaign and countermeasures by U.S., 122–23, 124, 126, 128, 129–30, 141–46; missiles and missile campaign, 113–14, 121, 122, 126; oil platform destruction by U.S., 126, 129, 133, 142–46; and oil revenues, 110; Ramadan offensive by Iraq, 145; Saudi Arabian riots, 123; and Soviet involvement in Middle East, 112, 117; *Stark* attack by Iraq, 114–15; tanker war, 109, 110–11, 112, 119, 121–34; U.N. Security Council Resolution 598, 116, 134; and U.S. access to oil supplies, 99, 109, 112, 119; U.S. role in, 100, 112, 119, 121–34
Iraq: arms sales to, 77, 78, 119; boundary dispute with Turkey, 9; British influence in, 8, 9; coup of 1941, 11, 15; coup of 1958, 67–68, 70; Kuwait invasion, 75; nationalist coup of 1958, 62, 63; petroleum industry development, 9, 12; pipelines, 9, 66, 111; security agreement, 61; Soviet relationship with, 119; Suez crisis effects, 66; threat against Kuwait, 69; trade embargo, xvii, xix; U.S. involvement in, 9, 117
Iraqi-Jordanian Arab Federation, 66
Iraqi Petroleum Company, 9–10
Iroquois, 156

Israel, 45, 87, 92, 98, 111. *See also* Arab-Israeli conflicts

Jack Williams (FFG–24), 143
Japan, 11
Jarrett (FFG–33), 126
Johnson, Lyndon B., administration of, 71, 75, 85
Joint Chiefs of Staff (U.S.): Joint Strategic Survey Committee, 27, 51–52; Middle East strategy review, 92–93, 99, 106; recommendations on commitments in Middle East, 21, 26, 27, 164*n*.19; strategic mobility study on Persian Gulf, 105
Jordanian crisis of 1970, 87
Joseph Strauss (DDG–16), 143, 144
Joshan, 143–44
Jufair, 38, 83

Karachi, 88
Kars, 22, 25
Kennan, George, 22, 23, 24
Kennedy, John F., administration of, 91
Kennedy, Edward M., 78, 79, 103, 170*n*.13
Khomeini, Ayatollah Ruhollah, 95, 134
Khorramshar, 13
Kidd, Isaac C., 81
Kingston, Robert C., 105–6
Kissinger, Henry, 76, 77, 86, 89, 94, 96
Kitty Hawk (CVA–63), 96, 173*n*.30
Knox, Frank, 21
Korean War, 47, 52, 57
Krug, Julius, 31
Khrushchev, Nikita, 168*n*.32
Kurdistan, 21–22, 133
Kuwait, 10: arms sales to, 111; British influence in, 8, 66, 75; Iran-Iraq war effects, 107–8, 110, 116; Iraqi threat against, 69, 75; Iranian terrorism in, 116; Mina al-Ahmadi terminal bombing, 126; oil development in, 12; reflagging of tankers, 112–13, 114, 116, 117, 122, 131–32, 176*n*.46, 177*n*.65; U.S. dependence for naval fuel, 124
Kuwaiti Oil Company, 10

Index

Lake Champlain (CVA–39), 57
League of Nations Treaty, 9
Leahy, William D., 27
Lebanon: civil war, 43, 67, 69, 107; French colonialism, 8, 43; U.S. intervention in, 67, 69, 70, 91, 93
Lee, David, 65
Less, Anthony B., 126, 142, 145
Levant crisis of 1945, 43, 107
Leyte Gulf, Battle of, 144
Liberty (AGTR–45), 72, 73
Libya, 11, 107
Longrigg, Stephen Hemsley, 12
Lynde McCormick (DDG–8), 142–43

MacDill Air Force Base, 91, 92, 106
Mahan, Alfred Thayer, 6, 34, 156*n*.18
Manama, 66, 88
Marshall Plan, 31–32, 34
Masjed Soleyman, 6
Massawa, 36
Mauritius, 88
McFarland, Stephen L., 28
McGhee, George, 47–48, 164*nn*. 18, 19, 4
Merrill (DD–976), 142–43
Middle East: arms race, 77, 170*n*.13; diplomacy by U.S., 3, 103; maps, 118, 120; oil reserves, 156*n*.19, 161*n*.2; ports open to U.S. ships, 88; security arrangement, 61, 77–78, 98, 135; strategic significance, 1, 6, 10, 11, 12–13, 25, 29, 41, 43, 51, 90, 135, 161*n*.4; U.S. planning for defense of, 44, 46–47, 53–54, 67–68. *See also specific countries*
Middle East Command (MEC). *See* Middle East Defense Organization
Middle East Defense Organization (MEDO): British responsibility in, 52; effects of, 62; formation of, 47–48; U.S. role in, 62–63. *See also* Baghdad Pact; Central Treaty Organization
Middle East Force, 59, 79: Arab hospitality to, 38–39, 70–71, 87–88; buildup, 90–92; chain of command, 147; commanders, 51, 148–49; deployment as a deterrent, 68–69; effect of British withdrawal on, 82–83, 85; establishment, 19, 34, 35–39; growth and strength of, 39, 97, 124, 169*n*.40; National Security Council recommendations on, 82; in Persian Gulf War of 1990–91, xvi; ports and bases, 36, 69, 82–83, 87–88, 98, 103; reconnaissance operations, 36–37, 39, 131; recreational facilities, 38; role of, 39, 70–71, 74, 136–37, 166*n*.50; support and logistics facilities, 36
Midway (CVB–41), 96
Mighty Servant 2, 134
Mine warfare and countermeasures, 122–23, 124, 126, 128, 129–30, 141–46
Missouri (BB–63), 23, 26
Mitscher, Marc A., 23
Molotov, Vyacheslav, 22
Moorer, Thomas H., 82, 122
Moran, Theodore H., 94
Morrison, Herbert, 165*n*.32
Mossadegh, Mohammed, 53–58, 165*nn*. 27, 35, 166*n*.42
Mubarak, Hosni, xvi
Muskie, Edmund, 100, 101
Mosul, 9
Muharraq, 66
Murphy (DD–603), 16
Murphy, Richard W., 109, 114, 116
Muscat, 3–4, 5, 155*n*.1, 156*n*.18

Nasser, Gamal Abdel, 48, 63–64, 65, 66, 69, 71
National Security Council policy statements: and Baghdad Pact, 62; and Iran, 49–50, 53, 56; Middle East Force strength, 82
Nationalism: anti-American, 62; Arab, 41, 42–48, 62; British politics and, 61; and defense of Middle East, 47–48; Egyptian, 61; Iranian, 22, 48, 49, 62; and Suez Canal crisis, 64; and Soviet intervention, 56–58, 165*n*.40; Turkish, 9; and U.S.-Arab relationships, 46–47, 48
Navy. *See* U.S. Navy
Nimitz (CVAN–68), 98–99, 104, 173*n*.30

197

Index

Nitze, Paul H., 54, 83–84
Nixon, Richard M., administration of: Middle East policy, 75–88, 95; Nixon Doctrine, 76, 81–82; Twin Pillars policy, 77, 106; U.S. presence in Persian Gulf and Indian Ocean, 81–82, 90
North Atlantic Treaty Organization, 47, 48, 62–63, 105
Northern Tier, 6, 29, 63, 167nn. 4, 5

O'Brien (DD–975), 143
Oil. *See also* Petroleum: demand, 6, 7, 31; embargo against Iraq, xvi-xvii; embargo of 1973, 86, 88, 89, 94, 116, 119, 161n.9; exports and imports, U.S., 31, 32, 33, 116; fields, 6, 32; pipelines/transport, 9, 157n.33, 158n.8, 162n.1; prices, 79, 89, 161–62n.15; production/producers, 6, 8, 10, 12–13, 29–30, 31, 156n.20, 157nn. 44, 2, 4; reserves, 7, 9, 30, 31, 33, 156n.19, 161n.2; scare of 1947–1948, 29–34; tanker reflagging by Kuwait, 112–13, 114, 116, 117, 176n.45, 177n.65
Oil industry: development in Persian Gulf, 1, 8, 9; exploration licenses/concessions, 8, 10; government-industry relationship, 13–14, 158n.8; nationalization in Middle East, 49; Red Line agreement, 9; U.S. diplomatic efforts for, 9
Okinawa (LPH–3), 125, 128
Oman, 12, 92, 111
Operations. *See* U.S. Operations in Middle East
O'Regan, William V., 36
Organization of Petroleum Exporting Countries, xvi, 89
Ottoman Empire, 4, 8

Pahlavi, Mohammad Reza Shah, 11, 22, 50, 52, 55, 63, 70, 77, 79–80, 95–96, 165n.27, 166n.41, 170n.15, 173nn. 22, 23
Pahlavi, Reza Shah, 11, 22
Pakistan: military aid to, 63; ports open to U.S. ships, 88; security agreements, 61, 63; strategic significance to U.S., 107
Palestine: British influence in, 8; partitioning of, 32, 44, 163n.13; resettlement of refugees, 45; U.S. oil exploration licenses, 8; U.S. policy, 43–44, 46, 47; U.S.–USSR trusteeship and occupation, 44
Peacock, 3
Pelletreau, Robert H., 108–109
Persia, 6–7. *See also* Iran
Persian Gulf: Arab hospitality, 38–39; early U.S. role in, 3–10; environmental conditions/heat in, 37–38; first U.S. warship in, 5; freedom of navigation in, 100, 109–10, 116, 137; Lend-Lease programs, 14, 16; oil production, 10, 30; reconnaissance by U.S. Navy, 36–37; refinery capacity, 13, 35; War of 1990–91, xv-xx; in World War II, 11–17, 31. *See also* Middle East, *and specific countries*
Petroleum: and the Arab embargo of 1973–1974, 86, 88, 89, 94, 119, 161n.9; and sea power, 7–8; security of Persian Gulf, 92, 99, 101, 103, 106; strategic significance, 8–9, 11–12, 27, 29–34, 161nn. 2, 4; and the U.S. Navy, 13, 35, 88, 124, 161–62n.15; and U.S. policy, 12, 19, 31–33, 98, 136, 158n.8; Western dependence on, 135. *See also* oil
Piracy, 4, 155n.1
Poland, 22
Port Louis, 88
Portugal, 3
Potsdam Conference, 19, 22
Preble, Edward, 3

al-Qadhafi, Mu'ammar, 107
Qatar, 12
Quayle, Dan, 122

Radford, Arthur W., 64
Rafsanjani, Ali Akbar Hashemi, 117, 134, 145
Ras Tanura, 13, 38, 162n.3

198

Index

Reagan, Ronald W., administration of: arms sales to Middle East, 108, 111–12; Corollary to Carter Doctrine, 108; international support for Persian Gulf role, 116–17, 124; Iranian policy, 101, 116; Iran-Contra affair, 111–12, 119; Middle East policy, 101, 116; military buildup in Persian Gulf, 124; retaliation against Libya, 107; Soviet policy, 101, 116; tanker reflagging in Iran-Iraq war, 112–13, 114, 116, 117
Record, Jeffrey, 104, 105, 174n.7
Red Line agreement, 9–10
Rendova (CVE–114), 38, 45, 46
Riyadh, 16
Roberts, Edmund, 3, 4
Roosevelt, Franklin D., administration of, 12, 14–15
Roosevelt, Kermit, 58
Rossow, Robert, Jr., 22, 23
Russia. *See* USSR
Ruthenia, 22

Sabalan, 142, 143, 144, 145
Sadat, Anwar, 107, 170n.9
Sahand, 133, 144
Said, Saiyid, 3
ibn-Said, Turki, 5
Samuel B. Roberts (FFG–58), 130, 133, 134, 141–42
Saud, Crown Prince, 38
San Remo Conference, 8–9
Saratoga (CVA–60), 81
Saudi Arabia: air bases, 16–17, 47, 92, 131; anti-British sentiments, 66; arms sales to, 80, 108, 111; British presence in, 16; Iran-Iraq war effects on, 110, 123; Iranian partnership with, 77–79; Lend Lease program, 16; military buildup, 80–81, 108; military defense of, 47; nationalization of oil industry, 49; navy, 80; oil embargo against U.S., 86; oil industry development, 10, 12, 16, 49; oil production, 157n.4; Peace Hawk program, 80; special fuels production, 13, 35;

strategic value to U.S., 31, 92; UAR relationship with, 70; U.S. military deployments to, 96, 108, 131; U.S. relationship with, xvii-xviii, 14, 15–17, 31, 36, 92, 106, 108, 135, 170n.9
Scan Bay, 143
Schwarzkopf, H. Norman, Jr., xvii, 158n.15
Schwarzkopf, H. Norman, Sr., 158n.15
Sea Isle City, 126, 129, 142
Seychelles, 83
Shatt-al-Arab, 5, 110, 111
Sherman, Forrest P., 39, 167n.4
Shufeldt, Robert Wilson, 5, 6, 7, 34
Shultz, George, 110, 111, 113, 117
Simpson (FFG–56), 132, 144
Sisco, Joseph, 169–70n.9
Slave trade, 4
Somalia, 11, 71
Soviet-Iranian treaty (1921), 57
Soviet Union. *See* USSR
Sri Lanka, 88
Stalin, Joseph, 14, 22, 24
Standard Oil Company of California, 10
Standard Oil Company of New York, 8
Stark (FFG–31), 114–15, 116, 121, 127
Suez Canal, 16, 29, 49, 70: British withdrawal from east of, 75, 77, 82, 85, 90, 135; crisis, 64–66, 67, 74, 91
Sykes-Picot agreement, 8–9
Syria: 8, 9, 43, 86, 107. *See also* United Arab Republic

Tabriz, 22, 24
Teheran, 23, 59
Teheran Conference, 14
Ticonderoga, 5
Tiran Strait, 68, 71
Trade in Persian Gulf; changes in, 4; embargo against Iraq, xvii, xix; U.S., 1, 3
Treaties and agreements (U.S.); commerce, 3, 4–5; with Iran, 4–5, 95; Muscat amity and commerce (1833), 3, 4; petroleum, 9–10; with Turkey, 4
Trenton (LPD–14), 142, 145
Trincomalee, 36
Trucial States, 12

199

Index

Truman, Harry S., 22, 52
Truman, Harry S., administration of: energy crisis, 31, 33–34; hard-line policy, 25, 160*n*.26; Iranian policy, 50, 51, 54, 56, 57; oil policy, 19, 31, 32, 34; Palestine policy, 43–44; Persian Gulf policy, 17, 26, 43–44, 63, 105; Soviet policy, 25, 29
Turkey: boundary dispute with Iraq, 9; nationalism, 9; oil pipelines, 111; security agreements, 61, 62, 63; Soviet expansion into, 19, 22, 25, 26, 168*n*.32; strategic significance, 6, 48, 61, 166*n*.2; U.S. relationship with, 4, 8, 25, 27, 28, 48, 61
Turkish Petroleum Company, 9
Turkish Straits, 25
Twin Pillars, 76, 81–82
Twining, Nathan, 67

U Thant, 71
United Arab Emirates, xvi, 110
United Arab Republic, 66, 67, 70
United Nations Organization, 26, 29
United Nations Security Council: Resolution 552, 109; Resolution 598, 116; Resolution 660, xvi
United States, xv-xx, 23–24, 27–28, 53, 56–59, 67–70, 91, 104, 142–46: Economic Cooperation Administration, 51; energy crisis, 31, 32–34; energy policy, 12, 31–33, 98, 136, 158*n*.8, 161*n*.2; exports and imports of oil, 31, 32; Foreign Production Program, 13; French cooperation with, 86; in Iran-Iraq war, 121–34, 142–46; isolationism policy, 35; in Lebanon, 67, 69, 70, 91; Lend-Lease programs, 14, 16, 160*n*.26; Near and Middle East Subcommittee of the State-War-Navy Coordinating Committee, 17; oil production, 6, 12–13, 29–30, 156*n*.20; oil reserves, 9, 30, 31, 33, 156*n*.19; Soviet containment policy, 22, 25, 33, 34, 35, 36, 74, 92, 101, 106, 116, 136. *See also specific presidential administrations*

U.S. military: Central Command (CENTCOM), 91, 92, 101, 105–7, 111, 124, 137, 141; CINCLANT, 91; CINCSPECOMME, 91; Joint Task Force Middle East, 124, 126, 131; Marine Air-Ground Task Force, 92, 103; Operation Crossroads, 26; Persian Gulf Service Command, 14, 158*n*.16; Petroleum Administration for War, 12–13; Rapid Deployment Force, 91, 98, 101, 103, 104, 105, 174*n*.7; Readiness Command, 91; SACEUR, 91; Strategic Army Corps, 67, 91; STRIKCOM, 91; terrorist attacks against U.S., 107. *See also* Joint Chiefs of Staff; U.S. Navy
U.S. Navy: Arab treatment of, 70–71; buildup in Persian Gulf, 92–93, 124; Carrier Battle Group Eight, 93; CENTCOM forces, 107; CINCNELM, 35–36, 51, 54, 59, 91–92; CINCUSNAVEUR, 91–92; Eighth Fleet, 23; exercises, 63, 122; in European waters, 21, 25, 36; Fifth Fleet, 92–93; Indian Ocean basin operations, 3, 35–39, 54, 63, 83–84, 91, 92–93, 97, 98, 103, 104; Iranian oil sales to, 172; first warship in Persian Gulf, 5; Libyan clashes with, 107; oil transfer for domestic use, 35–36; Pacific Command, 93; philosophy of operations, 130–31; ports open to, 88, 98; Political-Military Policy Division, 31; response to Six Day War, 72; ship modifications for environmental conditions, 37; Sixth Task Fleet, 36, 68, 136, 167*n*.4; special fuels production in Persian Gulf, 13, 35, 161–62*n*.15; support and logistics facilities, 36; Task Force 126, 35–36; transport of oil from Persian Gulf, 35. *See also* Middle East Force
U.S. Operations in Middle East: Ajax, 56–59; Bluebat, 67, 91; Desert Shield and Desert Storm, xv-xx, 84, 91, 136, 137; Earnest Will, 117, 120, 125, 131–32; Evening Light, 98–99; Praying Mantis, 133, 141–46; Staunch, 112; Whiplash, 64

Index

U.S. Policy in Middle East: Arab nationalism and, 46; commercial interests, 1, 3, 5, 12, 135, 155*n*.7; as counterforce to colonialism, 8, 28, 43; diplomatic missions, 3; Iranian policy of, 14–15, 25, 27–28, 29, 49–59, 62–63, 94, 101, 135, 170*nn*. 9, 13; oil concessions, 6, 8, 10, 14, 157*n*.33; oil industry development, 12–13; Open Door policy, 9–10, 13; "outer ring" security arrangement, 61, 167*n*.5; military aid, 25, 27, 28, 51, 62, 63, 80, 94; military presence, 12, 14, 16–17, 19, 23, 26, 27, 29, 34, 46–47, 81–82, 92, 97; protection oil interests, 23–24, 27–28, 53, 56–59, 67–70, 89, 91, 104; Soviet containment policy, 22–23, 27–28, 36, 92, 106, 116, 135, 174*n*.7; State Department Near Eastern and African Affairs office, 23, 27–28; strategic interests, 6, 12, 25, 27, 29, 44, 45; treaties, 3, 4–5

USSR, 11, 165: Afghanistan invasion, 94, 96–97, 107, 135, 137; aggression after World War II, 21–22; British confrontations with, 21, 29, 34; concerns about U.S. buildup in Indian Ocean, 169*n*.5; expulsion from Egypt, 170*n*.9; Indian Ocean military deployments, 75, 76, 77, 84–85, 90, 94, 104; in Iran, 19, 21–22, 23–24, 161*n*.9; Lend-Lease debt, 160*n*.26; Middle East opposition to, 45; military aid to Syria, 86; nationality tactics, 22, 166*n*.45; oil interests in Middle East, 27; oil production, 6, 156*nn*. 19, 20; in Palestine, 44; response to U.S. intervention, 69; in Somalia, 71; southern expansion, 4, 11, 19, 22, 25, 26, 34, 61; threat to U.S. interests in Persian Gulf, 9, 19, 47, 63; in Turkey, 19, 21–22, 25, 26; and U.S. containment policy, 22, 25, 33, 34, 35, 36, 74, 92, 101, 106, 116, 136

Valcour (AGF–1), 70, 71
Valley Forge (CV–45), 37, 38
Vietnam War, 71, 75, 90, 91
Vincennes (CG–49), 134
Virginia (CGN–38), 104

Wahabism, 4
Wainwright (CG–28), 143, 144
Webb, James H., Jr., 119
Weinberger, Caspar W., 103, 112, 113, 116, 117, 119, 121, 124
Willie Tide, 143
Woodhouse, C. M., 56
Woolridge, E. T., 162*n*.10
Woolverton, Robert C., 36
World War I, 7, 8, 11, 35, 156*n*.29
World War II, 11–17, 31
Wright, Edwin M., 23
Wright, Robin, 123–24

Yemen, civil strife in, 70, 71, 75
York Marine, 143

☆ U.S. GOVERNMENT PRINTING OFFICE: 1992 304–274

201